OPERATION EXODUS

ISBN 0-9778224-0-0
Publisher's Cataloging in Publication data:
   Nagel, Gerald S.
     Operation Exodus : the inside story of American Jews
   in the greatest rescues of our time / by Gerald S. Nagel.
     p. cm.
     Includes index.

     1. United Jewish Appeal. 2. Fund raising. 3. Jews--
United States--Attitudes toward Israel. 4. Jews--United
States--Politics and government. 5. Jews--Russia
(Federation)--Migrations. 6. Jews--Ethiopia--
Migrations. 7. Israel--Emigration and immigration.
8. Title.

HV3191.N23 2006   362.84'924
                QBI06-600037

Cover design by Stewart L. Nagel.
Type is Mrs. Eaves Roman, 11 point.

15 14 13 12 11 10 09 08 07 06   1 2 3 4 5

Published in the United States of America by Contemporary History Press,
New York, N.Y. 10001.

To Hadasa

TABLE OF CONTENTS

ACKNOWLEDGEMENTS

I am extremely grateful to Marvin Lender, Joel Tauber and Richard Pearlstone, three outstanding leaders of Operation Exodus, who encouraged me to research and write this book and provided important information and insight. I deeply thank Leslie Wexner, Max Fisher, Laurence Tisch, Andrew Tisch, Charles Bronfman, Charles Goodman, Peter May, Alan Greenberg, Lewis Rudin, Irving Schneider, Henry Taub and Joseph Wilf, legendary leaders in philanthropy and industry. They also provided important information and insight and, in particular, enabled me to constitute the chapter, "Breakfast of Champions." I am honored that former President George H. W. Bush, who eschews interviews at this juncture in his life, responded to my inquiry about the implication of Operation Exodus in international relations.

Morris Sherman, Marshall Jacobson and Harold Cohen, who played key roles in Operation Exodus, often behind the scenes, furnished important perspectives and details, and Harold Cohen provided wise counsel. They too have my gratitude.

Scores of others provided recollections or records or otherwise aided this project. I wish to thank Richard L. Wexler, Martin F. Stein and Morton A. Kornreich as well as Brian Abrahams, Robert Aronson, Shula Bahat, Yigal Barkan, Gad Ben-Ari, Jerry Benjamin, Michael Bennett, Sen. Rudy Boschwitz, Sandra Cahn, Shoshana Cardin, Gerald Carter, Marc Charendoff, Jerry Cheslow, Gen. Nehemia Dagan, Capt. Nir Dagan, Heidi Damsky, Amb. Simcha Dinitz, Irwin Field, Michael Fischer, Norbert Freuhoff, Darrell Friedman, Marina Furman, Rani Garfinkle, Victor Gelb, J.J. Goldberg, Yona Goldberg, Ari Goldman, Barbara Ribakove Gordon, Anita Gray, Blu Greenberg and Richard Gunther.

Also, Malcolm Hoenlein, Stephen Hoffman, Stanley Horowitz, Adam Kahan, Deborah Kaplan, Mendel Kaplan, Steven Katcher, Jeffrey Klein, Rabbi Doniel Kramer, Amb. Naphtali Lavie, Joel Leibowitz, Bud Levin, Judith Kaufman Levin, Jonathan Lichter, Jerry Lippman, Uri Lubrani, Rabbi Brian Lurie, Ernest Michel, Larry Moses, Seth Moskowitz, Dr. Steven Nasatir, Shimon Pepper, Fredi Rembaum, Dr. Howard Rieger, Susan Rifas, Russell Robinson, Rabbi Tzvi David Romm, Barry Rosenberg, Gary Rosenblatt, Stuart Rossman, Raphael Rothstein, Rabbi Jacob Rubenstein, Dr. John Ruskay, David Sacks, David Sarnat, Dr. Joel Schindler, Nachum Segal, Yale Septee, Barry Shrage, William Shure, Stephen Solender, Carole Solomon, Jacob Solomon, Allison Sommer, Susan Stern, Strobe Talbott, Alan Tigay, Leon Uris , Marek Web and Dr. Stephen Windmueller.

The writer Dan Carlinsky provided an abundant array of sagacious advice on book preparation and marketing. The photojournalist Zion Ozeri provided crucial advice on book marketing.

Several family members contributed significantly, not only with encouragement but also with professional advice and services. My wife Hadasa Nagel; our grown sons, Jason Nagel, Seth Nagel and Mark Nagel; my brother, Prof. Stewart Nagel; my sister, Dr. Ilene Allgood; and my close cousins, Edith and William Minick, have my personal appreciation.

I salute the valiant Soviet Jews who stood up to tyranny and demanded the freedom to emigrate to Israel, and the throngs of American Jews who demonstrated indefatigably in support of them, in the 1970s and 1980s. They laid the foundation for the narrative that follows.

I happily acknowledge the 1.2 million American Jews who gave of themselves and their resources in the 1990s to make Operation Exodus possible. Some of them said then that they wanted to write a great new chapter in Jewish history, but they meant it metaphorically. Now that chapter — this book — has been written literally. This is their story. And the name of each of them shines through on every page.

G. S. N.

NOTE TO READERS

This book is based on a myriad of facts, thousands of documents and more than a hundred interviews. Substantial care has been taken to stay true to all of them. Any errors or omissions are regretted.

CHAPTER ONE
Next Year in Jerusalem

For more than 2,000 years the Jewish people -- my people --
have been dispersed. But wherever they are, wherever Jews are
found, every year they have repeated, 'Next year in Jerusalem.'
Now, though I am farther than ever from my people, from my
wife Avital, facing many arduous years of imprisonment I say,
turning to my people, my Avital: Next year in Jerusalem.

*Anatoly (Natan) Sharansky, upon being sentenced to 13 years in prison by
a Moscow court in 1978 on trumped up charges of treason and espionage.*

The dawn of a new decade is often a time of hope, but when the 1990s began
the Jews were apprehensive in the three countries where most of them were
housed: the Union of Soviet Socialist Republics, Israel and the United States.
The decade's opening years would be defined, for Jews and others, by events
bubbling up within the Soviet Union, a vast and diverse empire of 15 republics
that spanned eleven time zones. There, Latvia, Lithuania and Estonia, fed up
with poverty and oppression, were threatening to secede, seemingly impervious
to the fate of Poland, Hungary and Czechoslovakia, where national yearnings
had led to brutal subjugation by the USSR in the 1950s and '60s. Those had
been foreign countries; the Baltic states were part of the Soviet Union itself, and
only a few hundred miles from Moscow, with its arsenals and tanks, at that.

In backward Central Asian republics like Uzbekistan, Tajikistan,
Kyrgyzstan, and Turkmenistan, food and fuel were in scarce supply, as they
were throughout that frigid country, and riots were becoming more common
and not suppressed by the local (hungry and cold) police. Dissent was growing
also in Russia, Kazakhstan, Georgia, Moldova, Armenia, Azerbaijan and even
Belarus, a rubber stamp for Soviet tyranny for years. Particularly nettlesome was
the simmering bitterness in Ukraine, where monumental Soviet incompetence
had caused a catastrophic nuclear explosion at Chernobyl, near Kiev, four years

earlier that Ukrainians widely believed had killed tens of thousands and that left the air, water and soil poisoned. Soviet Premier Mikhail Gorbachev was struggling to work his strategies of *perestroika,* or economic restructuring, and *glasnost,* political openness, through the Soviet bureaucracies, but the people's quests to live better than from hand to mouth, and in freedom, were growing faster than he could control.

The situation seemed ripe for the national government to blame the Jews and clamp down on them, as this had palliated restive populations before, under tsars and commissars. But that was not Gorbachev's inclination. Besides, the Soviet Jews had, incredibly, imposed their demands on his agenda: they wanted to emigrate. The pesky American Jews had helped them challenge him, with their years of rallies and letter writing campaigns, and were driving him into a corner on the issue. Gorbachev desperately needed American aid and, even more, arms reduction agreements to enable him to redirect rubles from guns to butter, and quell domestic disturbances. The national government couldn't pin the country's problems on the Soviet Jews even if it wanted to.

However, the ingrained canards about traitorous, devious Jews causing economic woe still played well in the countryside. Outside the big cities, lawless gangs were growing bolder as national power broke down. An anti-Semitic movement, *Pamyat* (Russian for memory), was founded and growing rapidly. Demagogues like Vladimir Zhirinovsky whipped large rural crowds into a frenzy, blaming the Jews for the country's ills. Often soldiers were few and the local police were not about to stick their necks out to protect Jews, and scores of Jews were beaten, and their homes were ransacked. The Soviet Jews were becoming more afraid of lawlessness than they were of Communism. Those who remembered Stalin's purges in the 1930s, and the rabid anti-Semitism surrounding the purported Doctor's Plot to kill Stalin in the early 1950s, feared pogroms.

Unlike the Soviet Union, Israel wasn't falling apart, but it was in the throes of a crisis of another kind: of its identity. Fault lines appeared in the fabric of the country that left it bitterly divided on important issues, including the perpetual question of how to achieve peace with security. The Intifada (Arabic for uprising), a low-level but tenacious rebellion against the Israeli presence in the West Bank and Gaza Strip, was entering its third year with no end in sight. When the Intifada had begun, with Palestinian youths throwing stones at Israeli soldiers, Israelis overwhelmingly supported a strong hand to suppress it. As Defense Minister Yitzhak Rabin warned, "We will break their bones." Israelis bristled at the horrendous symbol of the conflict, fixed by the world's news media, as David against Goliath. Except that Israel was seen as Goliath.

After thousands of years of being oppressed, the Jews were portrayed as the oppressors. Those supporting armed action argued that not only would it be inadvisable strategically to give in to the uprising but also immoral to abandon areas where Jews had lived over thousands of years. Nevertheless, as the strife continued, a formidable core of Israelis demanding settlement dismantlement as a reasonable risk for peace grew larger. Daily skirmishes continued, with Israeli deaths seen by one huge constituency as the price of security and by another as proof the policy was making all Israelis less secure. The mantle of morality was claimed by both sides.

Meanwhile, Israeli troops were bogged down in Lebanon. Eight years earlier the country had supported an invasion to protect its northern towns from relentless katyusha rocket attacks and cross border raids by the Palestine Liberation Organization and Syrian-backed militias. Israeli troops pressed northward, nearly to Beirut, and drove the PLO from Lebanon, but the militias remained formidable and the fighting persevered. Some Israelis urged more decisive military action as the practical thing to do, but others responded that the policy of the stick had failed and that Israel had lost its moral compass by being in Lebanon so long. The country was split almost down the middle. Each week, Israeli soldiers were being killed in Lebanon, hardening each side in its position.

The regional picture portended more gloom. Egypt stood behind the Camp David Accords, but a cold peace existed on Israel's southern front. Jordan maintained secret contacts with Israel, to limit their border clashes, but publicly condemned Israel harshly. Syria implacably demanded that Israel completely withdraw from the Golan Heights, West Bank and Gaza before any consideration of peace talks, a position no Israeli accepted. Saudi Arabia trained and financed radical anti-Israeli militias. Iran's mullahs threatened Holy War. Iraq's Saddam Hussein, still smarting from the Israeli raid that had destroyed his nuclear reactor, warned he would obliterate Israel. Eighteen of the 19 Arab countries, as well as the PLO, were pledged to Israel's destruction. Sporadic border clashes, kidnappings, bombings of Israeli commuters and schoolchildren, and even attacks on Israelis traveling in Western Europe, left Israelis uncertain and restless.

The country's divisions were reflected in its politics, which were interminably deadlocked. Neither Likud nor Labor had been able to achieve a majority in the Knesset for years and each needed the other to form a government. Likud's Yitzhak Shamir and Labor's Shimon Peres took turns as Prime Minister, serving alternately as each other's subordinate. The Knesset consisted of 120 members who represented a dozen parties. Coalitions had to be painstakingly pieced together for every important bill. Neither party was able to institute coherent long-term strategies. Shamir was at the helm again in 1990 but the threads that united Israelis politically decades earlier were rarely to be found.

Economically, the miracles of Israel's earlier years that had inspired people worldwide, such as growing crops in the desert as symbolized by a bronze-skinned kibbutznik in a patch of desert greenery, seemed as ancient as the Red Sea crossing. The country was mired in incessant nationwide strikes, high inflation, increasing unemployment, maddening bureaucracies, and fitful and incomplete thrusts toward efficiency and capitalism.

Israeli society was in transition. The State's early settlers, the battlers for Independence in 1948, the Holocaust survivors entering what felt like the Promised Land, and the massive waves of early immigrants fleeing persecution in Arab countries, were now old. There was widespread disagreement whether the axioms of their era should be the guiding principles in the 1990s. When Israel was established, draft exemptions were provided to those wishing to study Torah. But with religious Jewish settlers advocating that the Intifada be crushed, their opponents said yeshivah students should be drafted to fight the battles they support. Beneath the dispute was a growing chasm between Orthodox Jews and other Israelis. It spilled over into other issues, such as whether the national (money-losing) airline El Al should be allowed to fly on Shabbat, movie theaters in Tel Aviv could be open on Shabbat, and pork could be sold in Jerusalem. Should Israel be a Jewish state or a democracy?

Israel had arisen in a sense like a phoenix from the ashes of the Holocaust but surveys disclosed that Israeli pupils knew little about it. Some said the Holocaust must be an educational cornerstone, to show what happens when Jews are vulnerable. Others argued that Israel was gripped by a "Holocaust mentality," a sense of perpetual besiegement that obstructed it from taking prudent risks for peace.

Even the central Zionist principle, that Jews should live in Israel and build the Jewish State, was tottering. *Aliyah,* or movement of Jews to Israel, was at record lows, and *yeridah*, the movement of Jews from Israel, had grown so much that in some months it exceeded aliyah. The land established for Jews to move *to* had become the land that Jews were moving *from*. Where was this country going?

The United States was the only country that supported Israel. The United Nations regularly condemned Israel, even re-proclaiming annually, "Zionism is a form of racism and racial discrimination." A pervasive Arab-imposed boycott of Israeli products limited its exports mainly to the United States and Western Europe. A secondary boycott punished companies that traded with Israel. The United States stood with Israel against propaganda and boycotts, and provided substantial economic and military aid, but Israel's military response to the Intifada was unpopular with the administration of President George H. W. Bush. Shamir personally was seen as an obstacle to peace. Whereas Bush regularly telephoned Arab leaders, sometimes just to maintain good relations, he rarely telephoned Shamir, the diminutive fighter for Israel's independence and settlement builder, except on important business. Shamir was so disdained that Secretary of State James Baker once said in Congressional testimony that when Shamir wanted to talk peace he could call him, and then Baker announced his telephone number. Max M. Fisher, a venerated Detroit industrialist who was influential with Bush and Shamir, regularly ran interference between them. "I used to speak to George Bush on the phone every week or two and I got him to see Shamir when he came over here," Fisher said in one of several interviews for this book. "Bush wanted to ignore him completely, which wasn't right. But it wasn't easy to deal with Shamir. He was a tough old codger, very stubborn."

Of course, a year later it was the reviled Shamir who kept his military pilots strapped into their cockpits on the ground while Scud missiles from Saddam Hussein's Iraq fell on neighborhood streets in Israel, to enable Bush to retain his Arab military coalition in the first Gulf War.

Israel's best friend abroad was the American Jewish community. American Jews loved Israel and weighed in, without hesitation, on the panoply of issues affecting it. Israel welcomed this, in respect for American Jewish influence and philanthropic support, but even more so because it wanted all the world's Jews to feel they have a stake in Israel's future. Sometimes American Jews were as divided on those issues as were Israelis.

Then an issue that had been simmering for years flared again and threatened to divide American Jews *from* Israel. That was the status there of the Conservative and Reform movements. Orthodox Knesset members were preparing to reintroduce a bill that would deny recognition of persons converted by Conservative or Reform rabbis as Jews under the Law of Return, which guaranteed Israeli citizenship to any Jew who wanted it. The bill was important in itself but mainly was a domestic bargaining chip in the complex thicket of Israeli politics involving the role of religion in the democracy; the voice of the Diaspora in Israeli life; and coalition building for unrelated legislation. Fewer than a dozen Conservative or Reform converts applied for Israeli citizenship each year but many Conservative and Reform Jews felt, perhaps rightly, that the bill sought to delegitimize their movements. They wondered if Israel would soon reject them as Jews, even if they were Jews by birth. The question was posed as, "Who is a Jew?" and it was galvanizing Conservative and Reform Jews.

Domestically in America there were serious divisions within the religious movements. Orthodoxy was being pulled in opposite directions by the Hasidim, who took a literal view of Scripture, and the Modern Orthodox who sought to be true to Jewish law and traditions yet embrace aspects of contemporary life. Conservativism was cleaving toward more tradition on the one hand and toward greater egalitarianism on the other. The Reform movement found huge blocs seeking greater traditionalism at the same time that other large blocs advocated new applications of the liberal theology such as ordination of gay rabbis.

In the considerable world of American Jewry beyond the religious movements, where many American Jews were found, the Jewish community was assimilating. With fewer American Jews having been born abroad, or ever having experienced anti-Semitism, most thought of themselves as Americans and only tangentially as Jews. As thousands moved from the Northeast and Midwest in search of the jobs and sunshine of the West and South, they cut any ties they had to Jewish institutions and did not begin new ones. As the rolls of Jewish federations plummeted, fundraising became stagnant or declined. The growing assimilation didn't seem to matter that much to those not connected to Jewish institutions. Then there was a shocker on the horizon that was about to wake everyone up. The Council of Jewish Federations was completing the most comprehensive demographic study ever of the American Jewish community and it would disclose that one of every two American Jews was marrying out of the Jewish religion.

Yet all this was about to be pushed to the background, for there was one issue on which all Jews could agree: freedom for Soviet Jews to emigrate to Israel. On New Year's Day — the very first day of a decade in which Jewish destiny would largely be shaped by Jewish hands — three Israelis conferred by phone about rapidly accelerating developments in the Soviet Union. They were: Simcha Dinitz, Chairman of the Executive of the Jewish Agency and a former Israeli Ambassador to the United States; Mendel Kaplan of South Africa, Chairman of the Jewish Agency Board of Governors; and Baruch Gur, Director of the Jewish Agency Unit for the Soviet Union. Following the discussion, Dinitz placed a call to Stanley B. Horowitz, President and Chief Executive Officer of the United Jewish Appeal. UJA had been the preeminent American Jewish fundraising organization for more than 50 years and was the main source of funds for the Jewish Agency, which planned and implemented aliyah. Horowitz arranged a conference call the next day among Dinitz and Kaplan in Israel; Gur in Moscow; himself; Morton A. Kornreich of New York, the UJA National Chairman; Martin F. Stein of Milwaukee, UJA Chairman of the Board; Marvin Lender of New Haven, UJA National Chairman-Elect; and Joel D. Tauber of Detroit, a UJA trustee.

Crucial to that discussion was the report by Gur, who had established a modest field organization in Moscow for the Jewish Agency to encourage and facilitate aliyah. Gur informed the UJA leaders and others that the latest data showed that the aliyah could turn out to be much larger than expected. He said that by year's end thousands of Soviet Jews a week were declaring their desire to emigrate by filing a written request and informing the Jewish Agency. The Agency responded quickly, providing each applicant with a formal invitation, a prerequisite for Soviet consideration, within days. Often that had been as far as it got. But in recent weeks, he said, Soviet authorities increased their actions, in speed and scope, recognizing the invitation's validity, authorizing departure, providing applicants with permission to remove personal belongings from the country and designating a departure date. The endless process had been reduced to months.

Gur suggested that, whereas only 220 Jews had been able to make aliyah from all of the Soviet Union in 1986, and departures multiplied to 2,129, 4,379, and 17,239 in the next three years, that was the tip of the iceberg. He believed that a breathtaking 60,000 might be able to make aliyah in 1990.

More and more Soviet Jews were initiating the process because they feared lawlessness and pogroms, he said. This trumped their fear of Soviet retribution for seeking to emigrate. They were inspired by the example of Natan Sharansky, who defied Soviet power for years and won, and other Prisoners of Zion such as Ida Nudel, Vladimir Slepak and Iosef Begun, who had made it from squalid jail cells to Israel. Under *glasnost*, they were receiving word from relatives and friends in Israel that they would be welcome and happy there. They were motivated most of all, he said, by a yearning to be free, and to be able to live as Jews.

Publicly, the Soviet Union continued to take the position that emigration was bad because every citizen had an obligation to build the Soviet state, and that departures would drain it of persons with intellect and talent. It claimed that Soviet Jews were well treated and would find living in Israel unsafe and a hardship. Nevertheless, Gur said, harassment of those seeking to emigrate, a hallmark of Soviet response for years, had almost ended. Even more promising, the Soviet Union had begun to work directly with the Jewish Agency instead of through European intermediaries in the USSR, and allowed it to open more offices, indicating an expected expansion of the aliyah. He said all signs were that the nascent movement would accelerate.

Following the briefing, Kornreich, Lender and Stein advanced plans UJA had been developing to declare an additional campaign to fund the aliyah. Even the formidable UJA Federation Annual Campaign, which raised $750 million a year to aid Jews in the United States, Israel and 34 other countries, could not cover the expected huge additional costs. They agreed to present a resolution at the UJA National Officers' meeting in New York City on Monday, January 15, 1990 to declare the campaign. Seeking the highest possible turnout, to achieve a broad endorsement and energize the officers, they not only issued a written Call to Meeting but also telephoned each officer twice to urge him or her to be present.

Simultaneously, they briefed UJA's "sister organizations," the Council of Jewish Federations, American Jewish Joint Distribution Committee and United Israel Appeal. CJF provided services to the 189 autonomous American Jewish federations that raised funds with UJA, developed consensuses among federations and bridged differences between the overseas-focused UJA and locally-oriented federations. JDC, which received funds mainly from the UJA-Federation Annual Campaign, met Jewish needs in Israel and 34 other countries, providing food, clothing, shelter, medical services, cash grants and resources such as prayer books that allowed Jews even in remote hamlets to survive, and to experience life as Jews. UIA was a tiny American corporation that monitored Jewish Agency expenditures.

Meanwhile, Gur's written reports were disseminated to UJA lay leaders, the volunteers among the major donors who ran the organization, as well as to UJA professionals, the paid fundraisers, image makers and financial managers who made it work on a day-to-day basis. As January 15 approached, journalists were telephoned to advise them that a new UJA campaign would be announced shortly.

Three days prior to the officers' meeting, Stein, who had defied personal danger to visit and encourage Soviet Jewish dissidents in the 1980s, telephoned Dinitz from a Southwestern airport for an update.

"Where is this going, in terms of the numbers who will come?" Stein asked.

"No one knows," said Dinitz. "But it will be bigger than we thought. Maybe bigger than we dreamed."

With the new fundraising campaign taking shape, this writer, then the United Jewish Appeal's National Director of Communications, believed that it would attract more attention with a colorful and meaningful name.

I consulted communications practitioners who knew UJA well, and others available pro bono, and asked them to help think up a name. After individual meetings, I convened them as a group. The insiders seemed too close to the picture and coalesced around, "Aliyah '90." But the word aliyah was not known to many American Jews, and the campaign sought a broad base of support. Besides, there was no certainty the campaign would be for only one year. Worse, the name did not seem inspirational. "Project Deliverance" was preferred by the outsiders. However, it lacked a Jewish dimension, might have become confused with a recent best selling book, *Deliverance*, and was not exciting. I pointed out that many demonstrators at Soviet Jewry rallies said the struggle reminded them of the Jewish quest for freedom from ancient Egypt and that they even thought of Soviet Jews at their Passover seders. But the outside experts rejected that. One laughed that that imagery was "truly ancient for the world of today." "Another labeled it "too Jewish" for the general media. A third opined that the Passover linkage would make the name "seasonal." Project Deliverance received the most votes.

Dissatisfied, I considered the names of previous UJA rescue campaigns (please see Chapters 6 and 7). Most included the word "Operation." Operation Magic Carpet airlifted 51,000 endangered Jews from Yemen to Israel in 1949 and 1950. Operation Ezra and Nehemiah saved 111,000 Jews in jeopardy in Iraq and brought them by sea and air to Israel in 1950 and 1951. Operation Moses rescued 10,000 imperiled Ethiopian Jews and secretly flew them to Israel in 1984 and 1985. "Operation" connoted historic achievement and carried cachet.

Moreover, I had visited the Soviet Union many times on behalf of Soviet Jewry and was astounded by the operational challenge. Covering 8.6 million square miles, and significantly icebound in winter, the Soviet Union had surprisingly poor transportation and communications systems for a superpower, and a bureaucracy with legendary incompetence. The immigrants would have to be marshaled from across the country to staging areas in only three cities by Israelis, who had no diplomatic authority or rights. They would have to be flown to Europe, since direct flights from the Soviet Union to Tel Aviv were prohibited by long-standing Soviet policy. In Europe they would have to live in transit camps and be provided with all their necessities for weeks, if not months. Then they would have to be flown to Israel and helped to begin their adjustments to their new life. Meanwhile their belongings would have to be transported by truck and railroad to Baltic ports; protected along the way from loss, theft, and the vagaries of local inspectors; shipped to European ports aboard Soviet freighters; reloaded onto Israeli or European freighters; transported to Haifa; and delivered to them even though their destinations in Israel were not known when they last saw their personal effects. If that was not an operation, I thought, nothing was.

Much more difficult was conceiving of an inspirational Jewish component for the name. Since a celebrity culture was developing in America, I considered personifying the campaign with the name of a preeminent Jewish personality. But no Israeli figure was widely enough known and free from warts or contemporary politics to offer such a name. Names like Albert Einstein and Jonas Salk were widely known but unrelated to the cause. Reaching to antiquity, Abraham, Isaac and Jacob, the Jewish Patriarchs, were towering personalities, but many Jews knew little about them and I rarely heard them cited outside of religious circles for their words or deeds. Practically speaking, Operation Abraham, Operation Isaac or Operation Jacob did not sound likely to galvanize the contemporary market. Operation Moses was attractive, but taken. Operation Joshua held sway with me for a long time. Joshua had led the Hebrew people into the Promised Land and this was known to many American Jews from John Derek's portrayal of him in the annually televised Cecil B. DeMille film, *The Ten Commandments*. But Operation Joshua, like Operation Aaron for Moses' brother, and Operation Miriam, for Moses' sister, other names I had considered, seemed to be second choices to Operation Moses.

Interestingly, my favorite from ancient times was Operation Nachshon, for Nachshon ben Aminadab. When Moses raised his rod and ordered the Hebrew People to advance into the swirling Red Sea, everyone hesitated except Nachshon. When Nachshon plunged into the water, Scripture tells us, the Sea split. Nachshon's demonstrable leap of faith seemed to have foreshadowed the actions of Soviet Jewish dissidents like Sharansky, who strived to uncover for their people the path to Israel.

Then I began to think, more and more, that the transcendent drama of what might unfold in my day could not be encapsulated in the symbol of any individual or group. I found myself always returning to the theme of the departure from Egypt. It was a story all American Jews knew. It contained the profound roots of every American Jew's thirst for freedom and every Jew's identification with those unable to live freely as Jews. I knew that most Jews, no matter how unconnected to Jewish life, celebrated Passover in some way. I examined hundreds of photographs of Soviet Jewry rallies and noted that the most common message on homemade placards was, "Let My People Go." Late one night, after poring over texts, I picked up the document probably read by more Jews than any other, the Passover Haggadah. There I came upon words known to nearly every American Jew: "In every generation, every Jew must look upon himself as if he personally went forth out of Egypt." The meaning of the departure was universal yet personal, ancient yet newsworthy. It spoke directly to my goal in seeking the best name: for everyone to intuitively understand and respond to it. The word that best encapsulated the idiom of Jewish freedom, in ancient times and what we hoped would unfold in our own was: Exodus. I concluded the campaign should be named, "Operation Exodus."

In the end, I relied upon my own instincts. The UJA leadership wholly agreed with me. "Operation Exodus" was formally adopted as the campaign's name on January 15. Campaigns for Soviet Jewry in other countries adopted it. Presidents and Prime Ministers, journalists and scholars began to use the term. Soon it became the name of the period in Jewish history as well.

Israeli guides love to tell the story of the group of tourists they had taken to the Golan Heights in the north, Beersheba in the south and the high points of Jerusalem in between, when they arrived at the Mann Auditorium in Tel Aviv to hear an Israel Philharmonic Orchestra concert.

"By the way," one tourist asked as they entered the concert hall. "Who is the Mann Auditorium named for? Thomas Mann, the German writer?"

"No," the guide said.

"Then for a famous Israeli composer?"

"No," the guide said. "It's named for Frederic Mann of Philadelphia."

"*Frederic* Mann?" the tourist asked quizzically. "What did he write?"

The guide answered, "A check."

Philanthropies often say they want thinkers and doers on their boards, people of ideas and energy, but mainly they want people who will give them money. Ideas are not the exclusive domain of boards, and energy is the responsibility of the day-to-day professionals. The United Jewish Appeal board was different only in how many extremely wealthy people it attracted, and how extensively each of them gave.

There were over a hundred of them, UJA National Officers they were called, from large cities and small towns, leaders in their local Jewish federations and used to giving $50,000 and more, sometimes a lot more, to the UJA Federation Annual Campaign. As at most philanthropies, they were an undiversified lot. The UJA National Officers were all white, mainly over 50 years old and educated.

Most were men, although one in five was a woman. They were primarily self-made multimillionaires, or people who had been given a strong head start by their parents' business achievements who then built the family company into a huge enterprise that their parents could never have imagined. Most held the title of National Vice Chairman although ten past National Chairmen were officers too. The President and Chairman of the UJA Women's Campaign, which raised more than 20 percent of the Annual Campaign; the Chairs of the Young Women's Leadership Cabinet and Young Men's Leadership Cabinet that provided outreach to prosperous Jewish activists in their 30s and 40s; a rabbi, not in the high-donation league; and a student representative of UJA campus campaigns rounded out the group.[1]

Some officers had opened retail stores and built them into sizeable chains. Alex Grass of Harrisburg, Pennsylvania, positioned himself well for what he foresaw would be a growth industry in low-cost pharmaceuticals, opening five discount drug stores in the Northeast in the early 1960s. When Medicare became law in 1965, Grass opened several more stores, expanding to 200 by 1970. He called his chain Rite Aid. He brought Rite Aid onto the New York Stock Exchange, expanded across the country and by 1983 as Founder, President, Chairman of the Board and main stockholder, led the conglomerate to $1 billion in sales. When be began two years of service as UJA National Chairman in 1984, Grass presided over a network of 2,300 Rite-Aid stores, more than any other drug chain in the country.

Martin F. Stein began his career as a pharmacist in his hometown of Milwaukee. He opened one pharmacy in 1965, another the next year, a third the next until he owned 20 pharmacies in 20 years. Then he sold the chain to found two others, Stein Optical Care and Stein Health Services. He capitalized on the increasingly lucrative optometric and health care markets as he expanded in the Midwest. When Stein served as UJA National Chairman from 1986 to 1988, his chains were sufficiently large that he left them mainly in the hands of his executives and devoted nearly all his waking hours to raising funds for UJA and trying to free Soviet Jews.

Norman Braman of Miami Beach founded and owned automobile dealerships. You couldn't drive for ten minutes between Palm Beach and Miami

---

1 The Annual Campaign was also known as the Regular Campaign. Women's Campaign was earlier known as Women's Division and later as Women's Philanthropy. Hereinafter, the terms "Annual Campaign" and "Women's Campaign" are used. UJA applied the word Chairman generically, including for women. The National Officers ran the campaigns; a Board of Trustees, composed of people of similar background, discharged corporate functions. The National Chairman was the unquestioned leader although the Trustees head (who had different titles in different periods) maintained final legal authority. There were nearly 100 Honorary National Vice Chairmen whose roles were less specified but who maintained some influence.

without seeing his name on a vehicle in front.

Others were part of families that founded chains and helped lead the corporation. Sylvia Hassenfeld of Providence was a Vice President of Hasbro, Inc., marketers of G. I. Joe, Mr. Potato Head, Playskool, Monopoly, Scrabble, Clue, Parcheesi and Yahtzee; her husband Merrill's father, Henry, was one of the Hassenfeld brothers for whom the retailer was named. Arlene Zimmerman (later Kaufman) of Nashville, with Raymond Zimmerman, her husband at the time, were vice president and president respectively and the largest stockholders in Service Merchandise, the anchor store in many American malls; Raymond and his parents had founded the company in 1960. Donald E. Hess and his wife Ronne of Birmingham, Alabama, both National Officers, opened and owned Parisian, a cluster of Southern department stores. Sandra Weiner of Houston, with her husband Leon whose father had sold pencils on a street corner during the Depression, owned Weiner's Department Stores, 120 outlets and one of the largest clothing chains in Texas. (Ms. Hassenfeld, Ms. Zimmerman, Ms. Hess and Ms. Weiner were independent financially and philanthropists before they married.)

Most officers were household names in their home towns, some nationally, especially from real estate achievements. Albert B. Ratner of Cleveland, President of Forest City Enterprises, led a $3 billion family enterprise with large commercial properties in 20 states. Melvin Simon, President of the Simon Property Group in Indianapolis, built shopping centers across the Midwest. Burton P. Resnick, Chairman of Jack Resnick and Sons, built skyscrapers in New York City. Michael M. Adler of Miami, President of the Adler Group founded by his father Samuel, built office buildings in South Florida.

Several were venture capitalists. Richard L. Pearlstone of Baltimore and Aspen, scion of the prominent Meyerhoff and Pearlstone families of Baltimore, was such a businessman. One of the youngest National Vice Chairmen, born weeks after Israel was established in 1948, he possessed one of the longest exposures to UJA. His grandfather, the late Joseph Meyerhoff, had been a UJA National Chairman, and Pearlstone grew up hearing about the UJA and its mission. Although Pearlstone was a leader at cultural institutions, he never forgot his grandfather saying he was barred from such boards because he was Jewish. Pearlstone felt honored to carry on his grandfather's mission to ease Jewish suffering. Some officers were already speaking of Pearlstone as a future National Chairman but for Richard there was only one issue at the moment and that was to get the Jews out of Russia.

The names of the businesses they founded, owned or controlled sounded

Mom and Pop but were much more. S. Kornreich and Sons was a family insurance company that sons Morton and Matthew built into one of the biggest specialty insurers in the country. Mort, who was National Chairman from May 1988 to May 1990, and Matt insured things like the ankles of the Kirov Ballet dancers, fleet-footed thoroughbreds, and the life of the underwater explorer Jacques Cousteau. (Whereas some officers seemed able to replicate money, the Kornreich brothers also seemed able to replicate themselves and had fun doing so: they were identical twins. In one knee-slapper, Matt closed a deal in Los Angeles with clients who thought he was Mort (or so legend has it), while Mort was at an important UJA meeting in New York. Matt was an imposter for Mort at a UJA tribute dinner for Mort, playfully telling the crowd he hadn't really done very much for UJA when the real Mort rose from the audience, grinning, to say, "You sure didn't. *I'm* me!").

Heidi and Martin Damsky of Damsky Paper Company in Birmingham, Alabama provided paper stock for publishers across the South. Vic Gelb's Victor Gelb, Inc. in Cleveland sold fibers to industry. Joseph Gurwin's Kings Point Industries on Long Island manufactured textiles for the United States government. Rani Garfinkle's Gemini Industries of Franklin Lakes, New Jersey, manufactured electronics. And Steve Grossman's Massachusetts Envelope Company in Boston (he was to become Democratic National Chairman) was one of the world's largest stationery suppliers.

Several were outstanding lawyers. Stanley M. Chesley of Cincinnati was a dynamic class-action plaintiff's lawyer who helped win the silicone breast implant, Bhopal gas leak and Agent Orange cases. Richard L. Wexler of Chicago was widely respected in real estate law. Bennett L. Aaron, a Philadelphia lawyer, and Norman H. Lipoff, a Miami advocate, were well known in tax and business law. Sanford Hollander of Newton, New Jersey, the best orator among the officers, maintained a lucrative general practice.

And of course, as Jews, there had to be doctors among them. Julius L. Levy, Jr. of New Orleans, who had cared for radiation sufferers at Chernobyl after the explosion in 1986, was a surgeon. Dr. Conrad Giles of Detroit was a pediatric ophthalmologist. Dr. Saul Singer of Hollywood, Florida was a cardiologist. And Dr. Charles M. Rosenberg of Atlanta was an oral surgeon.

Religiously, most were Conservative or Reform Jews. Although Stein wore a large black skullcap at National Officers' meetings and other UJA gatherings which, with his jet black hair and full beard made him appear rabbinical, he was traditional, not Orthodox, and only wanted to represent that the UJA cause had an underlying spiritual dimension. Most officers subscribed to the idea of "Jewish Peoplehood," an umbrella phrase that welcomed Jews from all branches and those from none at all. One officer, Anita Gray of Cleveland, the Young Women's Leadership Chair, was a Jew by choice. She was aghast at the murder of six million Jews in the Holocaust and converted to Judaism to symbolically carry forward the life of just one of them.

The UJA National Officers had in common a remarkable sense of Jewish identity, not borne of religiosity so much as a sense of Jewish vulnerability, Jewish destiny. They felt a degree of collective guilt from American Jewish inaction during the Holocaust, even though they personally had been too young to help. With the confidence that made them enormously successful in business, they were aggressive in their determination to make life better for Jews. And they did not care who or what stood in the way. Although H. Irwin Levy knew in the 1970s that Boca Raton and Palm Beach County in Florida were inhospitable to Jews, he built four Century Villages there, marketed them exquisitely, and made South Florida the central retirement area for northern Jews.

The UJA officers could leave their businesses in the hands of highly paid managers while they went off for two or three days of UJA meetings or visits to Jews in Israel and remote countries. They were major contributors to their local universities, museums and concert halls which now gladly welcomed them and their money. They were giving to the range of local general causes that provided food, clothing, shelter, job training, counseling and crisis intervention. They had led local Jewish federations, day schools, Jewish community centers and houses of worship.

Yet they had been almost too successful in their careers in a sense. They had their exotic travel, their country estates, their boats, their luxury automobiles, their help around the house, yet it was no longer enough. There was a hankering in their souls to do more. It was no longer enough just to *have*, to be rich and well connected and fussed over wherever they went. They wanted to achieve something transcendent, that would outlast them, that would live forever in the history books, that money alone couldn't buy. They got their chance with Operation Exodus.

Mort Kornreich called the meeting of UJA National Officers to order at 1:10 p.m. on January 15, 1990, noting that 62 officers were present, the highest turnout in years. Indeed, most officers had come from across the country, and some from business trips abroad, to participate. He said the officers would consider a momentous resolution, to declare a bold campaign to finance the emigration of Jews from the Soviet Union to Israel. He said the officers, and this generation, could do for overseas Jews what American Jews during the Holocaust did not: save large numbers of Jewish lives. He asked the officers' indulgence while he took routine Committee reports. The presenters were brief and each said he too was eager to address the issue at hand.

Marty Stein, who had brought UJA into the Soviet Jewry movement beginning with a clandestine trip to the Soviet Union in 1986, could not have been more joyful. He delivered the *D'var Torah,* a lesson from Scriptures traditionally given on religious occasions but also at UJA and federation meetings. His words resonated with every officer. "In a few weeks we will celebrate Passover, the holiday that strikes the common chord among all Jews," Stein said. "As the Haggadah points out, 'Were it not for the Lord our God we, and our children and our children's children, would still be slaves unto Pharaoh in Egypt.' The Pharaoh has changed, but our sisters and brothers are still in bondage, and it is for us to be God's hand and get them out."

Simcha Dinitz, Chairman of the Jewish Agency Executive and one of Israel's premier orators, followed. Dinitz said that the Jewish Agency, which had been much criticized for inefficiencies, had improved its operations and was ready for the challenges ahead. "And challenges there will be," he said, his voice bellowing from start to finish. "Already 1,843 Soviet Jews arrived in Israel this month and the number keeps growing. The Jewish Agency will be ready to bring them in, but you must raise the funds to make that possible." Dinitz was questioned about the Jewish Agency absorption centers, insulated villages where immigrants lived and received all services. He noted these had been favored in Israel's earlier years but were criticized more recently as socialistic, inefficient and fostering dependency. He said that absorption centers would be available for immigrants who preferred them, but if immigrants wished direct absorption they would be offered an apartment in a city or town and provided with a stipend and an option for additional help. The officers said they favored direct absorption; Dinitz said most immigrants did too.

Ella Tsveyer was next. UJA officers often had a guest speaker from abroad, but few were like Ella. In her late 30s, speaking good English with a Russian accent, she was married with two daughters, eight and five. In Russia, she said, she had three roles: homemaker, teacher, and emigration agitator. Tsveyer described how she had continued to advocate for emigration despite fear of reprisal, even when she was followed by the KGB. Then two KGB agents came to her door in the middle of the night. "You like your daughters, don't you, Ella?" one said. "You like that they come home every day from school, don't you, Ella? You be careful, Ella. Be careful what you do." Trembling, she kept her daughters home from school while pondering how to reconcile her commitment to the freedom movement with safety for her daughters. She resolved to tell them why she had to continue her activism. Fortunately for Ella their exit visas came the next day. There wasn't a sound in the room, not a sound.

After a long pause, Marvin Lender rose to speak. Lender was a deeply committed Jew, a consensus builder, modest and deferential. He had confidence in his judgments, but had not wanted to succeed Stein as National Chairman two years earlier for just such a reason: Stein's articulate passion made him a tough act to follow. Now he had to follow Stein, the orator Dinitz and a woman who had stood up to the KGB.

Lender began haltingly. "Marty sounded the right note," he said. "The Jewish Agency will have things in hand. And what Ella said is what this is all about. We must get the Jews out of Russia." His confidence rose as he moved to his display charts. "Our piece of it is to raise enough money. Here is where things stand." He pointed out that in addition to a few thousand Soviet Jews who had departed, several thousand had secured final approval to leave, and tens of thousands had obtained preliminary approval. He showed that more Soviet Jews were declaring their desire to leave every day, noted that they were not harassed for doing so, and reported that Soviet authorities were granting approvals more quickly. "The departures are the tip of the iceberg," he said.

Lender said that cost projections were rising with the trend. He pointed out that the Israeli government had increased its commitment to $3 billion in tax levies, mainly for absorption, and that Keren Hayesod, the UJA counterpart in 30 other Diaspora countries, would likely set a $180 million goal.

Then he focused on the UJA Federation Campaign. "Two weeks ago we thought we would have to raise $350 million," he said. "Now we know we must obtain at least $400 million." He laid out the UJA Campaign Plan including major gifts events, trips to the Soviet Union and Israel to motivate major gifts donors to give maximally, a news media blitz, field visits by UJA leaders to help federations enhance local giving, speaking tours by dissidents like Tsveyer, and ready to use and locally-adaptable marketing materials. He emphasized that leaders, read that officers, must give to their capacity and persuade others to do the same.

Lender asked that he, Kornreich and Stein be authorized to determine the Campaign's final parameters later in the week when fuller data would be available. In their own businesses, these officers would never approve a major policy initiative based on uncertain data and delegate the decision to others, but they had been active in the Soviet Jewry movement for years, trusted the UJA senior leadership, and were favorably disposed. Nevertheless, some needed more information.

One officer asked Lender how he could rely on trends given that the Soviet Union was so unpredictable. "Anything can happen," Lender answered, "but we must proceed on what we know. The data indicate this will be a huge emigration." Some were eager for more details about major gifts events and said they would be happy to participate in them. A few asked about the capability of the Jewish Agency to usher so many Jews out of the Soviet Union, care for them in Europe, bring them to Israel and begin their absorption. Lender and Dinitz assured them the Jewish Agency would be able to do so.

Then one officer argued UJA should not declare a goal it could not achieve but should declare a much smaller goal. The question touched a raw nerve that had deeply perturbed UJA planners. UJA and federations had just concluded Passage to Freedom, a campaign to raise $75 million over nine months in 1989 to bring Soviet Jews to the United States, that raised only $49 million. Lender had been the Passage to Freedom Chairman and he himself judged it a failure. Now, UJA would try to raise more than eight times as much as it had, in the same basic time frame, from the same people. If UJA failed to raised a substantial sum in the early weeks an aura of failure could develop and become a self-fulfilling prophecy. The failure of two campaigns in a row would damage UJA-Federation credibility for future campaigns. Stein was on his way to the podium before the officer finished, and was pounding it with his passionate answer before he was recognized:

> We are at the opening moment of a great chapter in Jewish history. For thousands of years Jews had no place to escape to and now we have our own country. This is the glorious ingathering of the Jewish People in our time. We cannot be weak kneed. What are we going to say to those we don't get out? That we tried to raise *less* than what was needed to help them escape from communist tyranny? That we decided seven out of eight of them could rot in Russia? Would you want to be there waiting because nobody tried to raise the needed money? Neither would I.
>
> I am *against* the $400 million goal -- because I think it is *too low*. We should have *a billion dollar goal*. That's right, a billion dollars. I only *hope* that's what is needed. It makes no difference what it costs; we have to raise it. We can raise a billion dollars if we have to.

The pause that followed was pregnant, almost palpable; it hung in the air for about ten seconds. "Marvin," Joel Tauber of Detroit, said softly, "I'd like to read the resolution that Mort Kornreich alluded to and move for a vote."

Tauber read the resolution:

> With deep resolve and great enthusiasm about the historic aliyah of Soviet Jewry, and with a commitment to provide major financial support for their absorption in Israel, the Officers of the United Jewish Appeal call for an extraordinary UJA fundraising campaign. The campaign will begin immediately with individual consultations with major contributors, to be followed by a nationwide effort, to be known as Operation Exodus, which will coincide with Passover.
>
> UJA's federation partners will be requested to accept a commitment for their appropriate share of the overall dollar goal, which will be established by UJA in consultation with the Jewish Agency. The goal will be based on the best estimates of the dollar needs, together with the best assessment of UJA's fundraising potential.
>
> The dollar goal, specific timing, strategy, length of payout, etc., would be determined by February 6, 1990 by UJA's National Chairman, Chairman of the Board and incoming National Chairman.
>
> The UJA Officers by this action express their full solidarity with the people of Israel and their brothers and sisters in the Soviet Union, who will most certainly make a major contribution to building the State of Israel now and in the future.

The resolution passed unanimously by emphatic voice vote and Kornreich adjourned the meeting. Paragraphs one, two and four were useful, but paragraph three contained the real message. CJF and the federations were not on board. UJA planned to give them until their quarterly convention in Miami on February 6 to approve the campaign that UJA envisioned. This, even though no federation thought UJA's goal was feasible. Besides, nearly all the federations believed, even if the goal was tenable, achieving it would decimate the Annual Campaign on which local programs, funded mainly by the same donors, depended. The third paragraph recognized that UJA and federations were poles apart on every important decision about the proposed campaign. And it foreshadowed that there would be plenty of behind-the-scenes hardball politics between UJA and CJF, and UJA and federations, in the three weeks ahead. In any event, UJA reasoned, February 6 was too long to wait given the rising emigration rate. The clause, "The campaign will begin immediately with individual consultations," meant that UJA would begin to raise funds from the Annual Campaign's main prospects regardless of what the federations thought. In fact, UJA had already begun to solicit them, even though the battle with CJF and federations over goals, strategies and tactics had barely begun.

Marvin Lender was up before dawn the next day, thinking of his planned daylong meeting with his key advisers to determine the campaign goal. There was a lot to consider. He was disquieted by the fundamental uncertainties about how many Jews might be permitted to emigrate, over how many months and at what cost. He pondered whether the Jewish Agency, which had implemented massive waves of immigration in earlier decades but was perpetually perceived as inefficient, could lead the complex operation. He was aware that the goal could easily be exposed as foolishly high if the immigration peremptorily ended, or disappointingly low if it exceeded expectations.

Lender telephoned Mendel Kaplan in Israel, seven hours ahead on the clock, and reached him at the Jewish Agency. Kaplan was a South African who had made himself rich in the steel business, a humanitarian who opposed his country's policy of apartheid from within. Kaplan was an ardent Zionist who lived half of each year in Israel. As Chairman of the Jewish Agency's Board of Governors Kaplan, the organization's highest trustee, brought a strong business sense to the Agency's leadership. He and Simcha Dinitz, its chief professional, clashed bitterly, as would any two people used to being number one, but together they advanced the organization's efficiency and effectiveness.

"What are the numbers now?" Lender asked. Kaplan answered that nearly 300,000 Soviet Jews had filed requests to emigrate, that perhaps 200,000 might leave in the course of three years, and that costs could reach $3.6 billion. Kaplan said that both Shamir and Peres had provided assurances that Israel would commit $3 billion for absorption and that Keren Hayesod was confident its $180 million goal would be adopted. "The campaign leadership in Keren Hayesod countries will be voting on their shares of the goal within days," Kaplan said. "Those discussions are taking place in French, Spanish, Portuguese, Belgian, Italian, Danish and the like, but their substance is the same as yours."

"Can they raise it?" Lender asked.

"They have less financial resources than the Americans, and it is more difficult because of geography and communications to raise funds in some of the countries," Kaplan answered. "But they know what is at stake and are equally dedicated to helping the Soviet Jews as Americans are. They believe, and I believe, they can do it. The Jewish Agency needs UJA to raise $420 million as a necessary pillar of the package."

Then Lender asked about the Jewish Agency's ability to mobilize thousands of Jews from across the Soviet Union to disembarkation points, meet their needs and effect their departures. He wanted to know if it could keep pace with rising demand. He asked about management of the transit camps in Europe, the shipping of personal belongings, and the direct absorption initiative. He had been over this again and again with Kaplan in recent days and knew the answers, but wanted to hear them again for his reassurance and comfort. He had enormous confidence in Kaplan's leadership. But he wanted him to know, and to make it known to everyone in the Jewish Agency system, that UJA expected them to perform with excellence, every day and for months on end. Because he was convinced American Jews would give as they never gave before.

A few hours later, Lender convened the Committee on the Special Campaign for Soviet Jewry in his office at UJA Headquarters at 99 Park Avenue in Manhattan. The group would soon be reconstituted as his Campaign Executive Committee, or kitchen cabinet, but that day they were gathered to set the campaign parameters in advance of the showdown with CJF on February 6. The members were: Lender, as National Chairman-Elect and Operation Exodus Chairman; Kornreich, the National Chairman; Stein, the Chairman of the Board; Tauber, whose leadership at both CJF and UJA placed him in a crucial position to win federation support; Pearlstone, a crucial link to the increasingly prosperous but under-giving Jewish baby boom generation that had come of age; David B. Hermelin, a gregarious Detroit businessman, influential with major donors; Alan L. Shulman, an investor from West Palm Beach and a skilled gifts solicitor; Alan R. Crawford, a Milwaukee real estate investor who was new to UJA leadership; and Arlene Zimmerman, who was influential with senior level donors.

Although they were all ferociously independent and used to relying upon themselves and their own instincts, Lender began to wield them into a harmonious group. Harold Cohen, a UJA Assistant Vice President and a veteran of the Denver and Hartford federation campaigns, remembered the meeting. "The numbers were staggering," he recalled. "As the aliyah projections soared, the costs grew and so did the gap between what the UJA and federations thought could be raised. But the Committee, and all the officers, had a lot of confidence in Lender. He had command of the facts. He knew the situation in Russia and Israel, and fundraising in the United States. He had a quiet, deliberative approach but also a vision of what could be accomplished. They could see he did his homework and when he said what was needed, and could be raised, they agreed. His leadership was built from the ground up."

Cohen's minutes showed there was plenty of discussion, but mainly on how to achieve federation support; Committee members never wavered in their commitment to fund the best-case scenario. "The Committee endorses the $420-million challenge based on a projection that 200,000 Soviet Jews would be able to emigrate to Israel in three years," Cohen wrote. "There can be a three-year payout if necessary, but it must be a one-year raise."

The group, like UJA in general, had little patience for the CJF process of meticulous, painstaking consultations. While UJA agreed not to press federations yet for a full-fledged campaign, UJA would intensify its prospecting for senior level gifts, and announce the campaign publicly. In awareness of the need for the Annual Campaign to maintain its level of funding to JDC, UJA would urge federations not to reduce their Annual Campaign allocations to UJA.

"It was agreed that two key components must be accomplished if Operation Exodus is to succeed," Cohen's minutes concluded:

• "Successful solicitation of mega-donors; and

• A dramatic public relations campaign to achieve wide involvement of the Jewish community in Operation Exodus."

UJA was to achieve both.

The UJA called a news conference for 10 a.m. on January 19 in New York, presided over by Lender with Kornreich, Stein, Kaplan and Dinitz present. In front of a battery of cameras, microphones and journalists from the American news media, the Israeli news media based in the United States, and the American Jewish press, and amidst UJA video news releases and printed materials documenting and personalizing the quest of Soviet Jews to emigrate, Lender announced the establishment of the Operation Exodus Campaign.

Monday, January 15 to Friday, January 19: it had been quite a week for the leaders of the UJA. And yet the whole challenge was in front of them.

Daunting as it was to raise the unheard of sum, the immediate challenge was not the fundraising or the building of public awareness, both of which were underway, but to have the team engaged, all the players on board, the sales force ready to sell. That meant the 189 local Jewish federations that were committed to the cause but had other things on their minds. In announcing the Campaign publicly as $420 million, UJA placed itself on a collision course with federations. UJA's first challenge was the selling of the Campaign -- to the local fundraisers.

The relationship of UJA to federations was an odd one. UJA had the national name recognition and a professional staff second to none that had consistently raised funds no one had thought possible. Its Board of Trustees, National Officers and events chairs were some of the most successful business people in America. UJA could assemble the wealthiest Jews in the country, persuade them to go to Israel in wartime or to places like Ukraine to visit needy Jews in the bitter winter, and solicit them there for huge donations, but it needed the reach into the local communities that only the federations could provide. UJA always had moral sway, representing "those in need around the globe you can't see." Even when federations thought the case for overseas needs was overstated and knew of competing needs down the street from the federation that might have to be sacrificed to help Jews abroad, they could not stand up to the idiom of Jewish vulnerability in distant lands that burned unease into every Jewish soul. At least not since the Holocaust they couldn't.

But federations were more than UJA's local fundraising partners; they were service funders and providers. They bore legal, moral and often operational responsibilities for local programs. Their trustees knew the heads of the local agencies personally, lived near them, played golf with them, sent their children to the same schools. Federation trustees lived where the needs existed, in cities like Pittsburgh, Cleveland and Miami; no one lived in a city named UJA. The pressure on federations to maintain local funding levels was enormous.

Every year each federation, individually, negotiated with UJA how to divide the results of the Annual Campaign, which the federations collected. These sessions were often contentious, as federations argued vociferously to retain a greater share and UJA maintained overseas Jews needed the funds more. In the 1980s, the Annual Campaign was raising a total of $750 million a year, with 19 federations raising at least $8 million each, including the Big Daddy of them all, UJA-Federation of New York, which raised over $110 million a year.[2] That was enough to astound every other fundraiser in the country, but not those at UJA and federations. A lot of people depended on those campaigns and, on the eve of 1990, with needs at home and abroad growing faster than the Annual Campaign, federations were allocating less than half to UJA. That was the state of the relationship when federation leaders awoke one day in January 1990 and found that UJA declared a $420 million *additional* campaign — for overseas needs.

Federation chief executive officers, usually called executive directors, were the men (and most of them were men) in the middle. While UJA was getting

2 The 19 were: UJA-Federation of New York, Jewish Federation of Metropolitan Chicago, Jewish Federation Council of Greater Los Angeles, Jewish Community Federation of Cleveland, Jewish Federation of Metropolitan Detroit, The Associated: Jewish Community Federation of Baltimore, Combined Jewish Philanthropies of Greater Boston, Greater Miami Jewish Federation, Federation of Jewish Agencies of Greater Philadelphia, Jewish Federation of Palm Beach, Atlanta Jewish Federation, UJA Federation of Greater Washington, United Jewish Federation of MetroWest (N.J.), United Jewish Federation of Greater Pittsburgh, Jewish Federation of South Palm Beach, United Jewish Community of Bergen

worked up, and getting ready to work everyone else up, about the challenges and opportunities of Operation Exodus, the executive directors had many issues to ponder. Many of their donors had not yet recovered from the steep stock market decline of two years earlier, which contributed to flat (non-growth) campaigns. Their donor base had been alienated by Israel in the "Who is a Jew" controversy, and by Israel's inability to end the Intifada in a way responsive to their constituents' (mainly liberal) sensitivities. The bigger the federation the more money it raised but that didn't help because the greater was the local need. And then there was political pressure from all sides. On any given day, the head of the local nursing home, day school, family services center or vocational training institute could come into the executive director's office and demonstrate how many more people would be helped, or additional services provided, with more funds. Federation trustees even came in sometimes on their favorite local agency's behalf. Executive directors were paid professionals and their jobs depended on satisfying such people. When they explained about competing needs they were told, "Raise more money." Now, UJA was imposing a whole new demand that seemed impossible to meet.

The executive directors were typecast by Israelis as a parochial lot, but that was an unfair stereotype. While there was institutional conflict between UJA and federations, most executive directors possessed global understanding. For example, all the "Top 19" federation executive directors had visited Israel often, met with Jewish Agency, JDC and government officials and inspected campaign-funded programs there. Many had been to the Soviet Union where they met clandestinely with dissidents, risking danger to themselves and leaving with indelible accounts of fear and hope. Leaders such as Dr. Steven Nasatir of Metropolitan Chicago, Dr. Howard Rieger of Greater Pittsburgh, Stephen Hoffman of Cleveland, Robert Aronson of Metropolitan Detroit, Jacob Solomon of Greater Miami, Barry Shrage of Greater Boston, Stephen Solender of New York and Jeffrey Klein of Palm Beach intimately knew local needs but were among the most articulate local advocates of overseas needs. They were Zionists as well as localists who usually found ways to balance competing demands. Now, with a pending $420 million imposition, there

---

County (N.J.), Jewish Federation of St. Louis, Minneapolis Federation for Jewish Service; and Jewish Community Federation of San Francisco, Marin County and the Peninsula. There were 189 federations at the time of the inception of Operation Exodus.

In addition to the UJA Federation Campaigns, there were UJA-only campaigns in 400 cities and towns too small to need or sustain a federation. These "non-federated" or "independent" campaigns consisted of volunteers who raised funds, usually before Rosh Hashanah, Chanukah and Passover and in crises, often as gatherings in the local UJA Campaign Chairman's home. Collectively, they contributed $20-million annually, as much as a well-organized big city campaign like Detroit. Whereas federations collected all gifts and remitted a share, usually 45 to 50 percent, to UJA, the smaller communities remitted all funds to UJA.

seemed no way out.

The executive directors felt alone in January 1990. Ostensibly they were represented by both UJA and CJF but they were unable to turn to either for help in their dilemma. UJA had already declared a goal they might be forced to accept, and had begun one of its media blitzes to enlist public support, without heeding their complaints that the goal was unrealistic. They were exasperated by CJF's consensus building that seemed endless and that resulted in bland resolutions that failed to ignite anyone or raise a dime. Many in the Top 19 charged that CJF catered to middle-sized federations, which in turn felt CJF favored the Top 19, and the small federations felt left out entirely. The old joke, "Put three Jews in a room and you'll get four opinions," always seemed true. They felt alienated from UJA and CJF and their contradictory ways of doing business. The executive directors joked among themselves:

"This is UJA: ready... fire... aim."

"This is CJF: ready... aim... aim... aim... aim.........."

UJA had just declared a $420 million campaign, called a big news conference and got it into the newspapers and onto the air waves, and CJF was just beginning its consultations. It had happened again. Yet there was no doubt about it: the aliyah was underway and Soviet Jews were already arriving in Israel in spine-tingling numbers.

Hearing complaints from federations across the board about UJA aggressiveness, CJF was furious. Joel Tauber, who was UJA's main liaison with CJF, recalled:

> CJF felt we had gone too far, that the system wasn't capable of raising so much more money.... I was riding in a car with one CJF leader who had been my friend for years, and he was never as mad at me as he was then. He warned that pushing for a goal of more than $225 to $250 million was untenable. He was concerned that the federations would be exposed as having failed to achieve a publicly-stated goal. The CJF officers supported that view, which only made matters more tense. CJF took the attitude to UJA about a goal higher than $225 to $250 million, 'If you declare a goal above that you're on your own, you're flying on your own.'

Tauber persuaded CJF to allow UJA to make its pitch to the federations directly. With that green light, the UJA Soviet Jewry committee − Lender, Tauber, Kornreich, Stein, Pearlstone, Hermelin, Shulman, Crawford and Zimmerman − fanned out across the country. Each member carried a list of federations including collectively the Top 19 and as many medium sized federations as they could visit, in cities like Akron, Memphis, and Omaha. Other UJA officers assisted in their home towns and otherwise broadened the effort. At each federation, the UJA leaders presented the local leaders with the latest projections of immigration rates and costs and answered questions. Each federation was encouraged, then urged, then expected to support Operation Exodus and to guarantee the sum UJA decided represented its proportional share of the national goal. When a federation pleaded it could not raise such a sum, UJA said, "Borrow it."

The meetings took place in small groups, where matters could be explored and frustrations vented — and more easily controlled by UJA than plenary meetings. They were often heated. At some, UJA leaders telephoned Jewish Agency officials in Moscow and Israel who verified projections and emphasized the indispensability of the Campaign. Federation leaders were deeply concerned that there were no indications that the goals UJA urged them to embrace could be achieved. They said that even if they could be reached, the funds would be at the expense of the Annual Campaign which would wreak havoc on local agencies. They let UJA leaders know that, while news from the Soviet Union made them heady too, it was a lot easier to make promises to people in Israel and the Soviet Union from UJA headquarters in New York than to face local agency heads, and local Jews in need, and tell them their funding might be sharply reduced. No one opposed Operation Exodus, but few believed its goals were attainable.

Meanwhile, leaders in Philadelphia, Boston, Baltimore, New York and Washington, where Soviet immigrants had been arriving in need of language instruction, job training, housing, food and medical services, argued that federations with few new immigrants should help fund domestic resettlement. They maintained this was a national issue and not only the responsibility of port of entry cities. Communities with few new immigrants were reluctant to take on a new domestic obligation while beginning a daunting overseas campaign. Federations did not fight only with UJA but among themselves. As UJA pummeled them for Operation Exodus, CJF President Mandell Berman, Vice President Charles H. Goodman and Executive Vice President Martin S. Kraar sought to knit together a consensus to meet domestic costs.

One part of the UJA strategy to win federation support was an ambitious news media program that began with the well-attended January 19 news conference. The campaign announcement generated favorable coverage in *The New York Times, Washington Post* and other newspapers present and they transmitted their articles to newspapers and radio and television stations in their syndicates, which broadened placements. The *Associated Press* coverage of the news conference alone was published in several hundred newspapers. An article by the Jewish Telegraphic Agency was distributed to and published by its 151 member American Jewish newspapers which, according to the American Jewish Press Association, reached into 75 percent of American Jewish homes. UJA followed with news articles, feature stories, photographs, charts, statistics and other publishable materials dispatched directly to news organizations. Over the next several days, it secured local newspaper, radio and television interviews of Marvin Lender, architect of the dream. The radio interviews were live by telephone and those on television were by satellite. UJA's action to obtain local interviews without a green light from federations was an unconventional initiative to go over their heads to stimulate support in their communities. UJA was even able to obtain announcement of the campaign in news dispatches on international relations from Moscow and Jerusalem. Throughout, the media portrayed the Campaign as challenging and historic. The news media program gave the incipient Operation Exodus Campaign local visibility, making it a main topic of discussion and adding pressure onto those who would convene in Miami on February 6.

Meanwhile, the UJA-federation closed door debates continued and federation leaders began to do a number on themselves. Despite their realistic concerns, they felt a strong inner impulse to buy into Operation Exodus in a big way. Most had been active in the Soviet Jewry movement, some agitating since the 1970s to force the Soviet government to open the gates. Deep down they wanted to redeem their own longstanding commitment to Soviet Jews by maximizing the Campaign. They were proud that they had helped bring the Soviet Jews to the threshold of aliyah and they would not be able to face themselves if they fell short.

Simultaneously, Lender, Tauber, Pearlstone and the others began to persuade CJF that its concerns must be put aside, that a goal high enough to fund the full aliyah must be established. And many local agency heads became more enthralled by the prospect of the aliyah, for which they too had worked, than they were fearful of budget cuts; they started to let federations know the aliyah was the urgent priority.

Never delicate, UJA enlisted the Prime Minister of Israel to deliver the message directly to major donors with influence in their communities. On February 5 Israeli Prime Minister Yitzhak Shamir met with 110 major contributors at the Regency Hotel in New York to discuss the importance of Operation Exodus. This was the same Yitzhak Shamir who, six years earlier, had met with some of the same people under UJA auspices and told them Israel needed $60 million for a clandestine rescue of Ethiopian Jews, Operation Moses. The same Yitzhak Shamir who was then asked, "How can we raise so much money in secret?" and answered, "As you say in English, 'That's your problem'." Now UJA brought Shamir in to pump for a $420 million campaign.

The room was filled again for Shamir with Andrew Tisch, President of Bulova Watch Corporation whose family owned the Regency, seated next to fellow New Yorkers Peter May, whose Triangle Industries was the world's largest packaging company, and Lewis Rudin, whose Rudin Management Company owned Manhattan skyscrapers. Also present were Jane Sherman, a Michigan philanthropist whose father Max Fisher was an oil industrialist; Michael Adler, the Miami builder; and retired Air Force General Jerome Waldor of South Orange, New Jersey. The nonagenarian William Rosenwald of New York, one of the three signers of the agreement that had founded UJA in 1939 and a son of one of the four original investors in Sears Roebuck, was blind and infirm but present along with his daughter, the philanthropist Elizabeth Varet. So were most living past UJA National Chairmen: Irwin Field of Los Angeles, Herschel Blumberg of Washington, D.C., Robert E. Loup of Denver, Alex Grass, Marty Stein and Mort Kornreich. Senior professionals included Stanley Horowitz, Vice Presidents Morris Sherman and Raphael Rothstein, Assistant Vice Presidents Marshall Jacobson and Harold Cohen, Regional Operations Director Shimon Pepper and this writer who had scripted the program.

The luncheon had been called for noon but Shamir was an hour late. Horowitz expressed dismay that some participants might have to leave soon for business appointments. Finally Shamir arrived, at 1:10 p.m., with a party of thirteen, including his Soviet Jewry expert Shmuel Shinhar who had participated in an urgent meeting with UJA leaders in Lender's New York apartment weeks earlier. That was just after the PLO threatened to blow up European airplanes ferrying Soviet Jews bound for Israel so as to end the aliyah peremptorily, and before the U.S. warned that better not happen. That crisis served as an unintended backdrop to the UJA pressure on federations, showing that even if the Soviet Union wanted to open the gates wider they could be forced shut and that time was of the essence. As the UJA leaders greeted Shamir outside the room, Shinhar informed me that Shamir was hungry and wanted to eat before speaking.

The Prime Minister was announced and the guests rose with a loud round of applause as he entered and was escorted to his seat at the round table in front of the podium. He finished his salad quickly, then picked at the cold poached salmon. He took two forksful, seemed deep in thought, then said to this writer, who was nearby, "Let's get started. They all have to hear this."

Earlier, a small step had been placed behind the podium so the diminutive Prime Minister would convey a taller presence. Lender introduced him, standing behind the step, leaning forward into the microphone. But the Prime Minister did not need anything to give his voice volume or his words greater clarity.

"This is what it has been all about: all the demonstrations, all the pressure, all the diplomacy, over all the years," Shamir said, the side of his fist tapping on the lectern with each phrase. "We in Israel will still bear the main share of the costs, but you must do your share." Then, sounding the theme UJA had asked Harry Hurwitz, the Prime Minister's aide, to have Shamir include -- that Operation Exodus must be fully funded without reductions in other programs -- the Prime Minister declared:

> I know there are thousands of Jews you help already. You should not give them less than you do now. But Operation Exodus must be your priority. Four hundred and twenty million dollars is not a lot of money when Jewish lives are at stake.... No one knows when the gates will close. We must get them all out as soon as possible.

The showdown in Miami the next day was not the battle UJA had feared back on January 15 and had worked feverishly to avoid. It was not even contentious. It was more like the signing, in a hopeful spirit, of a prenuptial agreement whose details had been vetted previously by the parties. Stein set the tone by recalling his experiences during his clandestine visit to the Soviet Union in 1986 and said, "The Soviet Jewry movement has come very far but the aliyah is at its inception." Lender described fundraising events that UJA planned and exhorted federations to participate in them. Pearlstone reported on Shamir's charge at the UJA reception the previous day. Tauber spoke of the growing unity of federations, UJA and CJF behind the Campaign, careful to avoid mention of the eyeball to eyeball sessions that took place to bring it about.

For those who were not present for Shamir's call to action the previous day, or who as liberals did not like Shamir anyway, Kornreich brought a letter from former Prime Minister Shimon Peres, the Labor Party leader. In the letter, addressed, "Dear Morton," and dated and faxed the previous day, the UJA influence was again unmistakable. Peres asserted:

> I understand that the Council of Jewish Federations is meeting on February 6th. I understand there may be demands to satisfy local needs as for resettling Soviet Jews in America and other purposes. I would like you to impress on all involved the importance of taking the proper

decision to devote the resources necessary for the immigration and absorption of Russian *olim* [immigrants] in Israel. Moreover, these funds should not come from deductions from funds that would otherwise flow to the Jewish Agency for vital programs in Israel, which are already under severe strain.

With both Shamir and Peres hewing to its message, the UJA had all the rabbis it needed, except two: the Chief Rabbis of Israel. That came also on February 5 in this stunning fax from UJA's Director General in Israel, former Ambassador Naphtali Lavie:

The Chief Rabbis this morning approved the operation of flights on Shabbat in order to rescue as many Jews as possible. The intensity of the dangers to the Jewish community in Russia alarmed them to make this announcement. The whole aliyah movement is now turning into a rescue operation and a matter of *pikuach nefesh*.[3]

Lavie added:

The aliyah mood in the country is growing all the time. The people across Israel are all very excited, in very great anticipation.

On February 6 in Miami, there was humility at the magnitude of the goals, but no dissent as a four page resolution was unanimously approved. UJA won unqualified endorsement of everything it wanted for Operation Exodus, including from CJF. The resolution declared:

CJF calls on Federations to support enthusiastically the United Jewish Appeal's $420-million goal. The need is compelling and such support is consistent with the partnership between the UJA and Federations for over one-half century. This historic opportunity to bring Soviet Jews to freedom will also significantly build the State of Israel.

But UJA knew that pledges couldn't buy anything: only payments could. UJA persuaded federations to adopt an aggressive program of collections and remissions to UJA that would be pursued until UJA received every cent it demanded:

---

3 "Saving of souls," a Jewish obligation that supersedes virtually all other Jewish laws.

The federations are encouraged to transmit their agreed upon share of the UJA goal on a timely basis to signal to the people of Israel that we are indeed their true partners in this historic undertaking and that there will be no discrepancy between goal and achievement.

In line with the UJA position, the federations agreed that if their fundraising fell short they would borrow to meet their UJA-determined goals.[4]

And UJA induced CJF to call upon federations to halt the steady erosion of their Annual Campaign income for Israel:

In recognition of the even more stringent budget requirements that such steps will create, CJF and UJA join together in urging that federations maintain at least the present proportion of the proceeds of their Regular Campaigns which are allocated to the UJA.

The UJA victory was so complete that its momentum helped federations achieve agreement on a thorny domestic issue that had divided them for decades: whether one federation is responsible for Jews in another American community. Indeed, they declared that they were. The assembly demonstrated that by approving a formula in which every federation would share in the costs of Soviet Jews coming to the United States, expected to be 40,000 a year. UJA, the bull in the china shop, had become the catalyst for peace in the federations' home. Ready, fire, aim? Somehow, it turned out, they aimed at the right time and struck every target.

People often asked, "How did UJA leaders always raise so much money so fast?" The way they sold the Campaign to local fundraisers showed how. They had a clear vision and pursued it unflinchingly. They had a sound strategy and pursued it aggressively. They had access and did not hesitate to use it. They deployed their resources wisely. They created media buzz but focused on the point of sale. They were willing to take bold risks, even having no back up plan. They never doubted their ability to succeed. They believed in themselves.

---

4 Indeed, many of the best federations, including New York, Chicago and San Francisco, did borrow to remit funds quickly and according to the goals.

They knew their customers and what motivated them. Those from across the country who convened in Miami were in Jewish life because they wanted to help Jews—and UJA leaders showed them this was their opportunity of a lifetime. UJA helped them look deeply into their own hearts and to recognize what they themselves most desired was the greatest success possible for the Soviet Jews; this made the Campaign only a mechanism and UJA an instrument of their own desire. UJA leaders knew that every participant had dreamed of waking up one morning and reading the headlines in the newspapers that the gates were opening and that they would want to be counted on when that day came. UJA reminded them that this was their cause also, and that they wanted to be on the right side of history. In the end, no one could stand up to UJA's message of urgency. And soon, no one wanted to.

Then, too, what moved the issue to happy resolution was the promise of the immigrants themselves. Prisoners of Zion, whose photographs had been held aloft on placards at rallies, were getting out, and with them brilliant physicians, talented musicians, old widows, small children and young families with smiles of hope and tears of joy. Half a world away, on the same day that the wave of optimism buoyed federations, three more planes, filled with 611 previously oppressed Soviet Jews, arrived in Israel. And hundreds of thousands were moving through the Soviet emigration bureaucracy to line up behind them.

CHAPTER TWO
Breakfast of Champions

I have been trying to decide what to give. No one solicited
me for a specific sum. How much is enough? What is the
right sum? What says what I feel in my heart? I thought, six
million perished. I wanted to give something that responded
to that, that said something about them, to them, that
honored them, even each of them. Then I thought, move it
up to $6 million.

Leslie Wexner, Founder, President and Chairman of the Board, The Limited,
Inc., pledging at the opening of Operation Exodus, February 28, 1990.

Marvin Lender should have been pleased with himself but he wasn't.
He should have been pleased because he had brought the lumbering
United Jewish Appeal — Federation system along to where it agreed to
declare his goal even though it was far more than federations thought could be
raised. He wasn't pleased because he had not yet raised a penny for Operation
Exodus. Worse, he had heard grumblings, including from insiders, that UJA
might be past its prime, that the organization that raised millions to save
Holocaust survivors, help establish Israel and sustain the Jewish State during
five wars in four decades was no longer up to the challenge. And he was in the
fundraising off season, the months after Rosh Hashanah donations, Chanukah
gifts and the tax year cutoff when most contributions to Jewish causes were
given. But amid signs that the glass was nearly empty, Lender saw it as more
than half full. Even as he was trying to bring the local fundraisers on board he
was pursuing a plan to go for broke in fundraising.[1]

---

1 "Breakfast of Champions" is a registered trademark of General Mills, Inc., used in conjunction with a cereal product. It is also the
title of a book by Kurt Vonnegut. In this book, "Breakfast of Champions" reports on and refers to an historical fact, an important
United Jewish Appeal fundraising event named Breakfast of Champions, which was held on February 28, 1990. Its use herein is not
intended to indicate any association with General Mills, its product or Mr. Vonnegut.

Marvin Lender was all passion, passion for the cause of Jews, passion for something all his own.

Marvin was the son of Rose Lender and Harry Lender, a penniless baker from Lublin, Poland who came to the United States in 1927 and took a job at a bagel bakery in Passaic, New Jersey. Harry worked day and night making bagels for Jewish immigrants and, by 1929, saved $600. Then someone told him that a small, 800 square feet, bakery was for sale in New Haven, Connecticut. This was nearly twenty years before *Gentleman's Agreement* by Laura Hobson exposed institutionalized anti-Semitism in Connecticut. There were few Jews in New Haven, and that was no place for a Jewish greenhorn to stand behind the counter of a bakery and sell bagels. Nevertheless, Harry visited all the local bakery retailers and told them he would buy the bakery, make only bagels, and sell to them wholesale if they agreed in advance to buy his product. They would obtain product line variety and, more importantly, ensure that a retail competitor would not buy the bakery. They agreed. Harry had an idea in his head. He would begin selling bagels to non-Jews. He moved to a cold-water flat and set up shop.

By 1934 the business outgrew the tiny facility so Harry purchased a 1,200 square foot bakery on Baldwin Street in New Haven. He moved his family, including his wife Rose and their son Murray, born in 1930, into a two-story colonial in front of the bakery. Rose, and later Murray, came out back each day to help him make bagels and when Marvin, born in 1941, was old enough, he made bagels too. When Murray reached high school, he would go to school until early afternoon, do his homework, sleep for a few hours, then stay up all night baking bagels and making pre-dawn deliveries.

Murray went off to college and the army, and when he returned he heard about a new product, polyethylene bags. He bought thousands, filling the family's garage with them. Then he packaged his bagels into bags of six and expanded from Mom and Pop bakeries to New Haven supermarkets. Yet he still was getting up before dawn, which he disliked. One evening Murray began production early, froze the bagels, caught some sleep, then delivered the bagels defrosted on arrival. No one complained about the taste. So he did it for a few more nights. His father's recipe of boiling, then baking, high gluten flour, malt, yeast, sugar and salt stood up, even when the bagels were not served hot and fresh. Murray had an idea in his head. And with some preparation and production adjustments, in 1962, the frozen bagel industry was born. Murray began to market Lender's Bagels, with unlimited shelf life, not only in New Haven but everywhere.

In 1965, with his father deceased, Marvin returned from college and joined Murray in the business as the inside man. H. Lender and Sons moved to a 12,000 square foot plant, automated, and grew to six employees. The rags far behind them, the riches were in sight. Lender and Sons developed a variety of flavors including onion, poppy, sesame, egg, rye, pumpernickel, garlic, raisin and honey, raisin and wheat, and wheat and honey. Murray created several innovative marketing plans, including attention-getting gimmicks such as an oval bagel enjoyed by President Lyndon Johnson in front of television cameras in the Oval Office, and green bagels that were all the rage one St. Patrick's Day. By the time Murray marketed himself onto *The Tonight Show Starring Johnny Carson* in 1968, Lender's Bagels was a household name.

By 1984, Lender's was the largest bagel producer in America, turning out 750 million bagels a year and generating $50 million in annual sales. But Murray, who was 54, and Marvin, who was 43, decided to sell Lender's Bagels to Kraft, and retire early to be active in causes they espoused. In a fitting tribute to Murray's marketing genius, as well as his zaniness, Kraft staged a media spectacular: a preposterous mock wedding in which Murray and Marvin walked their nickname's sake, "Len," down the aisle, to be joined in matrimony with "Phyl," escorted by the heads of Kraft, maker of Philadelphia Cream Cheese. For all those who were reading that the Lenders' family business was becoming part of a conglomerate, Murray reduced it to the wedding of his bagel and cream cheese. The names of Kraft, and the company's subsequent owners, Philip Morris, Kellogg's and now Aurora Foods, have been kept off the packaging; the image of a family-owned business continues to this day.

While brothers in business often squabble, Murray and Marvin grew closer than ever. Marvin loved Murray, who was by all accounts an extraordinary older brother, and Murray loved Marvin, whom he treasured and kept under his wing. They were Damon and Pythias, inseparable personal friends. So they opened another business together in 1984, M&M Investments, mainly to invest their own funds. They stoked it a few hours a week, but they devoted their lives to their families and philanthropy. Murray's causes included Quinnipiac College in the Connecticut Valley. Marvin's was the UJA. Marvin had been a successful businessman, the executive who ensured the product would reach its markets; yet in the public eye he was in the shadow of Murray, something Murray was aware of but disliked. As Murray confided to this writer in late 1989, "I'm so happy Marvin will head the UJA. It will give him something truly, truly his own."

In January 1990, not yet UJA National Chairman, Marvin began to plan something no one had ever attempted in fundraising, or even imagined. In

Marvin's mind, it would get Operation Exodus off to a dramatic start and lay the basis for record fundraising for years to come. The idea was crazy. It was like Harry's idea to sell bagels to non-Jews, or Murray's to sell frozen bagels for breakfast.

Marvin Lender was in no one's shadow now, and he was poised, although unproven, to move from a wealthy young retiree with a big title, to center stage as a bona fide major leader in world Jewish history.

Marvin Lender had an idea in his head. He felt that the need was so great, the opportunity so extraordinary, the generosity of American Jews so grand, that anything was possible. As Passage to Freedom sputtered toward its inglorious end, Lender was studying the giving levels of the highest UJA donors.

Most philanthropies at the time experienced that 20 percent of the donors provided 80 percent of the income; in the UJA Federation system, ten percent provided 90 percent of the funds. Since UJA's main value to federations was its ability to secure major gifts, minimally $10,000 per donor per year, it raised very large sums from a fraction of one percent of campaign donors. But even UJA had a ceiling. Lender's strategy was to raise a huge sum early in Operation Exodus, but to do it in a way that would electrify the entire American Jewish community, causing everyone to take notice and give more. His idea was to assemble the wealthiest Jews in America, in one room, on one day, and soon, and have each of them pledge a million dollars to Operation Exodus. He was inclined to do this even though fewer than 30 in the entire country were giving to UJA at that level and they had already given that sum to the Annual Campaign; none had given near that for Passage to Freedom.

Beginning before the National Officers meeting on January 15, and continuing until the General Assembly of the Council of Jewish Federations in Miami on February 6, Lender sounded out others to see if they thought his idea could succeed. He presented it in early January to his Campaign Executive Committee, his kitchen cabinet: Joel Tauber, Richard Pearlstone, Morton Kornreich, Martin Stein, Arlene Zimmerman, David Hermelin, Alan Shulman and Alan Crawford. There was considerable discussion about Passage to Freedom. It had gone on for months and a main reason it never reached $50 million was the lack of blockbuster gifts. Lender said he felt Passage to Freedom was hampered by American Jewish misgivings that the Soviet Jewish immigrants were not going to Israel but were coming to the United States. He said Operation Exodus was consistent with the Zionist dream of building Israel and would appeal to every American Jew. He added that Passage to Freedom, which he himself chaired, had not attempted to mount such a head-turning event.

One Committee member asked Lender a pointed question: could he get major prospects to give him an appointment to discuss it with them? While the question might have sounded unimportant to outsiders, it cut to the heart of the challenge because in major gifts fundaising, securing an appointment was the linchpin to achievements. While givers of $10, $25, $50 and $100 might respond readily to the petitions of many charities, often not paying attention until tax season which organizations they gave to, major donors pooled their philanthropy into fewer causes. This gave their gifts more impact and established their presence at the charities where they could influence how the charities carried out their mission. To achieve that, major donors might turn down more telephone requests or direct mail than average donors. But major gifts required discussion and this meant solicitors had to meet with the prospects. Major donors did not like to turn down requests for significant money, so they turned down appointments -- unless they could not say no to the person who wanted to see them. When a major donor agreed to an appointment, it meant that a major gift would be on the way, even before what fundraisers called "the ask."

The question was pointed and embarrassed Lender who admitted he could not secure the appointments on his own. To the very rich, access holds high prestige and dependency of any type is a sign of weakness. However, Lender said he was confident others capable of giving a million dollars would open the doors for him to conduct one-on-one fundraising, or accompany him and help "do the ask" in two-on-two solicitations.

Lender's idea was so ambitious that few in his kitchen cabinet qualified to participate. They admonished him that it carried a substantial risk, for if the event failed to materialize it would not only fall short with the highest level donors but would set a negative example and depress giving at the lower major gifts levels. Since part of the psychology of UJA's success was that donors expected success and wanted to be part of it, the Campaign could be hobbled early on.

But the Committee members were impressed by the strength of Lender's belief in his idea. They reviewed the giving history of the highest level donors and what was known about their current financial picture, and how those donors felt about the UJA and Israel. In the era before the Internet and search engines, UJA always had shockingly detailed information on the finances and interests of major prospects, gathered and updated regularly from publicly available sources. They said they thought Lender's initiative would be worth the risk. They offered to sound out their own contacts who knew the top donors to ask if they thought it was viable.

Meanwhile, Lender pursued his explorations further. He met with UJA lay division leaders Bobi Klotz of New York, President of the UJA National Women's Campaign, and Roberta Holland of Providence, Rhode Island, the Women's Campaign Chairman. They encouraged him but said that, while women were gaining increasing control over their own and their family's wealth, they could not identify any woman yet who would qualify and give such a sum in her own right.

Lender turned next to the UJA professionals. Despite the smiling faces juxtaposed in annual reports of overseers, who were invariably major donors, and the paid professionals, in many philanthropies there is tension between them. Usually there is power to be taken; sometimes it is taken by the lay officers and at other times by the professionals. Some lay leaders try to operate independently of the professionals, imposing programs and policies styled on what they found effective in their businesses; others are obsequious to professionals, failing to provide leadership and oversight. Lender was extraordinary in his ability to achieve harmony with most professionals. He was comfortable meeting with almost everyone, not only those at his level of economic achievement. He enjoyed dropping into the offices of UJA staff members, sometimes just to chat, genuinely at ease with himself and others. He had already become a fixture in UJA offices to an extent that most of his predecessors had not. He had even bought an apartment on Park Avenue and 77th Street so he would be able to be at the nearby UJA headquarters whenever possible. Everyone called him Marvin, from the highest donors to the mailroom staff. Warmth was his middle name.

In his meticulous effort to gather all necessary information before deciding whether to proceed, and in his characteristic manner of embracing everyone on the same level, Lender met not only with lay leaders but also with several professionals. His decision to proceed followed a meeting with Morris Sherman, the UJA Vice President for Campaign, UJA's main fundraising executive. Sherman was one of the most respected fundraisers in Jewish life, having led federation campaigns in Los Angeles, Miami, St. Louis and Chicago. More than his impressive résumé showed, Sherman possessed enormous insight into people, something he learned as a boy in foster care, a teenager on the streets, and a social worker living in a home for deeply troubled youth. He knew how to explain the feelings of Jews in need since he himself had been a Jew in need. But he also knew his business, and how to find the hot buttons that motivated donors to give more than they themselves had expected.

Sherman did not whitewash the risks. He admonished Lender that if he attempted to mount such an event and it failed to materialize it could crush the crucial beginning of the Campaign; it could even destroy his National Chairmanship. Yet Sherman was impressed by Lender's idealism and courage and his placement of the cause above his future reputation. He liked Lender's boldness and thought the idea could have dramatic and measurable benefit. Lender felt kinship with Sherman's warmth, and recognized that Sherman sought to ground him in reality rather than discourage him. Sherman gave Lender pause, but not for long. As they discussed particulars, Lender grew more confident and said he was determined to proceed. Sherman assured Lender he would have all the professional advice and support he needed. It was the beginning of a beautiful lay-professional relationship.

Sherman pointed out that, to start, Lender had to develop a core of leadership from within the tiny cadre he could not yet penetrate. Lender was already thinking of a man he knew only in passing, a Midwesterner decades older than himself, born before Marvin's own father. He was the person Marvin knew he had to speak to next, who had the best view of the potential of his idea. He also knew that without that man's active support, nothing would materialize.

"Willy," someone asked Willy Sutton, the notorious 1930s bank robber, "why do you rob banks?" "Because," Sutton answered, "that's where the money is."

Those who stood in awe of the fundraising prowess of the United Jewish Appeal often asked, *How did they raise so much money so fast?* Another reason was simple: they asked rich people for a lot of money. But it was not easy to have them say yes. They knew first how to open the door; who should do the asking; how much to ask for; and how to ask, and negotiate, in the most persuasive way. And they knew, most of all, that the asker had to be giving personally as much as he requested of the prospect, because no one likes someone with less money to tell them what to do with theirs.

UJA was superb in all these techniques, which helped it raise sums again and again over the decades. Indeed, UJA's achievements astounded everyone. But it would be more difficult this time, especially to persuade donors who had already given large sums to match their sums and then give more. Many donors were alienated by what they felt was Israel's heavy-handed suppression of the Intifada. They were focused on local needs, and their own businesses, during the American economic recession. They were feeling less connection to Judaism. Many stagnated at the same, albeit high, giving level for years, contending they had reached their maximum for giving to UJA Federation Campaigns, even though they were contributing larger and larger sums to universities and museums. One such donor who had been giving a million dollars a year since the mid-1980s said this in 1989 when asked to give more: "I don't know why you think it has to be more. I think a million dollars a year is a lot of money. If you don't think so, there are others who do." Even among the wealthiest, UJA recognized, no gift, or gift increase, could be taken for granted.

Lender knew he had to make a 911 call to the man to whom American Jews had turned scores of times: Max Fisher of Detroit. Though 81 years old in 1990, Fisher was still very active and the dean of the American Jewish community. He was one of the most influential American Jews, in the panoply of causes he supported, and in the National Republican Party where he had been a main supporter in the years before anyone ever thought of campaign finance reform. He knew personally all those with the capacity to give a million dollars a year to Operation Exodus.

Fisher was a self-made industrialist. In Depression-era Detroit, he had devised a strategy to slash oil refining costs, then sold the plan to a local industrialist in exchange for a share of what proved to be significant profits. He came up with more strategies and encouraged people of means to invest in them. He parlayed his growing knowledge of oil production, then of automobiles and the overall industry, into huge sums, enough to enable him to become the primary owner of the Marathon Oil Company, the ninth largest in the world. A refurbished Marathon Oil gasoline station pump stood on display in the reception area outside his office on the 27th floor of the Fisher Building in downtown Detroit, a city he helped rebuild after the riots in the 1960s. Although he became a personal friend and close associate of Henry Ford II, years after Henry Ford, Sr. had made anti-Semitic diatribes and widely distributed the notoriously anti-Semitic *Protocols of the Elders of Zion*, he never felt quite comfortable as a Jew in an industry of gentiles, linked to Arabs.

Whereas most influential Jews adhered to the Democratic Party, whenever the President was a Republican Jewish leaders turned to Fisher. Fisher was appreciated by Richard Nixon, Gerald Ford, Ronald Reagan and George H. Bush for the millions he had raised for their campaigns but also for his acumen. They consulted him as a sounding board on Jewish issues, and he often smoothed the way between them and the more rough and tumble Israeli leaders. Israeli Prime Ministers turned to him when they needed an American to make their case at a Republican White House. Fisher played an important role in persuading Nixon in the Oval Office to provide vital aid to a besieged

Israel in the Yom Kippur War. Yet he never asked for anything for himself. He turned down Ambassadorships and Cabinet positions in several Republican administrations, explaining to several Presidents, "I only want you to take my call and do what is necessary if I call on behalf of people in need."

Fisher was respected by Jews for still more reasons. He saw poverty, destitution and hopelessness around him in Detroit during the Depression but, instead of shuddering and moving on, he resolved to devote an important part of his life and resources to ending human suffering. He never forgot stories of his parents and grandparents' fear of pogroms in tsarist Russia and remembered that Jews were invariably imperiled somewhere in the world. He frequently visited Jews in remote countries, to learn more about their needs and encourage them, and he spoke with a casualness that belied his wealth and status. He possessed a deep sense of community and a rare ability to bring people together. He was a leader at 35 organizations over the years including UJA, CJF, UIA, JDC and the Jewish Agency. At the American Jewish Committee he personified its missions of protecting Jews, and creating harmony among Jews and between Jews and others. Nothing major happened in national Jewish life without Max Fisher's agreement and participation. Whenever Fisher was in a room, the head table became wherever he sat. He was always the power behind the Jewish throne.

Lender did not think that Fisher knew him but Fisher recalled years later that he knew Marvin well. Although they had met only at a few events, Max recognized Marvin's honesty, his innate caring, his personal deferentiality, his complete lack of airs. He liked Lender very much, and respected his selfless devotion to cause. "I liked Marvin — loved him from the start," Fisher recalled in one of several interviews for this book. "He is a kind, sweet, decent, unselfish man." So Fisher was happy to meet with Lender in late January 1990.

Lender described his idea and asked Fisher if he thought it would succeed. Fisher said it could. He asked Fisher to serve as a co-chairman of the event and to play an active role; Fisher agreed. He asked Fisher if he thought that Leslie Wexner of Columbus, Ohio, and Laurence Tisch of New York City should be asked to serve as co-chairmen, to encourage their own maximum gifts and for their access to other senior-level donors; Fisher said yes. Lender said he had met Wexner and Tisch but did not know them well; Fisher said he would call them, emphasize the importance of funding the emigration, and encourage them to meet with Lender.

Marvin asked Max to personally solicit several major prospects to participate at the event. Max named some prospects offhand and took the names of a few others. Then Marvin asked Max if he would pledge $3 million at the event, "to set a good example". "Sure," said Fisher.

Leslie H. Wexner was one of the most successful businessmen in America in 1990. His achievements stirred the fantasies of MBA students the way Babe Ruth's captured the imagination of Little Leaguers.

His beginning, like his climb to the top, was legendary. Wexner grew up in Columbus, Ohio, the son of Bella and Harry Wexner who struggled for years as owners of a Mom and Pop women's clothing store. Leslie started to work at the age of nine, cutting grass and shoveling snow for spending money. In 1962, after he obtained his Bachelor of Science degree in business from Ohio State University and tried and left law school which he found boring, he minded the store for a week so his parents could take a vacation. When his parents returned, Leslie told his father his approach to business was all wrong. The conversation went something like this:

"Dad, you offer too much merchandise that doesn't sell, like dresses and coats."

"Those are my best selling items," his father exclaimed.

"They are your worst," Leslie answered. "Get rid of them. Specialize, like my friends are doing in areas of medicine and law."

"The department stores don't specialize, and they do just fine," his father noted.

"If your product line is limited, you'll be able to reduce costs, underprice your competitors, boost sales and make a lot of money," Leslie pleaded.

Exasperated, his father thanked him very much and said if Leslie thought that was a good way to do business he could open his own store across town and make it as limited as he liked. So he did. Leslie opened his own store in Columbus in 1963, with a loan of $5,000 from an aunt and $5,000 from a bank, and limited it to women's sportswear separates like blouses and skirts. He realized first year sales of $160,000. Three years later he owned two stores that grossed half a million dollars, then he had three, then five. He called his stores "The Limited." As shopping malls rapidly expanded across the country in the 1970s The Limited grew phenomenally with them. In 1982 Wexner brought The Limited onto the New York Stock Exchange and made it one of the decade's fastest growing companies.

While walking down a street in San Francisco in 1982 Wexner passed a ladies' lingerie shop. Since most ladies' underwear then was plain, white and cotton and sold in department stores, the business attracted his attention. He chatted with the owner, who had three stores and was on the brink of bankruptcy.

Wexner bought them for a price his critics scoffed at as too high: $1 million. He reconceptualized the product as glamorous lingerie, developed the line and built an ingenious niche marketing program. He changed everything except the name, with its titillating twitting of an English monarch's prudishness: Victoria's Secret. Before the decade was out, Wexner presided over Victoria's Secret stores in 400 malls that earned $1 billion annually.

Also in the 1980s Wexner established Limited Express to cater to young cost-conscious women, Limited Too for girls and Express Men for fashion-conscious males; bought an Henri Bendel store and built it into a national chain; and purchased Lane Bryant, Lerner, Abercrombie and Fitch and a few clothing catalog companies. By 1990 he sat atop a worldwide empire of 3,800 stores with gross sales of $5.2 billion.

While others slipped off to bars and restaurants after hours to bask in their glory, Wexner went to lead worthy causes like The Ohio State University and the United Jewish Appeal. It was always so with him. In 1959, when he was a student at OSU (he was to rise to become its Chairman of the Board), he was the UJA Campus Campaign Chair. In Jewish life, even as he was opening his first store in 1963, he chaired Jewish community groups and initiatives. In 1970, while conceptualizing The Limited's rapid expansion, he was a Board leader at the Columbus Jewish Federation. Soon he became a JDC Vice Chairman. He achieved prominence on the national Jewish scene in 1975 when he was elected Treasurer of the UJA Board of Trustees. In the early 1980s he was American Chairman of the International Leadership Reunion, an extraordinary gathering of 200 Jews worldwide who gave $250,000 annually to UJA and Keren Hayesod. He was also a board member of United Way of America, American Ballet Theater, Whitney Museum, Aspen Institute and the planned United States Holocaust Memorial Museum.

Yet, when Wexner was offered the UJA National Chairmanship he turned it down, saying he was unqualified because he did not know enough about Jewish history, values, thought and practices. "They couldn't run my business," he thought, "what made them think I could run theirs?" He consulted his friend, Rabbi David Hartman, a philosopher and founder of the Shalom Hartman Institute in Jerusalem, on how best to help. Hartman advised him, "Think about and work on the problems facing the Jewish People."

In considering this, Wexner noticed that there were many young people who were enormously committed to the Jewish future but lacked Jewish knowledge. At the same time he discovered that many young Jewish professionals knew little about the art of leadership. So in addition to learning all he could himself, he created the Wexner Heritage Foundation in 1985, with Rabbi Herbert A. Friedman, a former UJA Executive Vice Chairman, to provide both Jewish education and leadership training for promising young men and women entering Jewish life. He established the Wexner Graduate Fellowships in 1988 to do the same for Jewish educators, lay leaders, rabbis and cantors at a higher level. On his visits to Israel he met promising Israelis, who had begun careers in government but lacked leadership skills and sufficient knowledge of public administration, and funded the Wexner Israel Fellowship Program at Harvard University's John F. Kennedy School of Government in 1989 to help them. The Israel Fellowship program offers leadership training and leads to a Master of Arts in Public Administration.

"Good leadership can make or break a Jewish institution just like a business," Wexner reflected in an interview in his elegant Fifth Avenue duplex overlooking Central Park in Manhattan. "But leadership training sounded boring so no one else wanted to invest in it. Whenever money was available it was spent on other projects." He laughed as he came up with a Midwesterner's metaphor, "We've eaten the seed corn." In planting the seed corn to harvest tomorrow's leaders, Wexner began production in a vast untilled field in Jewish life.

When Max Fisher telephoned Wexner in January 1990, Les was tinkering with his latest vision, to develop a little store limited to health and beauty products he had just created into another chain: Bath and Body Works. "As you know, UJA is beginning an enormously important campaign to get the Jews out of Russia and into Israel," Fisher remembered saying. "They want to begin it with a new high level event, a million dollars or more apiece. I'm in for three. We need you to play a big role. The event has to get a lot of money in and set a never-before standard. Les, this is all about leadership."

"Good," said Wexner, who also recalled the conversation. "I am pessimistic about the fate of Jews in Russia. That place has been dangerous for us for centuries. Sooner or later things there always turn against the Jews. We must get as many out as possible."

Fisher asked Wexner to meet with Marvin Lender who would flesh out the plan. Lender telephoned later that day and met Wexner the next day in Columbus. Although they knew each other from a few UJA events, Lender remembered being unsure of himself, pummeled by those who doubted Operation Exodus could succeed and in awe of Wexner's accomplishments. But Wexner disarmed him. When Lender asked him to co-chair the meeting, Wexner quickly agreed. "I'll host it in my office in New York if you like," Wexner volunteered, to Lender's delight. They set the date and time: February 28, 1990 at 9 a.m. Still thinking he had to walk on egg shells, Lender approached the topic of Wexner's gift gingerly, but Wexner cut to the chase. "I'll give $3 million," Wexner declared. "Possibly more."

Laurence A. Tisch had been a leading American philanthropist for years. He was regularly donating a million dollars a year to UJA-Federation of New York and providing extraordinarily generous gifts to other causes and institutions.

In philanthropy, Tisch's name was most closely associated with non-sectarian causes, especially New York University, where he began a twenty year tenure as Chairman of the Board of Trustees in 1978. He oversaw the transformation of the institution from a sleepy school for the children of rich locals who had mediocre grades into a world-class university. Before he became Chairman, for example, high school students with grades in the 80's and Scholastic Aptitude Test scores below the national average gained admission to the College of Arts and Science. By 1990 the College was on the preferred list of the best high school students in America and 60 foreign countries, and required high school averages in the 90's, and SAT grades of 1300, the ninetieth percentile. Standards rose in all the schools of the university even though it expanded rapidly. The $30 million Tisch gave to NYU Hospital, renamed Tisch Hospital at the NYU Medical Center, propelled it to the national forefront in patient care. The $20 million for the arts school, renamed the NYU Tisch School of the Arts, made it a world class creative center; one student even won an Academy Award for a class project. Tisch not only donated tens of millions to NYU, he was a hands-on leader. He invited his wealthiest friends and business associates to join the Board of Trustees, then solicited them for millions. Tisch's generosity was visible everywhere in New York City, on a wing at the Metropolitan Museum of Art, at the New York Public Library, and in countless programs to help struggling New Yorkers. He gave generously elsewhere in the country and abroad.

Born in 1923 to Al and Sadye Tisch, who owned a garment business and operated two summer camps, Larry Tisch graduated from New York University with honors at the age of 18 and obtained a master's degree at 19 from the Wharton School at the University of Pennsylvania. In 1946, with capital from his father and a family friend, Tisch, later joined by his younger brother Preston (Bob), acquired a dilapidated New Jersey hotel, renovated it and earned a profit. They purchased and renovated another hotel, earning more profit. Then another, securing more profit. They identified other small businesses and turned them around too.

In 1959 the Tisch brothers invested $65 million to buy most of the Loews Corporation, a chain of formerly elegant one-screen movie theaters. Recognizing that the land beneath the theaters was more valuable than the theaters, they leveled most of the movie houses and constructed the Loews hotel chain. They obtained a majority ownership of the CAN Corporation and rebuilt it as CNA Financial Corporation, one of the world's largest casualty and life insurance companies. They invested in the Bulova Watch Company, of which Andrew Tisch, Larry's son, became President. They built Diamond Offshore Drilling, of which Larry's son James became Chairman. And they purchased large positions in CBS-TV and P. Lorillard and Company. With Bob's son Jonathan as President of Loews Hotels, the family's business sagacity built the Loews Corporation into one of the world's largest diversified corporations, employing tens of thousands worldwide. Yet, almost unheard of on Wall Street, the two powerful, independent, self-made men who started it all, Larry and Bob, remained Co-CEOs and friends throughout the decades of growth and change.

Although one of the world's most successful entrepreneurs, Larry Tisch lived a largely unostentatious life. He remained in the same apartment where he and his wife Wilma reared their four sons. There, he had set an example in philanthropy they had begun to emulate: Andrew was Campaign Chairman of UJA-Federation of New York, James was on the path to becoming Chairman and Daniel and Thomas were active in many causes. There too, without fanfare or public knowledge Tisch, a Reform Jew, learned Talmud weekly with a Hasidic rabbi.

Tisch and Lender enjoyed a pleasant conversation. They chatted about the cause and their families. Larry readily agreed to co-chair the event. He said most of his family would be traveling but that Andrew might be available. They agreed on the importance of a "leadership gift," a standard to set the bar higher for others, at an event whose ticket of admission was a million dollars. Tisch said his family would pledge $3 million. "We have to get the Jews out of Russia," Tisch told Lender. "Anything can happen there. We can't wait."

Lender was pleased with himself. It was still January. The UJA officers had enthusiastically endorsed Operation Exodus and provided him and his team with the authority to finalize the goal, and he was confident the federations would endorse the Campaign in Miami on February 6. But Lender was especially pleased because he had, rather easily, obtained the support of some of the most influential and wealthy Jews anywhere, Max Fisher, Leslie Wexner and Laurence

Tisch for his cornerstone event. He was assured of a few million dollars from them alone. Then he laughed as he said to Tauber, "This is great. Now how many few million dollars do I need to make 420?" He had begun the daring process, but the challenge of the event, and of a successful $420 million Operation Exodus Campaign, still lay in front of him. Whom should he invite next?

"United Jewish Appeal records show there are 27 gifts of $1 million or more to the (Annual) Campaign," UJA President Stanley Horowitz wrote in a letter to Lender dated January 17, 1990, long before Internet search engines and private firms consolidated and made information on personal wealth easily available. The 27 were not all from individuals, Horowitz wrote, but included "gift units," from families that pooled their gifts to reach that level. Perhaps individuals who contributed to gift units might give a million dollars on their own. Conjecturing about individuals within families who might be able to do so, Horowitz said the number could be as high as 59. Listing others giving from $750,000 to $950,000 a year who might be "upgraded," as the fundraisers put it, Horowitz found that the "universe" was 81. Horowitz made clear this was a wish list, that many of the 81 could not reach the million dollar level, and that others had recently pledged to the Annual Campaign and could not yet give so much more. But Lender resolved to try with every one.

In the late afternoon drop from the UJA mailroom on February 6, while federation leaders were flying home from their endorsement of Operation Exodus in Miami, among the hundreds of letters were 81 signed by Marvin Lender. Lender wrote he was extending an invitation on behalf of Fisher, Wexner, Tisch and himself "to a small, possibly historic, meeting on Wednesday, February 28, at 9 a.m.," at Leslie Wexner's New York office. The letter made clear the aliyah was underway and that the situation for Jews in the Soviet Union was dangerous. He wrote that he, Fisher, Tisch, or Wexner would telephone soon to discuss the meeting and a substantial gift to the planned Campaign.

Each day for three weeks, the UJA staff issued an updated insider's document titled, "Potential Invitees." A tracking sheet, it listed in columns on the left the names, addresses and telephone numbers of 81 persons, and a simple "Yes/No" column on the right. It could have been a guest list for a party. However, the middle columns listed the prospect's giving history and potential, and the name of one of the richest people in America who would be calling to recruit the prospect personally. A regular party, except that each guest would be required by the hosts to bring along a million dollars or more.

Lender knew that those who did not attend could still be solicited but he needed as many as possible to be present at what was still planned, as late as February 14, as a meeting at Wexner's office. That was because when someone announced a million dollar gift in almost any venue it would seem like a lot, but amidst many donations at that level and higher, it might not seem quite enough. As at synagogue Yom Kippur appeals and other public pledgings, there was substantial social pressure to give maximally.

Lender knew that the number of 81 was soft, since only 27 had given individually at that level and nearly all of them had just given to the 1990 Annual Campaign that had begun in the fall of 1989. Nevertheless, he was committed to pursue everyone on the list aggressively. Lender, Fisher, Tisch and Wexner telephoned, then visited, as many prospects as they could. They sounded out each based on his "rating," how high UJA thought he would go, which usually meant doubling his Annual Campaign commitment. They welcomed, encouraged, urged, cajoled, coaxed, presumed, summoned, inveigled, inspired, shamed, coerced and did whatever it took to persuade the prospect to attend. By February 14 all 81 had been contacted; a few had agreed to be present, many could not. The process was underway but no one yet knew whether the event would have the critical mass to raise a collectively huge sum and draw wide attention to the Campaign.

With events abroad unfolding fast, Lender left for the Soviet Union and Israel to obtain the latest data and vivid personal observations to persuade more people to participate. As he departed from UJA offices for John F. Kennedy International Airport, Marshall Jacobson, the UJA Senior Assistant Vice President for Campaign, handed him the status report. All too quickly, the number of prospects had been whittled to fewer than 40.

Below is most of the text of a memorandum to Wexner that Lender dictated en route to the airport on February 14, two weeks prior to the event. All those named were to give generously, some with participation at the event, others not. With first names like Sam, Ted, Lester, Frank and Mel and last names like Goldman, Hirsh, Stone and Rosenwald, it could have been a list for a fiftieth wedding anniversary gathering for elderly Jews in the Bronx. Except that Sam built office buildings in Miami. Ted owned Carnival Cruise Lines. Lester owned skyscrapers in Chicago and the biggest chunk of the New York Yankees this side of George Steinbrenner. Frank had co-founded Automated Data Processing, Inc., and was a United States Senator. Mel owned the luxurious Fairmont Hotel in San Francisco. Goldman owned a large insurance company and was part of the Levi Strauss family. Hirsh owned office buildings in Los Angeles. Stone was Founder and Chairman of American Greetings Corporation. And Rosenwald, who began to give UJA a million dollars a year in 1947, "in the years when a million dollars meant something," he used to laughingly say years later, was part of a family that founded Sears Roebuck.

The memorandum, issued with the notation, "dictated/not read," gives a sense of what it was like to try to secure critical mass at a million-dollar-a-guest event. Except for one passing reference to a dollar sum, the memorandum breathtakingly whizzes past what the guests were being invited to do.

To: Les Wexner
From: Marvin Lender
Date: February 14, 1990
Re: Meeting prospects

Les, here is where we stand with recruitment for the meeting and what I think we have to do in these pressure-cooker days remaining.

Sam Adler. He cannot attend the meeting but will encourage Ted Arison of Miami to participate. They are very close friends.

Ted Arison. I made that call when I was in Miami. My sense is that he will come to the meeting. I will call him from Israel to try and get a final commitment.

Edgar Bronfman. Edgar will not be at the meeting but his brother Charles will attend.

Lester Crown. He will be at the meeting.

Max Fisher. He will be there.

Richard Goldman. I have to get back to him when I'm in Israel. If he comes he will do what has to be done for himself and representing the Levi Strauss family.

Alex Grass. Hopefully he will be available and able to attend the meeting. I will follow up again.

Alan (Ace) Greenberg. Definitely coming to the meeting.

Peter Haas. Hopefully he will be represented by Richard Goldman, his brother-in-law. Mrs. Walter Haas will also be represented by Richard Goldman, her son-in-law.

Stanley Hirsh. Hopefully if he comes he will announce the $1 million. I have asked him to invite Bram Goldsmith and if Bram comes as his guest, Hirsh will definitely come.

Chuck Hoffberger. I've put a lot of time and effort into this, and I hope he will attend. He understands the minimum.

Mort Kornreich. He will be there.

Frank Lautenberg. I have not yet been able to speak to Frank. He's out of the country. However, he is calling my assistant Maureen when he returns.

Marvin Lender. I will be there with bells on.

Joe and Mort Mandel. They cannot attend.

Peter May. Peter May is a Max Fisher call. I am not sure whether he is planning to come or not, but a call from you wouldn't hurt.

Bud Meyerhoff. Meyerhoff is not sure if he can come. I have to call him on 2/23. A call from you in advance might be helpful. He is a key figure and I know he wants to be there. Please call him.

Lowell and Michael Milken. They won't be coming to the meeting. I am setting up an appointment to solicit them mid-March.

Milton Petrie. Petrie is assigned to Larry Tisch and Larry promised me he would call him.

Lou Rogow. Lou is 91 years old and I'm following on this gift. He cannot be at the meeting.

William Rosenwald. He is in his 90's and I've been working with Elizabeth Varet, his daughter. He may or may not be able to come.

Lew and Jack Rudin. If you know them, please give them a call. If not, then they will be assigned to Max Fisher.

Irving Schneider. I'm on that one and will be seeing him again in Israel. He is definitely coming to the meeting.

Mel and Herb Simon. They are on your list. I know they will respond to you.

Marty Stein. He will be at the meeting.

Irving Stone and Morry Weiss. I'm on this one and will follow up from Israel.

Mel Swig. I was in his office a couple of weeks ago. I am continuing to work on it hoping he will come.

Henry Taub. He will be at the meeting.

Larry Tisch. He will be there.

Jack Weiler and Bob Arnow. Weiler can't come. If you know Bob Arnow, his son-in-law, give him a call.

Harry Weinberg. Weinberg probably will not come to the meeting. However, he is waiting to see what the big guys are doing before he makes his gift. If we get big numbers out of our meeting on the 28ᵗʰ, it might require you and me flying to Baltimore to talk to him, but we will have to wait and not push that one just yet.

Leslie Wexner. I have a feeling you will be at the meeting. By the way, I will be flying into New York on the 27ᵗʰ and if you like, we can meet along with Stanley Horowitz, Marshall Jacobson and Morris Sherman that evening for dinner, just to review what is in place for the meeting. I have an apartment in the City and I think we can meet there for a late snack. Please let them know.

Joe Wilf. I have spoken to Joe and I am going to get back to him from Israel. There is a possibility he will come.

Raymond Zimmerman. At first I thought Raymond was going to attend, but I received a call from his office today saying he can't be in attendance. This is a guy you could have great influence on. Try to make the call. Also, Zimmerman can influence Mel Simon.

I am dictating this as I'm driving to the airport to depart for Russia. I'll be in touch just as soon as I can get through to you, either from Russia or Israel.

Again, thanks for all the help.

Sincerely,

Marvin

ML/jdk

Dictated/Not Read.

No one knows who came up with the idea to move the meeting from Leslie Wexner's office to a nearby hotel, change the time from 9 a.m. to 8 a.m. and make it a breakfast. But someone did. For a million dollars a person, someone paused and said, "Let's give them breakfast."

For half of January and most of February, Wexner, Fisher, Tisch, and Lender descended on prospects like an armed invasion by men in suits. They contacted each prospect personally, often twice. Sometimes two of them solicited a prospect in succession. Sometimes one solicitor contacted two members of the same family. Lender telephoned a few from Russia. None of the effort was haphazard; considerable thought led to careful decisions as to who should call whom, where and when. The UJA's maxim, "People give to people," meaning that the relationship between the solicitor and prospect was key to a gift, had been proven repeatedly over the decades and that was at the core of the strategy.

The event leaders believed the cause was urgent and clear, but they were still meticulous to adhere to the methods that had won rapid, dramatic campaign achievements in the past. They were emotionally committed to the planned Campaign and knew a lot depended on the Breakfast, yet they proceeded in a coolheaded, businesslike manner. Every few days they held conference calls, evaluated the responses, and decided how to proceed with each prospect. Initially they sought to place the germ of the idea of participating and, where this was viable, followed to secure it. If the prospect responded readily, they used the million dollar pledge as a platform to build for a higher commitment. People who negotiated brilliant business deals often were no match for solicitors from the UJA.

The atmosphere during the calls was strictly business with the proven UJA twists. Whereas universities, museums and cultural centers solicited with the promise of a naming opportunity such as a building, wing or concert hall, UJA solicitors never promised anything in return. Nothing. All that donors received, in fact, was a letter of appreciation, prepared by the public relations department and signed by the National Chairman [actually signed by this writer in the name of the National Chairman]. UJA's approach to what in business terms would be called sales was absurd: it asked monumental sums and promised nothing in return. Even more, whereas other philanthropies tried to make prospective donors feel comfortable, UJA made them feel *uncomfortable*. They let the prospect feel comfortable only when he or she reached up to the level UJA had in mind for the donor in the first place. Preposterous. But it worked.

Soliciting for a million dollars, however, was never easy. From January 17 through February 13, Lender alone personally spoke to almost every prospect and met with most, living out of suitcases and hotel rooms. But the case for giving to Operation Exodus was strong. Increasing signs of destabilization in the Soviet Union, more incidents of anti-Semitism, and growing Jewish fears of pogroms were being reported in newspapers and magazines and on radio and television broadcasts. Tisch, Fisher, Wexner and Lender needed to persuade each prospect that he or she personally had to do something about it. They did not appeal to them as businessmen, but as Jews. For, in the last analysis, despite their enormous wealth and influence, they all still felt vulnerable, even in America, as Jews.

Most people named Baker are not bakers and most named Miller are not millers, but in the case (no pun intended) of the Bronfman family, distiller is their family name. ("*Bronfman*" means distiller in Yiddish.) In 1889, Ekiel and Mindel Bronfman fled tsarist Russia for Canada. Their family held nondescript jobs there for decades, their son Samuel delivering cases of liquor. However, when Prohibition was instituted in the United States in 1919, Sam formed his own company, Distiller's Corporation, Ltd., to serve the throngs of visitors from south of the Canadian border. He had plenty of customers. By 1928, he was strong enough to acquire the relatively modest Joseph E. Seagram and Sons. He not only sold his products but also amassed an ample stock of aged whiskeys so that, when Prohibition ended in 1933, he had an insatiable supply of customers in the United States. He prospered enormously. Over the next decades, he and his sons Edgar and Charles built Seagram into one of the world's largest suppliers of liquors, wines and spirits. In 1971, Mr. Sam, as he was known in his company, divided his holdings among his sons Edgar, who moved to New York to manage the United States operation and became an American citizen; and Charles, who remained in Montreal to run the central business.

Edgar, who had begun to make a reputation for himself as a colorful fighter for restitution to Holocaust survivors as President of the World Jewish Congress in the 1980s, was the original prospect for Lender to visit. But Brian Lurie, a Reform rabbi who was Executive Director of the Jewish Community Federation of San Francisco, Peninsula, Marin and Sonoma Counties, was a friend of Charles Bronfman's and suggested that Charles be invited. Lurie helped Lender obtain Charles Bronfman's participation and gift and Charles agreed to aid recruitment. A prospect facing a line-up of Wexner, Tisch, Fisher, Bronfman and Lender was like a pitcher facing Ruth, Gehrig, Mays, Mantle and Aaron.

Lender telephoned Charles H. (Corky) Goodman, President-Elect of the Council of Jewish Federations, who played a crucial role in persuading federations to endorse the Operation Exodus Campaign. At the same time, Wexner telephoned Lester Crown, Goodman's brother-in-law and partner.

The Crown name was prominent and visible in Chicago, on properties the family owned including hotels, theaters and office buildings. The family invested outside the city too, for example owning the second largest bloc of New York Yankees stock. But it was best known in Chicago, and not just for its properties. The family was known for philanthropic leadership in every major local cause, supporting self-help and antipoverty programs, and cultural, educational and health institutions throughout "secular" and Jewish life. Indeed, "the Crown

Event," an evening at Lester's residence at which guests pledged $100,000 or more to the Annual Campaign, had been the foundation of the Jewish Federation of Metropolitan Chicago's fundraising for decades; and similar Crown Events raised funds for special and ongoing campaigns across the philanthropic spectrum. The family donated to national and overseas causes as well.

In rather short order, Goodman and Crown established a formidable level of generosity and agreed that Corky would represent the family at the Breakfast. In addition, the presence of Goodman, soon to be head of CJF, while of little interest to outsiders, underscored the image of federation commitment to Operation Exodus.

Whereas some Breakfast participants had benefited from a financial head start in life, Henry Taub began from scratch. Taub was a child of the Depression. His parents were immigrant mill workers from Poland who impressed upon him that a college degree was his ticket out of poverty. Henry graduated from high school in 1944 at the age of sixteen and won a partial academic scholarship to New York University. His mother brought him to freshman registration by train from their cramped apartment in Paterson, New Jersey, the $300 in tuition crumpled in her hand. When Henry emerged from the Registrar's Office onto Washington Square Park, his mother sobbed for joy. "This is the happiest moment of my life," she told him. Little did Mrs. Taub know that Henry would not only emerge from poverty but also that he would embark upon a path to immense prosperity beginning in just a few days.

Henry found a job after class keeping the books for a small firm in a SoHo loft near the university. When he noticed that other firms in the building were too tiny to support a full-time bookkeeper he offered to do their books for them. Soon he noticed that factories nearby had seasonal employees. He offered to be their bookkeeper, and increase and decrease his hours based on their needs, so they could concentrate on their business. "Big companies did not need me, but small entrepreneurs did and were willing to pay me to relieve them of those functions," he recalled years later in an interview. "I had that idea and expanded on it."

Taub graduated from college at age nineteen and, with his brother Joe, rented a small office in Paterson to expand their fledgling business. They became friendly with a tall, lanky kid in a marketing department down the hall, another son of immigrant mill workers. With your business sense and my marketing savvy, the kid in effect told them, someday we'll be rich. They decided to be a threesome. The kid's name was Frank Lautenberg. They called their company

Automatic Data Processing.

In 1961 they bought an IBM 1401 computer. They persuaded brokerage houses, swimming in paperwork, to let them computerize their stock transactions and soon they processed a million trades a day. As automobile accidents increased they began to process some collision claims, then nearly all vehicle insurance claims. Then they were processing nearly all American automobile sales, computerizing auto parts inventories for Detroit manufacturers along the way. Soon they processed paychecks for millions of workers and issued their year-end tax statements. By 1982, when Lautenberg went off to the United States Senate, ADP had become the pioneer in outsourcing and the world's undisputed data processing leader. ADP was a $1.6 billion global enterprise when Lender called Taub to recruit him for the Breakfast.

Taub was more successful than his mother dreamed but he did not hunger for wealth. He had remembered how he hungered for food as a boy. He knew that money was something to be shared, including with the truly hungry. He served as President of the American Jewish Joint Distribution Committee, the UJA Federation Campaign's lifeline of food packages, clothing, medicine and other life sustaining aid to Jews in need on six continents. He was an architect of Project Renewal, a UJA Federation anti-poverty initiative that benefited hundreds of thousands of poor Israelis. He fought poverty in Paterson. And he was current President of United Israel Appeal, which helped the Jewish Agency squeeze out more funds for its worthy programs. An insider, Taub knew about the planned Campaign and was expecting Lender's call. He only needed to know where and when the opening event would be held. "Yes," he told Lender in the briefest of conversations. "I will be present and give."

"Of course I'll be there," Andrew Tisch told Marvin Lender. Andrew was not one to stand on ceremony and Andrew's father Larry, an event co-chair, had already invited him, but Marvin wanted to show Andrew the respect he deserved as a high level donor in his own right. So Marvin telephoned Andrew himself to invite him to the Breakfast. The main difference between Andrew and Larry may have been that, in his earlier years, Larry had to spend most of his youth building his businesses, and gradually provided time and huge sums for philanthropy; Andrew was able to provide pacesetting gifts and volunteer leadership from an earlier age. That he did. Barely 40 in 1990, Andrew was already a national leader as Chairman of the UJA Prime Minister's Council, consisting of $100,000 donors. Andrew told Marvin he had high hopes that the Breakfast giving would inspire others to give generously, and that he and his family could be counted on to undertake solicitations as Operation Exodus progressed.

Charles and Sarah Hoffberger arrived in Baltimore in 1881 to escape from poverty in the Austro-Hungarian Empire. They struggled for years to establish themselves, though, and their seven sons sold coal, ice and wood by horse and wagon to help make ends meet. Later, their children founded the Hoffberger Insurance Company. The couple's children and grandchildren built the company into one of the country's largest family owned full-service insurance agencies, with expertise in horses and photography. Jerold (Chuck) Hoffberger purchased the St. Louis Browns, a Major League baseball team, in 1953, brought it to town and renamed it the Baltimore Orioles, in one of baseball's first franchise relocations. The Orioles became the pride of Baltimore, reaching the World Series five times during Chuck's ownership. Chuck served as Chairman of the Board of Governors of the Jewish Agency from 1980 to 1987 and Charles and other family members were active in many causes, including at The Associated: the Jewish Community Federation of Baltimore. Both Chuck and Charles agreed to participate at the Breakfast.

Peter May received his call from Charles Bronfman. Though May was a long-time New Yorker and Bronfman a Canadian, the two were neighbors in Palm Beach, Florida. May was easy to persuade to give to Operation Exodus; in fact, he even encouraged Bronfman to be as active as possible in the cause.

Blessed with a financial background, outstanding organizational skills and a sense of vision, May and his partner Nelson Peltz had gained control in 1983 of a relatively small packaging company, Triangle Industries, that had $264 million in net sales. Within five years they achieved $4.5 billion in net sales, building Triangle into the world's largest packaging company and the 98th largest industrial company in the United States. Having achieved their business goals, May and Peltz sold their business and began to spend more time with their families.

While serving on a committee of the prestigious Fieldston School in Manhattan, May met Elizabeth Varet, another Fieldston parent, who had long been a leader at UJA-Federation of New York. Varet encouraged May to become active at UJA-Federation too.

May was a third generation American with no family Holocaust background. He was not religious, and felt little vulnerability as a Jew in America. However, he always admired his mother who was active in their Reform Temple and on behalf of the Anti-Defamation League. He went to UJA-Federation, but found the assignments too particularistic and began to drift away. Peggy Tishman, a past president of UJA-Federation, met with him and, as he recalled, "described the mission more completely to me and encouraged me to return."

May exuded an infectious energy, demonstrated exceptional leadership skills and was willing to build a financial commitment. Stephen Solender, New York's Executive Vice President, and Adam Kahan, New York's Vice President, recognized May's leadership potential. They recommended him to be Chairman of the federation's Passage to Freedom Campaign and he was about to become Chairman of the New York Operation Exodus Campaign.

May was enthusiastic about Operation Exodus from the start. He was a substantial Annual Campaign donor already, with gifts of $300,000 in 1988 and $360,000 in 1989. But he did not flinch at the challenge of moving above the level of one million dollars, as he promised Bronfman, and told Max Fisher that when Fisher telephoned him in phase two. May offered to help recruit others to attend and did so. As he recalled in an interview for this book, "I was very excited about the Breakfast, about the idea of a huge amount being raised at one opening event. I thought it was a brilliant idea and had enormous potential to invigorate a new Campaign at all levels of giving."

By the time Leslie Wexner telephoned in phase three, gift closing, May was ready with his answer. He said he would pledge $2 million over the morning's coffee and Danish.

In a City that loves to hate landlords, Lew Rudin was the landlord who was truly loved. He helped build a family real estate business begun more than 60 years earlier by his parents, Samuel and May Rudin, and the Rudin plaque on New York skyscrapers showed what the family owned. But the existence throughout the City of hundreds of neighborhood programs, playgrounds and centers to help struggling New Yorkers, including abandoned youth, the unemployed, the aged, the infirm, the homeless and single mothers showed what they gave away.

Lew Rudin was best known as the Chairman of the Association for a Better New York, which he founded in 1971. From that perch he led countless civic projects and became the City's biggest businessman cheerleader. In the dark days of New York's fiscal crisis, from 1975 to 1983 when it needed help in establishing budgetary independence and fiscal stability, Rudin was regularly featured on television asserting the City would survive and prosper. It was a tribute to the man that, while he stood to gain in real estate values as the City would be rebuilt, no one doubted his love for the City and his belief that wealth within it had to be shared. This mirrored his commitment to share with Jews in need, wherever they lived, and with others. Lew's brother and business partner Jack Rudin was equally active and generous, including as a major contributor to UJA-Federation for decades.

Lew received the call from Larry Tisch, and a follow up from Leslie Wexner, but he said from the start he would attend the Breakfast and that the family would give more than a million dollars. As he recalled years later in an interview, "Jack and I talked about it, and then I spoke with my wife and with Irving Schneider and we all agreed we had to increase our gifts. The one million dollar level just was not high enough for the challenge. We felt this was the right thing to do."

Irving Schneider was Co-Chairman and Chief Operating Officer of Helmsley-Spear, Inc., an owner, among other properties, of the Empire State Building. Schneider began his real estate career in 1946 after graduating from City College of New York and serving in the military during World War II. From early on, he was able to conceptualize imaginative real estate ventures and presented them to Harry Helmsley who implemented them. Schneider's ideas and Helmsley's formidable capital led to handsome profits for both, and Schneider became one of the premier property owners in New York City.

But Schneider continually felt a need to give back, to a wide range of causes, and was especially moved to alleviate children's suffering. He established the Schneider Children's Hospital at Long Island Jewish Medical Center, and the Schneider Children's Medical Center near Tel Aviv, world class institutions that served children of all religions and backgrounds.

Long active in the UJA-Federation system, Schneider raised significant funds as Chairman of Project Renewal; helped create the more efficient UJA-Federation of New York by merging two, sometimes competing, agencies; and was active on finance and budget committees. He readily agreed to participate at the Breakfast at a level similar to that of the Rudins. "We had to get the Jews out of the Soviet Union and to Israel," he recalled. "There was no question about that."

When Alan C. Greenberg was 31 in 1958 he was diagnosed with colon cancer. He said that if he survived, he would live every day his own way. That is pretty much what he has done. However, Greenberg, who grew up in Wichita, Kansas, was already doing that, at least since he was a sophomore at the University of Missouri. When he was accepted by the University, well-meaning friends recommended he change his name so as not to stand out as "too Jewish." So he registered as Ace Gainsboro. But he did not feel he was being true to himself and after a year resumed using Greenberg. He said if Greenberg was good enough for his parents it was good enough for him. He kept the nickname Ace, though, because he was determined to be a winner. He took his belief in himself to Bear Stearns on Wall Street where he worked his magic in the capital markets. He earned huge profits for his clients, the company and himself, and soon became the company's public face and Chairman of the Board.

Greenberg did his philanthropy his own way too. He was unabashedly supportive of UJA-Federation Campaigns, not only chairing the Wall Street Dinner, a main annual fundraiser, but conducting an annual UJA-Federation Campaign on top of the United Way Campaign at Bear Stearns, personally soliciting the top brass. He also has been a major source of scholarships for Danish students in the United States for years, a cause to which he had no personal connection. "The Danes stuck their necks out to save thousands of Jews from Nazi ovens," he said in an interview. "We have to remember those who help us." Queen Margaret II of Denmark remembered him too, and knighted Greenberg—that's Greenberg, not Gainsboro—into the Order of Dannebrog in 1984.

A professional quality magician, Greenberg delighted in visiting hospitals, performing for sick children, often on Saturday nights when visitors were few. He was an enthusiastic bridge player who won a national championship. He reads avidly about animals, intrigued by how some species survived for millennia while others died off quickly.

"That's the way it is with the Jews," Greenberg said in the interview, explaining why he agreed to give a million dollars at the Breakfast on top of the million dollars he had just given to the Annual Campaign. "Life is an illusion and you don't always know who will survive and who not. We Jews have to take care of our own."

The Meyerhoff family is one of the most prominent and philanthropic in Baltimore, in American cultural life and in American Jewish life. During the pogroms in Russia in the early twentieth century, a pivotal development that led tens of thousands of Russian Jews to flee to the United States, Oscar Meyerhoff stayed to fight as long as he could. He protested the atrocities and was imprisoned. When freed, with the cause apparently lost, he bought steamship tickets and took his family to America. He was determined that his family would become financially secure and use its resources to help others. His son Joseph Meyerhoff realized that goal for him, prospering in the construction business and devoting half his time to philanthropy. A chapter in Joseph Meyerhoff's biography is called "50/50," for the 50 percent of his time provided to each. In the 1970's, Joseph Meyerhoff became UJA National Chairman and was close to Yitzhak Rabin during Rabin's first term as Israel's Prime Minister. Richard Pearlstone, a member of the Committee on Soviet Jewry, who would later become National Chairman, was Joseph Meyerhoff's grandson.

There was no question that the family could be counted on again, and for considerably above the million dollar admission fee for the Breakfast. Harvey (Bud) Meyerhoff, Joseph's son and Richard's uncle, would represent the family at the Breakfast. Although heavily committed as the founding Chairman of the United States Holocaust Museum in Washington, Bud Meyerhoff said Operation Exodus must be supported generously despite commitments to other worthy causes.

The next time you slip behind the wheel of your automobile, think of William Davidson of Detroit. Chances are, when you are looking at your windshield, especially if it is a General Motors or Chrysler vehicle, you are looking at his product. A longtime friend of Max Fisher, Davidson took over his uncle's windshield business in 1957 and made it into the fifth largest glass manufacturer in the world. Guardian Industries was his company, and Davidson was its Chairman of the Board, President and Chief Executive Officer for decades. Davidson also made Guardian into one of the world's leading producers of flat glass and fabricated glass for the construction industry, and of fiberglass insulation.

Davidson managed operations in 80 markets in 17 countries on five continents and had 17,500 employees, but he was best known as the owner of professional sports teams. He had been the principal owner and managing partner of the Detroit Pistons in the National Basketball Association since 1974. He also owned the Detroit Vipers and Tampa Bay Lightning hockey teams, and the Detroit Shocks in the Women's National Basketball Association. He was the majority owner of Palace Sports and Entertainment, a mammoth complex in Auburn Hills, Michigan, which was the home court and arena of his teams. The Pine Knob Music Theater, a Midwestern showcase for quality cultural programming, also was at Palace.

Yes, he said to Fisher after a brief conversation. He would be glad to join him at the Breakfast.

Milton Petrie loved bridge and he played it as often as he could at the Regency Whist Club in Manhattan with the boys: Larry Tisch, Ace Greenberg, Al Taubman and Jack Dreyfus. Tisch and his family ran the Loews Corporation. Greenberg ran Bear Stearns. Taubman, the Chairman and controlling stockholder of

Sotheby's, built and operated twenty upscale regional malls including the sprawling Woodfield Mall, the largest mall in Metropolitan Chicago; the Beverly Centre in Beverly Hills; the Montreal Centre; and The Mall in Short Hills (New Jersey). Dreyfus began with the idea in 1951 that if people without enough capital to invest in the stock market could gain low-cost access to a diversified portfolio of stocks they could begin to do so. This would help them build their assets and enable companies to obtain capital for growth. He came up with a mechanism for them to do this and called it a "mutual fund." He named his company the Dreyfus Fund, built the Dreyfus Corporation around it, and spawned an industry that revolutionized investment for 100 million Americans.

Petrie was good at bridge, but he was really good at pleasing women interested in specialty apparel. Beginning in Cleveland in 1927 with $5,000, half of which he was said to have won shooting craps, he opened a small hosiery shop that he expanded into a small chain. Petrie was forced to declare bankruptcy in the Depression, but he reimbursed every creditor, a dollar on the dollar, which made it easier for him to obtain credit when he resumed his business. That he did in the 1940s. He offered low-to-moderately priced women's clothing, choosing variety over high fashion, and keeping costs down with simple designs and no advertising. He hired women to work for him, asked their advice, listened to them, and moved them quickly into executive positions. "They are women," he said. "They know what women want." He began to open stores in the new suburban malls that were beginning to develop, and purchased small related family chains to keep pace with the opportunities from the fast rising suburban population.

By 1990, when Larry Tisch spoke to him at the Whist Club about the Breakfast (Max Fisher made the follow-up call), Petrie Stores Corporation was an empire of 1,500 stores in 48 states, with more than 12,000 employees and net sales of $1.2 billion. Petrie's own published net worth was approaching a billion dollars. He had just given $10 million for the Carroll and Milton Petrie Sculpture Court at the Metropolitan Museum of Art, and a million dollars to Just One Break (JOB), his favorite charity, which provided job training to promote self-sufficiency. But he couldn't say no to the invitation from his New York bridge partner Larry to be present at the Breakfast, and assured his Detroit neighbor Max that he would give above the minimum.

Joseph Wilf was born into a family of Zionists near Krakow, Poland as Hitler rose to power in neighboring Germany. When the Nazis invaded Poland in 1938, he fled to the Soviet Union, soon being separated, forever, from most of his family. When Hitler invaded Russia in 1940, Wilf moved east, to frozen but safer Siberia. Later in the war, he made his way south to Kazakhstan, which was heavily Muslim but secure from the Nazis. There he survived as a slave laborer, including in construction which, despite the horrendous conditions, attracted his interest.

After the war, Wilf emigrated to New Jersey where he, and his brother Harry, who also survived, knew that no financial risk could measure up to the human risk they had experienced in the Holocaust. Knowing a little about construction, they bought vacant land and built houses on it, bought more vacant land and built some more. Soon their business, Garden Homes Management, was a major New Jersey real estate company. They began to build condominiums and then office buildings, shopping centers and hotels, expanding into 37 states and Israel, where the five-star Ramada Renaissance hotels in Tel Aviv and Jerusalem were among their properties.

The Wilf brothers never forgot the idiom of Jewish vulnerability. They gave generously to Jewish causes such as Yad Vashem, the Holocaust memorial and education center in Jerusalem; Yeshiva University, where Jewish knowledge was preserved and Jewish leaders were prepared; and the United Jewish Appeal and Central New Jersey federation, which met urgent needs. "Of course, of course," Joe Wilf told Lender, as he recalled in an interview. "I'll be there." Joe Wilf would become the voice of the Holocaust at the Breakfast, now less than a week away.

What do you serve at a million-dollar-a-plate breakfast? This:

Freshly squeezed orange juice in a cut crystal goblet, garnished with a cluster of champagne grapes. On the bread and butter plate, baby fresh croissants accompanied by honey butter rose on a lemon leaf. A Queen Anne: delicately poached pencil asparagii on a toasted English muffin, topped with a poached egg with stilton cheese sauce and a light spray of caviar. Platters of warm freshly baked rugelach and miniature oval prune and cheese Danish. Coffee and tea with skim milk and clotted cream.

Most guests arrived at the Tent Room at the Regency Hotel in Manhattan a few minutes before 8 a.m. Wexner, Fisher, Lender and Larry Tisch were there first, eager to begin. Some gifts were not locked in at only a million. They hoped participants would be encouraged to give more as they heard the sums that the others pledged. They did not want the timetable condensed. They warmly greeted Charles Bronfman, who knew few of the guests at the time. Bronfman was introduced to them by Tisch, who knew most, as the guests arrived. Goodman, May, Rudin, Greenberg and Taub came in quick succession and soon the room was filled.

By 8:20 a.m., breakfast, the culinary part, was well underway. The program was about to begin. Heightening the historical drama, Wexner, the official host, asked those on one side of the long table to stand behind those seated on the other for a group photograph. And so they were assembled and recorded:

• Standing, top row, left to right: Lewis Rudin; Peter May; Marvin Lender; Mendel Kaplan; Andrew Tisch; William Davidson; Laurence Tisch; Charles Bronfman; Morton Kornreich; Henry Taub; Joseph Wilf; Charles Goodman; and UJA President Stanley Horowitz.

• Seated, left to right: Max Fisher; Harvey Meyerhoff; Leslie Wexner; Irving Schneider; Alan Greenberg; Charles Hoffberger; Milton Petrie; and Jerold Hoffberger.

Dishes were cleared except for coffee, tea and desserts, and the program commenced.

Wexner spoke first.[2] He thanked the participants for coming and said they would begin that morning to write a great chapter in Jewish history. "We have in front of us the most important opportunity in Jewish life since the founding of the State of Israel in 1948," Wexner said. "We can rescue as many as 200,000 Soviet Jews in the next three years, if we establish this Campaign at the right level. We can save them and, in doing so, enrich Israel with thousands of doctors, scientists, musicians, artists, dancers and engineers."

He introduced Lender, who reported on his visit days earlier to Moscow and Kiev. "I have been to the Soviet Union three times in the past year, and felt the excitement building among Soviet Jews," Lender declared. "I heard it in their voices. They are fearful to remain and hope to reach Israel. Years ago when I was at the *Ovir*, the visa office, there was no line. A year ago, the line was out the door. Two weeks ago, the line spun down the block and around the corner. The numbers are burgeoning at all steps in the emigration process. They want to leave and are emboldened to declare their intentions to Soviet authorities. They will get out if we come through with the dollars and lay the basis for the Campaign this morning."

Mendel Kaplan reported for the Jewish Agency in his full South African accent. "Marvin has given you the picture in the Soviet Union," he said. "I can tell you what we are doing for transit and in Israel." He spoke of the movement of thousands of people to three airports, of moving their belongings to ports, and the more difficult task of moving the Soviet bureaucracy. He spoke of

---

2 Nearly all Breakfast of Champions participants were interviewed for this book. Direct quotations were taken from those interviews.

the need for translators, social workers and child care personnel to help the immigrants; and said the immigrants would find jobs and adjust well in Israel. "We must bring the Soviet Jews to Israel," he declared. "Today is the day to establish it is going to happen."

Leslie Wexner returned to the small podium at the head of the long mahogany table covered by a fine-linen tablecloth. Tall, slim, well built and immaculately dressed in business attire, although fair in complexion and soft in voice, Wexner cut an impressive figure. "The Jews are becoming more vulnerable in the Soviet Union every day," he declared. "They yearn to leave. Jews in the Holocaust had no place to go, but these Jews do: Israel. It is our responsibility to get them there." He paused, then stated:

> I have been trying to decide what to give. No one solicited me for a specific sum. How much is enough? What is the right sum? What says what I feel in my heart? I thought, six million perished. I wanted to give something that responded to that, that said something about them, to them, that honored them, even each of them. I thought, move it up to $6 million.
>
> But I worried that, if I did that and said that, it might be seen as a dollar a person. That might seem paltry, might be disrespectful, might say a Jewish life is worth little. But the total would be high.
>
> And a dollar for each of them, every single Jew, every one, every man, every woman, every child, in every concentration camp, in every city, in every field, everyone pulled out of bed in the middle of the night and murdered, it is a way of saying, 'Yes, every Jew killed in the Holocaust counted. Every Jew killed in the Holocaust has to be remembered and honored.'
>
> I would like to pledge $6 million to Operation Exodus.

Lender recognized Max Fisher who said:

> I've given a lot to UJA over the years, as have you. But the issue is what is needed now. We have to get the Jews out of Russia. Out of danger. The situation is unstable. Anything can happen.... None of us are that far away from it, you know? These were our parents or grandparents, or in some cases us, not that long ago. I am pledging $3 million. And I don't need and won't take three years to pay it up.

Then Fisher told them he had spoken to an old friend who could not be present, but who was making a gift to Operation Exodus. His friend was Walter Annenberg, a man few present knew personally but all had heard of. Annenberg, who would turn 82 in a few days, a few months before Fisher, had grown up in privilege in Philadelphia and made the most of it. As editor and publisher of the *Philadelphia Inquirer*, he found readers craving more specific information than newspapers provided. So in addition to improving the *Philadelphia Inquirer*, he founded a series of specialized publications beginning with *Seventeen* magazine in 1944 and made *TV Guide* into a national publication in 1953. He began or bought newspapers, magazines, radio and television stations, amassing great wealth. Like Fisher, he was close to several Republican Presidents and Presidential candidates, especially Richard Nixon. Nixon appointed Annenberg as Ambassador to the Court of St. James's, a position he loved. Annenberg was one of Nixon's few close friends, and hosted him at his estates often during and after Nixon's Presidency.

Annenberg had pioneered private funding of public education and educational television, and founded the Annenberg School of Communications at the University of Pennsylvania, but had not been giving as much to the UJA cause as had others in his economic bracket. In fact, the Jewish Federation of Greater Philadelphia advised Morris Sherman, UJA Vice President for Campaign, only days earlier that the best UJA could expect from Annenberg was $850,000. Fisher had been informed of that but was unfazed; he felt Annenberg's heart contained more than his giving history showed.

> I told him, 'Walter, this is no different from when your parents were in that part of the world. They were lucky to get out. But we have to make sure the others, there now, can get out too.' He said, 'You're right, Max. That's the nub of it.'
>
> He asked me, 'How much do you need from me?'
>
> I told him, 'Walter, I need $15 million.'
>
> He said, 'OK, Max, you've got it.'
>
> I said, 'Fine, Walter, thanks. You have three years to pay it, five million a year. But if you can pay the first five real quick, and follow up with the rest as fast as you can, we will be able to put that cash to work right away.'
>
> 'OK, Max,' he said. 'I'll do that.'
>
> So, gentlemen, I am pleased to announce a gift of $15 million from Ambassador and Mrs. Walter H. Annenberg of Philadelphia to the United Jewish Appeal's Operation Exodus Campaign.

Fisher's announcement electrified the gathering. Even among the extremely wealthy and incredibly generous, there was room to be impressed by wealth and generosity. Suddenly, a gift of a million dollars from those who had not yet pledged seemed low.[3]

Then, continuing the technique UJA had perfected over the decades, of softening everyone to give at higher levels than they intended, Charles Bronfman rose to announce his gift. "I had not had the pleasure to meet most of you until this morning," Bronfman said. "But I do know *of* you, and that you are generous and dedicated people." The slim, soft spoken and bespectacled Bronfman added:

> If ever we are to be generous, gentlemen, this is the time. This is an historic opportunity in Jewish history. That is why we are assembled here, all of us — just us. How much we give today is very important. After 70 years of Communism, we have a chance to get the Jews out of the Soviet Union. We didn't do enough for European Jews during the Holocaust and look what happened. Do we have to wait until a tragedy to act, until there is Jewish blood on the streets? Today we have a chance to rescue Jews rather than cry over their spilled blood. Edgar and I are proud to announce our gift. We pledge $10 million to Operation Exodus.

Larry Tisch was brief but direct. "The scars of the Holocaust are still fresh on all our minds," he asserted. "We have to get the Jews out of Russia -- before it is too late." He pledged $2 million.

Andrew Tisch spoke:

> The rescue of Jews in danger is the obligation of every Jew in every generation. It has always been that way, and always will be. Will ten thousand be able to get out? A hundred thousand? Two hundred thousand? We don't know. However many can, we must see to it that no barrier that we can tear down should stand in their way.

He pledged $1 million.

Peter May spoke of his experiences visiting Jews who had recently emigrated from the Soviet Union and were in transit camps in Italy and Austria:

> I am moved by how personal the immigration is. It is a question of thousands, of tens of thousands, of hundreds of thousands, and also of ones. One child I saw learning Hebrew. One father who told me how much he wanted a better life for his family. One mother trying to hold three

---

3 Fisher did not say that morning what he disclosed in interviews for this book: "What a mistake I made. I should have asked him for more. He agreed so easily."

generations of her geographically-split family together. This is very exciting. I pledge $2 million. We are leaders. Now is the time for us to lead.

Charles Goodman said that he and the Crown family understood the urgency of Jewish emigration from the Soviet Union from their visits there and their meetings with many officials. On behalf of himself and the Crown family, he pledged $3 million. Irving Schneider pledged $3 million. The Hoffbergers, Charles and Jerold, pledged $2.25 million. Harvey Meyerhoff pledged $2 million. William Davidson, $1.5 million. Milton Petrie, $1 million. Alan Greenberg, the man who kept his Jewish-sounding name and still made it in the secular world, said he was in for a million dollars. Marvin Lender, on behalf of himself and his brother Murray, the baker's sons, pitched in a million dollars. Henry Taub, the mill workers' son whose mother had prayed only that he would someday escape from poverty, gave away a million dollars.

Lew Rudin pledged $3 million on behalf of the Rudin families. He seemed to summarize the participants' personal identification with the plight of Soviet Jews:

My grandfather left Russia in 1883 because of the pogroms. I can understand how the Jews there today want to get out for a better life. Just as my grandfather did. Just as your grandparents or parents did. We have to get them out, get them out while there's still time. We're not that far removed from it, you know? One or two steps from the shtetl. That's all.

Maybe fewer. Joe Wilf added this coda as he announced his million dollar gift:

I spent years hiding from the Nazis. I never forget, even for a moment, what can happen. As a Jew, I never feel safe. Never. No Jew can ever feel truly safe. Not even us -- we in this room, with all that we have -- here in America.

After all donors had pledged, Wexner rose with a sheet of paper in his hand, listing the names of the donors with penciled in numbers next to each name and a sum at the bottom of the page. "I am pleased to announce that we have raised $58,750,000 this morning to begin Operation Exodus. Please pay as soon as you can. Thank you. This meeting is adjourned."

Most participants went to their offices, or to airplanes to take them to their home towns. Kornreich and Lender returned to UJA to review and discuss the next steps. By 10 a.m., the room was empty. The table was cleared, the tablecloth removed, the chairs stacked, the carpet perfunctorily vacuumed. There remained neither track nor trace physically of what had transpired that morning in the Tent Room of the Regency Hotel in Manhattan.

However, word of the achievement spread quickly. Within hours, UJA contacted all federations, and donors who could give close to a million dollars, and positioned the results for further giving. The photograph of participants, and the total they gave, was published on page one of every American Jewish newspaper, alerting nearly all American Jews that the Campaign was underway. The Breakfast of Champions was a fantastic triumph. A head-turner it was - - the single greatest fundraising achievement of all time. Operation Exodus, the breathtaking quest to implement the largest voluntary movement of Jews since the Exodus from Egypt, had begun!

CHAPTER THREE
The National Campaign

The State of Israel will be open for Jewish immigration and for the Ingathering of the Exiles... We appeal to the Jewish people throughout the Diaspora to rally around the Jews of Eretz-Israel in the tasks of immigration and upbuilding, and to stand by them in the great struggle for the realization of the age-old dream--the redemption of Israel.

Israel's Declaration of Independence, May 14, 1948

For most fundraising campaigns $58 million denotes success and that the campaign is happily over. But for Operation Exodus it meant it had only begun.

And it was a good thing too. The signs of growing instability in the Soviet Union, of the type that had led Simcha Dinitz to telephone Stanley Horowitz at home on New Year's Day only nine weeks earlier, were becoming more ominous. No one had any idea where things were headed. Political instability has never been good for the Jews, certainly not in Russia, the Ukraine, Central Asia, the Baltic States, the frozen eastern regions and other parts of the Soviet Union. Israeli government and Jewish Agency officials there were sending home dispatches warning that it was increasingly urgent for the Jews to get out.

Hope was the theme, tempered by fear for those still behind, as in this excerpt published the day of the Breakfast of Champions:

> The word hope is repeated time and again in a conversation with Nahum and Natalia Simonovsky, two weeks after their arrival in Israel from Leningrad.
>
> Hope that both of them will find good jobs as pediatricians; hope that they will find a comfortable apartment; above all, hope that their children will grow up to be real Jews.

'We always hoped that one day we could come and live in our homeland,' says Nahum. 'Our hopes have served us well. We Jews have only one country we can call our own. That's why we came here.'

'The situation in the Soviet Union is not healthy,' Nahum says, 'especially for young Jews like ourselves. Perestroika and glastnost have so far been all talk. The economic situation has, if anything, worsened. The only change brought about by liberalization has been an increase in nationalism and anti-Semitism. Such a development is dangerous for Jews. At least here in Israel our children will grow up as real Jews.'[1]

But the dread of what could happen sobered those most closely engaged in the nascent immigration movement. At the end of February Kaplan, Dinitz and senior Israeli government ministers received information that the number of Jews who had declared their desire to emigrate had reached a million. They kept the news from the public, for fear that the Arab countries and the Palestinian Liberation Organization would pressure the Soviet Union to slam shut the gates.

Their fear was well founded. After all, Arab countries had briefly coerced the Soviet Union just a few months earlier to cease issuing visas to Soviet Jews traveling to Budapest and Bucharest, the way stations en route to Israel; and the PLO temporarily forced Hungary and Romania to end their role in the aliyah. The Arab countries had warned that they would reduce the flow of oil to the Soviet Union and client states. The PLO had threatened to blow up Hungarian and Romanian airplanes and kill citizens on the ground in Hungary and Romania. Pressure on the Soviet Union from the United States turned out to be even greater. But for a few tense days it looked as if the Soviet Jewish emigration movement would end soon after it began, and no one was sure that the Soviet Union, Hungary or Romania would be able to stand up to future economic and terrorist threats.

Marvin Lender, Leslie Wexner, Charles Bronfman and Max Fisher had not embellished the dangers at the Breakfast of Champions. They had barely left the room when it began to look as if they had understated them. For the Union of Soviet Socialist Republics, for decades a behemoth on the world stage, whose name struck terror in the hearts of people from CIA headquarters to its own population, was indeed collapsing.

During the very hours of the Breakfast, protests against Premier Mikhail Gorbachev for not moving fast enough to lift the Communist yoke erupted in every one of the 15 republics and drew one million demonstrators. And the

1 Simon Griver, "Hope is the key word for Leningrad couple," *Jerusalem Post*, February 28, 1990, p. 3.

protesters were not asking the Soviet government to institute reforms; they were demanding that it step aside.

March went in like a lion and left like a pride of 15 lions. Utilizing virgin democratic processess and defying fulminating warnings from Moscow, the previously moribund republics moved rapidly toward independence from the Soviet Union. On March 4, 1990 tiny Estonia, with a population far less than one percent of Russia's and only 200 miles from the Soviet legions assembling near Moscow, elected 78 candidates of the independence-minded National Popular Front Party to the 105-seat legislature, turning out 78 Communists from office. One week later on March 11, pugnacious Lithuania, similarly small and only six hours by tank from Moscow, declared itself an independent country. As Gorbachev planned a response, especially to the most egregious threat in Lithuania, the Supreme Soviet, the national parliament that had rubber stamped the plans of Nikolai Lenin, Josef Stalin, Nikita S. Khrushchev, Leonid Brezhnev, Yuri Andropov, Konstantin Chernenko and heretofore Mikhail Gorbachev, voted 1,817 to 133 on March 13, to end the Communist Party's monopoly on political power. On March 20 the Soviet, or legislature, in Stalin's birthplace Georgia declared independence. On March 24, Soviet tanks rumbled into Vilnius in a massive display of military might by a Cold War superpower in the streets of a defenseless citizenry. But the Lithuanians were not dissuaded. On March 28, the Estonian Communist Party disaffiliated from the Communist Party of the Soviet Union. On March 29, Moscow sealed the Lithuanian borders and ordered foreigners to leave the republic, an ominous portent that had preceded the crushing Soviet invasions in Hungary in 1956 and Czechoslavakia in 1968. Moscow's rage was palpable, but the republics remained defiant, as *The New York Times* reported from Vilnius:

> The Soviet authorities sent a column of tanks and paratroopers rumbling past an all-night session of the Lithuanian parliament early this morning, in what witnesses described as the strongest attempt yet to intimidate the republic into abandoning its declaration of independence.
>
> More than 100 tanks and trucks and more that 1,500 soldiers armed with automatic weapons thundered by the parliament building in central Vilnius at about 3 a.m. as legislators worked through the night to complete the creation of an independent government.[2]

---

2 Esther B. Fein, "Moscow's Forces Step up Pressure Across Lithuania," *The New York Times*, March 25, 1990, p. 1.

But protests erupted in the other republics in support of an independent Lithuania and the Soviets did not act. Gorbachev was heir to Lenin who imposed Marxism on an agrarian society; Stalin who mercilessly killed millions of his own countrymen in the Purges; and Khrushchev, who brazenly crushed freedom fighters in Hungary and Poland in 1956 and Czechoslavakia in 1968, introduced missiles into Cuba in the early 1960s and threatened the United States with the infamous words, "We will bury you." But he found his arsenal reduced to vain words. Gorbachev condemned the parade toward independence. Yet his strategy was to scramble to the front of it, control it, and lead the mushrooming movement rapidly through the thickets of *glasnost* and *perestroika* before it consumed the whole Soviet Union.

It did not work. As Gorbachev railed, and Russian President Boris Yeltsin rose, Latvia, Moldova and even Ukraine, the largest republic other than Russia and the breadbasket of the country, moved quickly and in democratic fashion toward independence. The movement was not only in the legislatures; it was fortified in the streets. Newspapers began to report on and promote independence movements and flyers advocating independence were circulated everywhere. The pen was proving mightier than the sword. Gorbachev spent most of March trying to control the pace of change and the rest of it pulling troops out of Eastern Europe, which only made him appear weaker at home.

When he and his ministers and generals stood atop Lenin's Mausoleum in Red Square during the May Day celebration a month later, the enduring icon of Soviet military might that sent chills up the spines of Americans for decades, they were subjected to 25 minutes of catcalls and insults before leaving, visibly shaken by how direct, brazen and "in your face" the proliferating independence movement had become.

Before the year was out, every republic was restive for sovereignty. Boris Yeltsin was elected Chairman of the Russian Supreme Soviet on a pledge to abolish the Soviet colossus. Gorbachev visited the United States to seek capitalist investments to help save the Soviet Union. Press freedoms, and even private land ownership, anathema for decades, were approved in Soviet law.

This was a titanic and complex battle and the Soviet Jews were in the cross hairs. Everyone wanted a better life and most minorities wanted to leave the country entirely. The difference was that Jews had a place to go: Israel. That in itself made them unpopular.

Not that in a thousand years Jews had ever been popular in Russia. After centuries of periodic attacks by tsars and cossacks and all manner of local vigilantes, a wave of pogroms drove hundreds of thousands to America at the turn of the twentieth century. It was only the century's first installment of Russian anti-Semitism. Lenin denounced Zionists and other Jewish parties, Stalin purged Jews and held them responsible for threatening his life in the Doctor's Plot. Georgi Malenkov, Nikolai Bulganin, Khrushchev, Brezhnev and Kosygin ostracized and suppressed them. At various times Jews were accused of undermining the November Revolution of 1917; blamed for genocide in the Civil War between the Whites and the Reds, for the failures of collectivization, and for the Purges; denounced for destroying Russian churches and historical monuments; and generally suspected of treason and of corrupting Russian traditions as clandestine agents of Western culture. Even the medieval charge of murdering Christian children to use their blood to bake matzah sometimes resurfaced.

But the Soviet rulers had never tolerated violence of any kind (except when inflicted by the government itself) because it threatened stability. Thus they put a lid on unofficial anti-Semitism along with other public opinion. However, as Gorbachev moved forward with *glasnost* and *perestroika*, Soviet repression eased. Ironically, *glasnost* made it easier for Soviet citizens to openly attack Jews for foisting economic and social ills on their neighbors, and *perestroika* made it easier to throw them out of their jobs.

Instability and uncertainty grew, not only in Moscow, Leningrad, Kiev, Odessa, Dnepropetrovsk, Kharkov, Minsk and other large cities, but even more so in rural areas, including the Asian Republics of Kazakhstan, Uzbekistan and Azerbaijan where Moscow's secular authority was thousands of miles away and the local populations were overwhelmingly Muslim.

These were fertile areas for the growth of Ku Klux Klan-type groups that trumpeted patriotism, remembered the good old days that never were, and blamed all problems on the Jews who, locally, were almost completely unprotected. With erosion of Soviet authority, Jews in Central Asia, for example, found that they depended on local Muslim policemen for protection, the policemen being as hungry and cold as anyone else in the disintegrating Soviet Union and as ignorant and willing to turn the Jews into scapegoats.

Public movements dedicated to scapegoating the Jews took root. Of these, the most infamous was *Pamyat*. *Pamyat* thugs beat up local Jews and torched synagogues. Under *glasnost* Pamyat was allowed access to national television several times to air its canards that Soviet Jews were part of a worldwide conspiracy headquartered in New York and Tel Aviv, and that Jews were making money on everyone's misery. By early 1990 *Pamyat* had established hundreds of local chapters and was attracting thousands of new members every month.

There was no twentieth century precedent for an empire as large and powerful as the Soviet Union unraveling from within, and no one knew what would happen. *Pamyat* worried the Soviet Jews. *Glastnost*, even more than *Pamyat*, scared the Soviet Jews half to death. The number of Jews declaring their desire to emigrate, swollen beyond one million, grew by thousands every month.

Meanwhile in Israel 17,569 Soviet Jewish immigrants arrived in just the first three months of 1990, easily exceeding the 12,721 total for all of 1989. Some went to absorption centers, the separate villages or dormitories where immigrants lived temporarily, learned Hebrew and benefitted from a variety of government and Jewish Agency services. However, social planners no longer favored the centers, and the new immigrants didn't want them either, so Israel found them apartments in cities and towns where immigrant services could be provided. The immigrants were welcomed everywhere. Municipalities hired Russian-speaking staff, painted Russian words on street signs (already written in Hebrew, Arabic and English) and set up welcoming committees. As Ze'ev Bielski, mayor of Ra'anana near Tel Aviv told me then, "We are trying to help them learn how to be Israeli, how things get done in this country, how to shop, find a job, get a driver's license. We want them to feel welcome. We have more residents signed up to help immigrants than we have immigrants." In April, their first Passover in freedom, 97 percent of all new immigrants in private housing and 100 percent in absorption centers were invited to a seder, and an overwhelming majority accepted the invitation.

Israel's heart was in the right place, but its bureaucracy wasn't. Although Shamir had announced a year earlier that housing for incoming immigrants would be the priority, an analysis in January concluded that there were only 19,100 empty apartments in the whole country, including 2,600 in rural areas.[3] If rooms in fleabag hotels, youth hostels and guest houses were counted, a full 100 percent occupancy would still be reached in another two or three months. Shamir knew there wouldn't be a room at an inn before long.

Shortly after Passover a few greedy landlords, tempted by the saturated market and the government's willingness to pay rent a year in advance to settle newcomers, raised rents and evicted hapless Israelis priced out of the market. Fourteen tent camps sprouted around the country, including one in front of the Knesset.[4]

Shamir called onto the carpet those ministers whose turf battles were holding up progress and knocked their heads together, but they were only part

---

3 "Report on the Activities of the Inter-Ministerial Committee on Absorption Chaired by Deputy Minister of Finance Yossi Beilin," as summarized in an internal Jewish Agency document issued by Moshe Nativ, Jewish Agency Director-General, February 13, 1990. The Committee was coordinating the absorption effort.

4 "'Tent Cities' Spread Through Israel," *Jewish Telegraphic Agency*, July 11, 1990, p. 2.

of the problem. The Construction Workers Union, a powerful component of *Histadrut*, the umbrella labor organization in the still semi-socialist Israeli economy, was balking over work rules. The Construction Industry Council, a powerful builders' organization, was seeking to extract more favorable incentives. Bureaucrats throughout the ministries adhered to arcane regulations. As late as June, even when all approvals were obtained, it was still taking six months for a shovel to pierce the ground.

Something drastic had to be done or thousands more would be on the streets before long. There was only one knight, even his fiercest opponents agreed, who could slay the Israeli bureaucratic dragon. Ariel Sharon, an outcast since 1982, when he did not prevent the Sabra and Shatilla massacres in Lebanon, returned triumphantly from the dustbin of history. Sharon wasn't nicknamed "The Bulldozer" for nothing. With broad emergency powers, he took office as Minister of Housing and immediately imported 45,000 prefabricated homes over the objection of Histadrut. He obtained Knesset approval to transfer the Israel Lands Administration to his ministry, to provide faster access to vacant tracts where the homes could be erected, over the objection of the Ministry of Agriculture. He persuaded Shamir to suspend the income tax landlords paid on low-rent apartments, which provided an effective ten percent increase in profit and muted inducements to seek evictions. He broke ground for the first 3,000 units of prefabricated housing in early July, thrusting the first shovel into the ground himself. Later in the year, he used his reborn influence to help obtain budget realignments to maintain a building pace that kept supply ahead of demand. True to his word, Sharon built all units within the Green Line, none on the West Bank or in Gaza.

But not everyone welcomed the new immigrants:

> I want to say clearly: open fire on the new Jewish immigrants, be they Soviet, Falasha or anything else. It would be disgraceful of us if we were to see herds of immigrants conquering our land and settling our territory and not raise a finger. I want you to shoot, on the ground or in the air, at every immigrant who thinks our land is a playground and that immigration to it is a vacation or picnic. I give you explicit instructions to open fire Do everything to stop the flow of immigration.[5]

The United Jewish Appeal's Young Leadership Cabinet was founded in 1964

---

5 Yasser Arafat, quoted in the Lebanon weekly newspaper Al-Mohar, reported in Martin Gilbert, *A History of Israel From the Rise of Zionism to Our Time*, New York: Random House, 1996, p. 544.

by Rabbi Herbert A. Friedman, then UJA's Executive Vice Chairman and Chief Executive Officer, to introduce the next generation of Jews to UJA giving. In general the Cabinets (Young Women's Leadership was later added) showed wealthy Jewish activists in their 30s and 40s that UJA provided access to power brokers, other committed Jews of means and experience not otherwise available to them.

Their main event was their joint biannual Young Leadership Conference, the seventh of which was being planned for March 11-13 at the Washington Hilton. The Conference offered the 2,200 participants from 37 states who checked in on a cool but sunny afternoon a program featuring talks by senior Bush and Shamir administration officials, small-group lobbying sessions with Senators and Representatives on Capitol Hill and workshops with leading Jewish thinkers.

Fundraising was not on the formal agenda, but the issue of Soviet Jewry was on everyone's mind. The savvy participants knew about the increasing flow of Jews to Israel; most had seen the photo of Breakfast participants and read of the fledgling Campaign in their local newspapers. The issue of Soviet Jews quickly took over the Conference as participants peppered nearly all speakers with questions about what was happpening and how they could help.

They got their answer from a slim, five-foot-tall, 27-year-old former Soviet dissident who addressed the plenary. Marina Furman had met with Cabinet leaders in Leningrad in 1988, and her quest for freedom had become their cause. Finally free, but representing those who were not, Furman, wearing a high-necked brown dress, without jewelry or makeup, kept the Grand Ballroom enraptured in silence for 20 minutes, without notes or pause. This is part of what she said:

> I don't have enough English to tell you how happy I am to be out of Russia. From a small child I knew I was to suffer because I am Jew. The teacher in my class told children, "Marina is Jew. She comes from people who used to drink blood of Christian children for Jewish holiday...." My grandfather dreamed to be buried in Israel but even this simple dream did not happen. He died day we received refusal [denial of emigration]. But I dreamed to live in Israel....

> I was able to meet Americans on a UJA mission who visited me and knew of my plight. UJA Young Leadership came back to United States and conducted a campaign for me and my family to leave Russia.

> Policeman arrested me for wanting Jews to be able to be free and put me in cell with 30 drunkards who beat me and put me in coma for three months. I woke up in hospital and found I had problems in my heart.

I met Lev who taught Hebrew, which was against the law. We fell in love and married and I became pregnant. When I was two months pregnant I was sick and taken to hospital in Leningrad. KGB officer came to me in hospital and said, 'It is time for you to decide what you want. If you will continue your struggle for Soviet Jews, if you continue your struggle to go to Israel, if your husband continues to give Hebrew lessons, then when you come into hospital to have your baby, and you know you must because government says women must have babies only in hospital, you and your baby will not leave hospital alive. When you both die no one will have anything to say because you have heart problems.

'And if you think your dear friends in United States will help you you are very wrong. They cannot reach into hospital to help you. No one will cry that you are dead and your child is dead. Think, Marina. You will die and you will make your baby die if you continue to do this for Soviet Jews.'

But we did not give up hope. When came time for child to come, I went into hospital. They did not give me medicine for the pain and they told the staff they could not help me in any way. The pain was great, but I thought about the six million Jews killed in Holocaust and the one million children. There were one million mothers who could not save their children. That was a pain a thousand times childbirth.

A physician passed by my room and thought this crime was too big to participate in. He saved me and my child. He was fired for saving Jewish lives.

I named my baby Aliyah in hope that our dream of aliyah would become reality.

Still KGB came to me and said, 'Even if every other Jew leaves Russia, you and your family will die here.' Lev and I were imprisoned for resistance, but they knew American Jews were watching. They released us on Chanukah. Our freedom was a miracle that UJA Young Leadership made happen.

But I cannot be happy without freedom for million more Soviet Jews. Someone I knew from Russia asked, 'Why are you going to talk to the American Jews? They live a life of safety and privilege and have never been persecuted. How can they understand?' I said, 'I will tell them. They will understand. They will help more.'

I say to you tonight, this could be the biggest exodus of Jews of all time - - and willingly. Every one of you can be a Moses, to lead the Soviet Jewish people to freedom in Israel. The gates are opening. You must help.

Furman held aloft two photographs, one of Moscow, one of Jerusalem. Pointing to the first, she said, "This is our past." To the second, "This is our future."

As Heidi Damsky of Birmingham, Alabama, a Conference Co-Chairman, recalls, "Spontaneous fundraising broke out. Well, orchestrated spontaneity." Although the UJA Young Leaders did not decide to fundraise until after the Breakfast of Champions fewer than two weeks earlier, when they did, as always with UJA, nothing was left to chance.

"We needed more intimate groups so people could be motivated by others' enthusiasm, others' gifts," Damsky said. "We rented all available meeting rooms in the hotel but couldn't fit everyone in. So we solicited many gifts in the hallways, in corners of the Ballroom. We had placed a Cabinet leader or UJA professional at every one of the 200 tables before we broke so that no one got lost. We didn't surprise or pressure anyone to give. It was a natural outgrowth after Marina's speech."

"There was tremendous pent-up emotion to help the Soviet Jews," recalls Brian Abrahams, the Cabinets' director. "There was a sense, 'We lobbied for this; now we have to deliver on the second half of what we started.' Everyone wanted to help and the quickest and easiest way was to give money, to give it fast, as much as they could. They felt it was the least they could do. The fundraising was like a coiled spring that had a chance to be expressed. There was a real sense of moment in Jewish history."

None of the angst that had gripped the Breakfast donors was present: the shadow of the Holocaust, collective guilt over inadequate American Jewish response years earlier, worry about Jewish fate under Communism. The Young Leaders focused solely on the future. Idealistic, they expected that they would have their way on the grand stage because truth can stand up to power. They were convinced that the Soviet Jews would reach Israel because the Young Leaders themselves would make it happen. They were aware of past American Jewish lethargy, and some feared for the Jews as the Soviet Union was collapsing, but their unbridled emotion was hope.

The participants reconvened in the Grand Ballroom. Stuart T. Rossman of Boston, a Conference Co-Chairman, announced that Conference organizers had received 1,400 gifts (some participants came as married couples) and that $3.5 million was raised, most of it paid in checks submitted on the spot. He tried to continue, saying that many people had promised to give more once they were home and that many solicitations for $25,000 and more had begun at the Conference and would be completed in coming days. But the participants drowned out his words. They applauded lustily, rose, whisked away chairs to provide dancing room, waved for Furman to take a seat within a circle, held her chair aloft and shook the rafters with a raucous rendition of, *"Heveinu shalom aleichem"* ("We bring peace to you," or in context, "Relax, you're welcome and safe here"). Within hours, news of the fundraising achievement and the chord Operation Exodus had struck was spreading in their home cities and towns.

Marvin Lender was on the dais when Marina Furman spoke and was astonished by the breadth and depth of support for Operation Exodus. This, even though he had come up through Young Leadership himself. There had been no indication that so many high gifts could be obtained without basic fundraising groundwork and private solicitations.

Lender was especially encouraged because he knew that seeing and hearing Jews *who yearned to get out* would raise even more funds than seeing and hearing someone *who had already emigrated.* If prospects went to Russia and met many Marina Furmans, he knew, they would give even more to Operation Exodus. UJA was arranging such a trip. Lender set the pledge requirement at $100,000, dropping the major gifts bar from a million dollars to aim at a wider market of prospects—seven hundred as opposed to fewer than a hundred. UJA insiders below that level were invited to join in the trip too; he wanted to inform and ignite the cadre of 70 National Vice Chairmen, 178 federation Campaign Chairmen and 50 local Operation Exodus Chairmen and hedge UJA's bets if it could not secure 100 other participants. Most of them were able to give only $25,000 or $50,000, but, of course, you could make another million with twenty $50,000 gifts.

Richard Pearlstone of Baltimore was named Chairman of the Mission, which was billed as the UJA Inaugural Operation Exodus Mission to Russia and Israel. Pearlstone's proven financial support gave him credibility both to recruit Jews at the $100,000 base, far below his own gift level, and to solicit them for more once they were overseas, the crucial twin requirements of a UJA mission chairman. As a veteran mission leader in Russia, Pearlstone could allay fears about travel in a crumbling, hostile empire. As an experienced solicitor, he could make an excellent fundraising pitch. He did not disappoint.

One hundred and twenty of the wealthiest Jews in America were aboard the Swiss Air McDonnell 1011 as it taxied down the runway from John F. Kennedy International Airport on March 24, soaring into the black sky on its way to the boiling cauldron of the Soviet Union. Many of those who settled in for the long flight had been on prior UJA missions to Israel and to the decimated but surviving Jewish communities in Poland, Hungary, Czechoslovakia, Romania and Austria. Some had visited the Soviet Union. A few had undertaken clandestine trips in the 1980s, and even the 1970s when the cause was just emerging in America, and met with "Refuseniks" like Natan Sharansky, Yuli Edelshtein, Ida Nudel, Vladimir Slepak and Iosef Begun, Soviet Jews who risked everything for the right to emigrate. The visitors had risked their own safety to encourage the Refuseniks, and to let Soviet authorities know the Jews had important friends in the United States. They brought in outlawed religious articles as well as electronic equipment that the dissidents, who had lost their jobs because of their protests, could trade on the black market for food. Pearlstone and Lender knew the Russian Jews they would meet would provide valuable perspectives.

The word "mission" can have religious or even evangelical connotations, but at UJA it simply meant a trip with a purpose. For participants, the purpose was to meet Jews in remote countries and glimpse what their lives were like. UJA's purpose was fundraising. Few things raised money for UJA like overseas missions, the Breakfast of Champions being a notable exception. Donors can participate in twenty missions and still be moved on the 21st. Every time they went they gave more than the huge sums they pledged before departure, more than they anticipated, more than they imagined. This always happened. They went again anyway.

As the cabin lights dimmed after dinner, Pearlstone and Lender clicked on their overhead reading lights to review the latest faxes from their team on the ground in Moscow. They were looking for assurances that the prospects would have sufficient personal contact with Jews in need. They knew that no donor could plead financial difficulty after visiting courageous Jews striving to emigrate. This was the first of dozens of UJA Operation Exodus missions, projected to bring 6,000 donors abroad in the year, every one to be asked to give more than he or she had promised.

In Moscow, the first stop was the Chorale Synagogue, a 160-year-old building similar in appearance to other synagogues built in the nineteenth century in Eastern Europe and Russia. The participants filed in past rows of mahagony-stained pews and sat down in the front. Before them was a large *bimah*, the platform where the Torah was read on Mondays, Thursdays and Saturdays and from where their first host was about to speak. Behind the bimah, steps led to a higher platform in front of the Holy Ark, which contained Torah scrolls. An Eternal Lamp hung in front of the Holy Ark. Off to their right was a large illuminated panel with hundreds of words written in Russian. It was a prayer asking blessings on the Soviet authorities -- just in case soldiers or police barged in and were suspicious of the murmurings in Hebrew. Until 1917, it asked blessings for the tsar and his family. In two more years it would ask blessings for the post-Soviet Russian authorities. The Jews lived on.

The pews provided seating for a thousand, but hosted fewer than a hundred on an average Shabbat, and a few hundred on major Jewish holidays. But the sanctuary had also long served as a place for Jewish dissidents to gather, in a country where the congregation of even three persons on the street without a permit was against the law. In the past, dissidents whispered to avoid detection by the Soviet listening devices. Now, with the Soviet Union crumbling, there was no longer need to whisper. The participants received an earful from Rabbi Adolf Shayevitch, Chief Rabbi of Russia, about the growing anti-Semitism.

"We have scattered instances of Jews being beaten by small mobs," said Shayevitch, bearded and dressed in Orthodox garb. "Jewish children are criticized for Israeli policies at school. Cemeteries have been vandalized. Flyers say Jews are responsible for the economic problems. A gang broke into a meeting at the House of Writers in Moscow and beat up the Jewish writers, claiming a Zionist conspiracy. Pamyat is behind some of this, but not all." He added ominously, "*Glasnost* is the ironic culprit. It has made it easier for people to express themselves and what more and more are doing is expressing their view that Jews are responsible for all the ills of Mother Russia." He added, "I know many people who never wanted to leave but now they want to get out. You call it immigration. I call it flight."

As participants filed out, near the rear an old Russian man with thinning white hair, deep wrinkles, a gold front tooth amidst dental gaps, a white shirt so worn it was gray, asked visitors as they passed by, *"Fershtaist Yiddish?"*

"No," the first three said.

This writer was next and said, *"Ich fershtai a bissel* (I understand a little)."

The old man seized my arm above the elbow and held tightly. His eyes were wide and fearful, his voice trembling. *"Du iz nisht gut fur Yidden. Ich hub moira."* He clenched his jaws and blurted, *"Nem mich tse Israel."* (Here it is not good for Jews. I am afraid. Take me to Israel.)

Later, at a restaurant, participants heard from Michael Chlenov, President of the Va'ad (the "Board," formally known as the Confederation of Jewish Organizations and Communities of the Soviet Union, a nascent secular authority). He said Jews were filled with fear as Soviet authority crumbled, and wanted to make aliyah. He stressed, though, that many of the estimated two million Jews in the country would not leave; therefore, Jewish life in the country must be rebuilt. The participants were seated around fourteen tables, each with a Va'ad member present. During the meal one visitor asked, "How else can we help, beyond giving more?" The Va'ad member answered, "Teach us how to make business. Teach us how to make money to take care of ourselves like you Jews in America."

In late afternoon, participants arrived at the Soviet Foreign Ministry to meet with Ambassador Yuri Reshtev, Commissioner of Human Rights and Humanitarian Affairs, who said the government was aware of Pamyat and anti-Semitism but that the Jews were safe. Reshtev also said that once Jews were processed they could leave for wherever they liked.

Martin F. Stein asked pointedly, "Does the government believe that Soviet Jews should be allowed to go to Israel?"

"The *Ovir* (emigration office) has been processing more and more applications and many more Jews have been approved to leave," Reshtev replied.

"We have heard there might be a deliberate slowdown in the processing; is that going to happen?" Stein asked.

"I will look into that, but we have no such plans," Reshtev answered.

"Right now, Jews who wish to move to Israel can only obtain visas for Europe where they must remain for months of further processing," Stein said. "Isn't it time for direct flights from the Soviet Union to Israel?" He knew the issue was sensitive. The Soviet Union was under ferocious pressure from American Jews and the American government to allow direct flights, which would rapidly increase immigration to Israel, and under ferocious pressure from the PLO and Arab countries to do no such thing.

Reshtev conferred in Russian with his aides and responded, "I do not know enough about this. I will look into it."

Shoshana Cardin, Chairman of the National Conference on Soviet Jewry, asked why Gorbachev did not strongly condemn anti-Semitism. Reshtov answered, "We have about 100 nationalities in the Soviet Union. If Gorbachev made a statement in favor of one nationality, I don't know if it would be a good course, especially when other groups are in bad shape and even in civil war. A new human rights bill for all citizens will be signed within months and it will further protect the Jews."

Victor Gelb of Cleveland spoke up, using a tactic that had helped Sharansky, Edelshtein, Nudel, Slepak, Begun and other Refuseniks--citing their names in direct appeals to Soviet authorities. "Even though the gates have opened somewhat, there are at least 100 Refuseniks," Gelb said. "Anatoly Genis has been waiting since 1976. When will he have permission to leave?"

Reshtev said, "I know his case. I will look into it."

There is no way to know how much meetings like this helped chip away resistance by the government, but Soviet policies soon changed. Gorbachev issued his first statement condemning anti-Semitism the next month. Genis was allowed to emigrate in July. The old man in the synagogue made it to Israel in August. Direct flights were instituted the next year.

In any case, the tough questions the participants raised unquestionably helped Operation Exodus and the mission members themselves. The participants were wealthy and influential in the U.S., but they had never had access to the sanctuaries of Soviet power from which threats to bury the United States had emerged for decades. Now they had the opportunity to say the things they dreamed they could say to help Soviet Jews emigrate. UJA empowered them greatly, and they would remember it.

They assembled for a relaxing dinner at a Russian restaurant and went to bed early. Pearlstone, Lender, Stein, Rani Garfinkle, Alan Shulman and other UJA solicitors met into the night, reviewing the 120 5x7 index cards, each contain the name and giving history of a participant. During the next day they would begin to take donors aside, starting with those rated for the potentially highest gifts, invite them to reflect on their experiences, and begin to float large numbers for them to consider donating. There are, of course, skeptics in every group, and this was so on the mission. But not for long.

Everyone was down to breakfast at 7 a.m. on their second morning in Moscow. The few who were kosher or distrusted Soviet food ate crackers and tuna fish from pop-open cans they had brought from the United States, while the rest sipped good coffee and consumed bread with spreads. None touched the swigs of vodka they were served even before morning coffee, a Russian custom.

By 8 a.m., the participants arrived by bus in an open area behind a Jewish Community Center, where they were met by more than 50 Russian drivers. They were divided into groups of two or three, given a translator and driven to the homes of nearby Jews. There the case for leaving, and the need for giving, was brought home to them. They had expected to be moved on their visit, to enjoy the access to political power, the synagogue visit and meetings with local Jewish leaders, but they underestimated the power of meeting Soviet Jews privately in their living rooms. For there, rich comfortable, secure Jews from America, they were face to face with Soviet Jews who could not yet get out.

Half an hour from downtown Moscow, one driver stopped near a large courtyard and the participants walked gingerly across large patches of frozen snow into a massive, block-long, battleship gray building. Inside, they were uncertain about the elevator, fearing no one would come if it stopped between floors. They took the darkened staircase winding around it, guided by daylight from small windows on landings. A dusty breeze greeted them as they climbed when the creaky lift passed by, its walls open and separated from the surrounding staircase by a curlicue metal grating.

Inside an apartment they met Georgi and Tatiana, a couple in their late thirties who served them coffee and cake (provided in advance by UJA). They proudly showed their visitors photographs of their children, Zygmundt, II and Nita, 8, who were in school. Georgi was a civil engineer known to the authorities as "Georgi the Jew," because he had defied warnings not to seek to emigrate. Despite three years confinement in a Siberian jail he came back even more determined, and encouraged others to try to leave too. Tatiana was a Hebrew teacher; she had not been imprisoned although the teaching of Hebrew in the 1980s was illegal, but she was harassed. Zygmunt and Nita were each beaten by other children in school because their family wanted to move to Israel. The word zhid (kike) was carved onto their door; they had painted it over but did not scrape it away, leaving it faint enough to be invisible to passersby but clear enough to remind them never to stop trying to emigrate to Israel.

"The lines at the Ovir are growing," Georgi said through an interpreter. "There are thousands more like us, tens of thousands across the Soviet Union. This is no land for Jews. Sooner or later it always gets worse. We deserve a better life.

"We have children," Tatiana added, speaking English with a heavy Russian accent. "You are a mother?" she asked a woman present, who nodded. "You understand," Tatiana said.

William Shure visited an old woman who had lost her husband in the battle of Stalingrad and was alone in the world, except for a Jewish community volunteer who visited her daily, and food packages from the American Jewish Joint Distribution Commmittee. "She said she was too old and too sick and too used to her way of living to move," Shure recalls. "She made me realize that that as large as the aliyah was going to be, there would be a million or two left behind. I think of that woman very often even though many years have passed. She lived there. She probably died there. But it made me think while I was sitting on her old couch, and looking at the faded photographs of her husband in his World War II uniform, that every day delayed was making it too late for somebody. It was 50 years too late for her and shouldn't be 50 minutes too late for someone else. That's when I really understood how important Operation Exodus was."

Lois Zoller of Chicago visited a mother whose son was bloodied by classmates after an anti-Semitic diatribe by his teacher. Alan Shulman visited a family that had obtained permission and they described it as their dream come true. Marvin and Murray Lender met a frail, blind, 93-year-old man whose quest to make aliyah had endured for years (they met him soon in Israel); they were motivated by his determination. Pearlstone visited a scientist who had lost his professorship years earlier because he sought to make aliyah; now he had neither a professional position nor permission to leave. Norma Buxbaum of Des Moines, Rabbi Matthew Simon of Rockville, Maryland, Rani Garfinkle of Franklin Lakes, New Jersey, Joel Leibowitz of Parsippany, New Jersey and 130 others had similar experiences.

Marshall Jacobson, recalled the mission well:

I remember it as clear as day. Discussions among the participants, and in the few solicitations we were able to squeeze in in those hectic days in Russia, showed we had two distinct clusters on the mission. One was older, not very old but old enough to remember Jewish vulnerability say before the Six-Day War in '67. They knew they were in the vanguard of something historic and that they were in on the ground floor. They were overwhelmed and inspired, as everyone always is on a mission, but they felt the fear, the danger, the chance it could all unravel and none of them would get out. They were primed to give because they knew that life was at stake.

The other group was younger and was skeptical. They almost did not want to be moved but wanted to see if it was real, if they would find a Sharansky and they doubted that they would. And they were right. Sharansky was Sharansky. There was only one of him. But they did find something else. Behind Sharansky, and Nudel and Slepak and the others in the vanguard who had made it out, were people named Arkady and Irina and Andrej and Serge. They weren't as charismatic, but they were Jews and they were suffering because of it.

I remember having discussions with the younger participants about this. They thought before they left the U.S. that once the glamor was stripped away they would find nothing, but what they found was just as compelling. Everyday people, struggling for a better life. Struggling to live a Jewish life. These people had hope and their visitors felt it. It was like the hope their grandparents had when they left Russia or other countries of oppression decades earlier. Then they identified with them and saw that these Russian Jews were like them, wanted the same things, and couldn't get anything without help. That's when they knew, one by one, discovering for themselves, that their job was to give and help them get out.

And the mission was only half over. At 11 p.m. on March 24, their flight departed for Tel Aviv, two hours by air but five hours by flight plan to avoid flying over Iran, Iraq and Syria. In Israel, the participants visited Soviet Jews in their homes and work places in Ra'anana, Beersheba, Ashkelon, Carmiel and Mevasseret Zion; they learned that Israelis were delivering on the promise to help them build a better life. They met with Prime Minister Shamir and Defense Minister Rabin as well as Jewish Agency and JDC officials. They were offered a lavish smorgasbord of Middle Eastern cuisine near poolside at the King David Hotel and had a chance to walk around the Old City of Jerusalem and pray at the Western Wall. Each programming component reinforced the mission's motivational theme, the preciousness and precariousness of Jewish freedom.

The mission culminated, as UJA missions always did, with a caucus, which is a speech by an Israeli leader followed by a forum in which participants rise one by one, express what moved them most, and state how much they would give to the United Jewish Appeal. Of course, the UJA fundraising team had managed somehow, in one intensive week of 12 to 15-hour days of programming amid the rigors of constant travel to and around two countries, to open, develop and close every gift. The speaker was Finance Minister and former Prime Minister Shimon Peres, who spoke of the aliyah as a defining moment in Jewish history and an opportunity for American Jews to express their support for Israel and Soviet Jews. The caucus took place at the Knesset, before three huge tapestries by Marc Chagall portraying the flow of Jewish history. One by one the donors rose and announced their gifts (largest givers first). The caucus was good therapy; it allowed everyone to bring the experience to an emotional close before the flight home later that night. It also was good fundraising. The UJA raised $11,041,000 for Operation Exodus.

"A billion here, a billion there; before you know it you are talking about real money." In the 1960s Senate Republican Minority Leader Everett M. Dirksen was decrying the easy outflow of funds from excessive government spending. But in the first days of March Marvin Lender and his team could not get out of their minds the easy inflow of funds, and how fast *a million here, a million there* were adding up to real money for Operation Exodus. The Breakfast of Champions had no sooner ended, and the Young Leadership Conference and Inaugural Mission were still being planned, when solicitations *continued* at the million-dollar level.

After the Breakfast, Leslie Wexner headed to LaGuardia International Airport where he boarded his private plane, ate lunch, and made a stopover in Indianapolis to meet his friend Melvin Simon. Simon had been born a step above poverty in New York, to a tailor and a homemaker. He graduated from the prestigious Bronx High School of Science and was able to study real estate at City College of New York because it offered free tuition. Simon joined the Army in 1953, was assigned to Fort Benjamin Harrison in Indiana, liked the area, and decided after discharge to live there. He gained exposure to the local real estate market as a leasing agent and made good initial investments. In 1959 he formed his own company, Melvin Simon and Associates, and persuaded wealthy investors to pool their money with him to leverage their potential. He began by developing small strip centers, anchored by groceries and drugstores. By 1967 his company owned and operated three million square feet of retail property, and was adding a million square feet more every year. Within 15 years, Simon was opening three malls a year.

Mel and his brother Herb, his business partner, loved Indianapolis, and were the ultimate home town boosters. For example, they always bought season tickets to see the Indiana Pacers, the National Basketball Association team, play. When Mayor Bill Hudnut told them in 1983 that the Pacers might be sold to a conglomerate that would relocate the team, the Simon brothers bought the Pacers to keep the team in town.

Mel was making decisions regarding his company's management of the Mall of America under construction near Minneapolis, Minnesota, soon to become the nation's largest mall, when Les stopped by to chat about Operation Exodus. Les had already spoken with Mel, and Mel and Herb had spoken and they knew that whether or not they could be in New York for the Breakfast, the cause had to be supported. "We met for a short while," Wexner recalled. "They gave a million and a half."

Wexner said thanks, boarded his plane and flew to Atlanta where he met the next morning with Arthur Blank and Bernard Marcus. Arthur had grown up in one-bedroom apartments in Queens and Bernie had lived in tenements in Newark before they moved to Atlanta and found jobs in the Handy Dan home improvement chain. They rose to the top of Handy Dan but a corporate raider took over in 1978, concluded he could do better without them, and fired them both. So Blank and Marcus opened their own stores, losing a million dollars in 1980. But they honed their understanding of what homeowners needed, and built a staff they empowered by selling them shares of the business. Soon they recovered. When Les arrived on behalf of Operation Exodus, few in America knew the name of Handy Dan but everyone knew the name of Arthur and Bernie's company: Home Depot. Blank and

Marcus pledged a million and a half dollars.

Wexner remained in Atlanta for the evening where he addressed a major gifts gathering and obtained hundreds of thousands of dollars more. He then flew to St. Louis where he solicited prominent donors such as Bud Levin, a UJA leader in the Prime Minister's Council who owned gas stations across Missouri, obtaining more huge gifts. Then it was off to Cleveland where Wexner conducted several similarly successful major gifts solicitations including of Albert B. Ratner and his family, whose Forest City Enterprises was one of the country's largest developers.

Meanwhile, Max Fisher headed from the Breakfast to his office in Detroit where he telephoned his close friend A. Alfred Taubman. Taubman was a Detroit native, a product of local schools and the University of Michigan. He had begun his career in real estate with a $5,000 loan he parlayed into stores, shopping centers and then a string of upscale shopping malls that dotted the country from coast to coast. Taubman had been pre-solicited by Larry Tisch. Taubman had told Tisch, his bridge partner when in New York, that he couldn't make the Breakfast but he was in for at least a million. Taubman met with Max Fisher afterwards for further discussions. This is a memorandum in March from Stanley Horowitz to Morris Sherman and Marshall Jacobson on what to expect for the "close:"

> Max Fisher reports that Al Taubman's solicitation is probably finished at $1.5 million for Operation Exodus. He says that if Taubman goes on the plane with Wexner from Finland to the Soviet Union in June, he is sure to improve it, but otherwise he thinks we've had it. Please enter this in the data base at least temporarily.

Taubman went on the short plane flight and agreed to Wexner's request to increase his pledge to $1.8 million.

Henry Taub, the mill worker's son who had founded Automatic Data Processing with his brother Joe and another mill worker's son, Frank Lautenberg, visited Lautenberg in Washington in early March. Lautenberg did not need any persuading about the dangers to Jews in the Soviet Union. Since his election in 1982 he had often pressured the Soviet Union to open the gates and, from the Senate floor, warned the USSR of economic and political consequences if the Prisoners of Zion were harmed. Lautenberg also did not need any explanation of the importance of funding the aliyah, although Marvin Lender had briefed him a few days before. After all, 15 years earlier Lautenberg had been Lender's predecessor as National Chairman of the United Jewish Appeal. Frank agreed to provide an extraordinary gift.

Corky Goodman, Lester Crown and Steven Nasatir conducted several solicitation sessions with their fellow Chicagoans, Jay Pritzker and his family, the main owners of Hyatt properties. The Pritzkers had revolutionized the hospitality industry in the late 1960s, building hotels with atriums and an emphasis on open space that proved popular with business travelers and vacationers alike. By 1990 the Pritzkers' properties included the Hyatt Hotels and Resorts, Hyatt Regency, Grand Hyatt and Park Hyatt. Larry Tisch began the solicitation process with Jay Pritzker in February and Max Fisher conducted the closing in May. The Pritzker family gave $5 million to Operation Exodus.

In San Francisco, Melvin M. Swig, Chairman of the Board of Swig, Weiler and Dinner, owner of the Fairmont Hotel and other companies, gave $1.5 million. He also hosted a fundraiser for donors of $100,000 and over, and went on the road for UJA soliciting major donors in other cities. Other million dollar donors like Jack Weiler and Robert Arnow, who owned Manhattan skyscrapers, and Walter Haas of San Francisco's Levi Strauss family, gave enormous sums and solicited for Operation Exodus too. Larry Tisch's sons Andrew, James, Daniel and Thomas and Larry's brother Preston Tisch were among those who did the same.

Most solicitations took place in the prospect's office or home, on the golf course, at a country club, or over dinner in an elegant restaurant. San Francisco Giants owner Bob Lurie was solicited in April during a baseball game; Mel Swig closed Lurie's gift before the Giants closed their victory over the Los Angeles Dodgers. Ted Arison of Miami, owner of Carnival Cruise Lines, was solicited aboard his private yacht. In a rarity, Barney Gottstein was solicited over the phone; he lived in Alaska. Sheldon Adelson lived in Boston but was solicited at the Sands Hotel in Las Vegas; he owned the place.

The cause was compelling and, on top of that, it was difficult to say no to someone like Tisch or Bronfman who were giving millions themselves. It was downright impossible to say no to Tisch, Bronfman, Wexner, Fisher, Crown, Goodman, Lender, Taub and Swig in any combination. Especially if you knew that *they* knew that you could indeed find the million or million and a half or whatever they said you should give.

By the end of March, UJA had closed 30 gifts of $1 million or more. It wasn't finished seeking gifts at that level, but Passover was approaching so the Campaign simultaneously moved down, down, down, to those who, try as they might, would not be able to give more than a few hundred thousand dollars to Operation Exodus. UJA picked up a bunch of $25,000 and $10,000 gifts too.

If the market of million dollar donors is at the top of the UJA fundraising pyramid, the base is the mass market where donors give at any level. Although most donors think campaigns begin only when they hear of them, this is the public phase and not the beginning. The private phase precedes it with events like, at the acme of acmes, a million dollar a plate breakfast. That's why newspaper accounts "announcing" a campaign often report that substantial sums have already been raised and that the goal is on its way to being met. The theory is that donors like to be part of a success story and that organizations should devote resources to fundraising among smaller donors only after larger givers have been solicited.

Mass campaigning for Operation Exodus began on April 4, 1990, five days before Passover, with an event named Freedom Seder for Soviet Jewry, a model seder in Washington, D. C. at which there was *no* fundraising. Held at the cavernous Departmental Auditorium at the Commerce Department, the largest facility available on short notice, the Freedom Seder attracted 500 leaders including Vice President Dan Quayle, 15 United States Senators, 65 Members of the House of Representatives, scores of diplomats from the U.S. and abroad, the heads of many philanthropies and the vanguard of Operation Exodus fundraisers.

Ostensibly the Freedom Seder sought to cast a spotlight on the plight of Soviet Jews, but the spotlight had shone brightly and long enough on them for the gates to have been pried open. The Freedom Seder's main purpose was to set a national tone to bolster local Operation Exodus campaigning. UJA wanted federations to broaden the fundraising to approach potential donors at all levels. Furthermore, aware that some federations were mired in their Campaign's planning stages and that a few were reluctant to begin theirs until autumn when their Annual Campaigns would be completed, UJA wanted to jump-start campaigns in the planning stages and dissuade through isolation federations insisting on holding off campaigning for months. UJA also wanted to give fundraisers present who had not been on a mission an experience they could relate to and discuss in their speeches and solicitations. The Freedom Seder was UJA's way to broaden the Campaign quickly to the mass base, and ensure every federation would be enthusiastic and on board. UJA had invited heads of other fundraising organizations to persuade them to not to object to Operation Exodus fundraising in the spring, when UJA Federation Campaigns were usually dormant and the season was traditionally ceded to other organizations.

The Freedom Seder was co-sponsored by the National Conference on Soviet Jewry, a small but savvy group chaired by the charismatic Shoshana Cardin of Baltimore, which had held the torch of freedom high for Soviet Jews and was a reliable listening post for developments affecting Jews in the Soviet Union.

When the crowd quieted, the entertainer and Jewish activist Theodore Bikel directed the audience's attention to a 32-page Haggadah, tailored for the occasion by the UJA Rabbinic Cabinet. The Cabinet, chaired successively during Operation Exodus by Rabbi Matthew Simon, Rabbi Michael Zedek of Cincinnati and Rabbi Jacob S. Rubenstein of Scarsdale, New York, raised modest funds among rabbis, a cadre perpetually besieged and broke. But the Cabinet's main value was in writing and distributing materials that articulated the religious underpinnings of UJA campaign themes. As Rabbi David A. Wortman of Philadelphia, the Haggadah editor, wrote in the introduction:[6]

> Over 3,000 years ago, a mixed multitude defied the Pharaoh and began an Exodus process that continues to this day.... This Haggadah is dedicated to the miraculous extension of (that) ancient process.... It is dedicated as well to all those who struggled that our Soviet brothers and sisters might make the transition from tyranny to freedom.... (T)he unsung heroes of our saga are the thousands of Soviet Jews who flooded the offices of *Ovir* with applications for exit visas (and) the hundreds of thousands mobilized in every Jewish community who remain ever vigilant in their advocacy.

The motif continued throughout the Seder. In answers to the Four Questions, the matzah was deemed a reminder of the haste with which Jews wanted to leave the Soviet Union; the bitter herbs were emblematic of their acrid confinement; the herbs were dipped twice, in salt water and charoseth, a sweet mixture, to commemorate their struggle and prayer for its successful end; and participants reclined as a symbol of the freedom Soviet Jews hoped to achieve.

The Haggadah likened the ten plagues, visited on the Egyptians to admonish Pharaoh to let the Jews go, to the signposts of the Soviet Jewry movement, like the Jackson-Vanik Amendment in 1972 that made sale of American wheat to the Soviet Union contingent on some emigration for more than a decade; the Helsinki Accords promulgated by 35 countries in 1975 that cast an international spotlight on human rights; and Freedom Sunday for Soviet Jewry, the rally of 250,000 in Washington in 1987 that was instrumental in opening the gates.

The celebratory nature of the Freedom Seder was dramatized in quotations from three freed Prisoners of Zion, read aloud by legislators:

---

6 Haggadah quotes from *"The Exodus Haggadah: From Tyranny To Freedom: A Celebration,"* Rabbinic Cabinet, United Jewish Appeal, 1990, various pages (unpublished).

The pride of being a Jew, the pride for our State of Israel after the Six Day War, made me feel free.... I felt myself free from that big Soviet prison. I was free even before the very last day of my leaving the Soviet Union.

—Natan Sharansky

It is like being reborn. Until I die, I'll never forget this morning, when I woke up and looked out at the sun rising over the Judean Hills, and the Old City in front of me.

—Vladimir Slepak, on his first morning in Jerusalem.

A few hours ago, I was almost a slave in Moscow. Now, I am a free woman, in my own country. It is the moment of my life. I am at home in the soul of the Jewish people. I am a free person among my own people.

—Ida Nudel, upon arrival in Israel
after years of imprisonment in Siberia for seeking
the right for herself and others to emigrate.

Since those at the Seder were not physically visiting the homes of Jews in the Soviet Union and Israel, as had mission participants, a family of overseas Jews was brought to them live by satellite. A 77-year-old botany professor in Moscow named Irina Voronkevich, who was denied permission to emigrate to Israel, was able to see and speak to her son, daughter-in-law and grandchildren in Israel and see her great granddaughter Katrina, age one, by satellite for the first time. On one huge screen Ms. Voronkevich was seated alone at a Seder table in the austere studio of Glostelradio, the Soviet Union's state television network, while her family was at a Seder table in an apartment overlooking the Western Wall in Jerusalem. Their plaintive words and tears, and participation in the Seder by blessing cups of wine, dramatically illustrated the unfulfilled yearning for family reunification, unmistakable to the audience in Washington.

After Lender briefly reported on the Campaign, the Haggadah ended with this conclusion, read aloud by those assembled:

We have come to the end of our Passover Seder. We have completed the requirements of our tradition and Law. As we have been worthy to celebrate together this year, may all Jews be so worthy in future years. Creator of the Universe, gather Your people from the four corners of the earth, restore the congregation of Israel to oneness. Speedily guide each of us to Zion in joy.

For all Jews of the Soviet Union, for all Jews everywhere. L'shanah haba'ah b'Yerushalayim: Next Year in Jerusalem.

With that affirmation that Jewish destiny would be fulfilled, the participants burst into singing, *"L'shanah Haba'ah B'Yerushalayim,"* nearly everyone clapping to the beat, most singing the simple lyrical refrain.

In his speech following, Quayle expressed support for a wide range of issues of interest to American Jews such as direct flights from the Soviet Union to Israel. He denounced anti-Semitism at home and abroad; and advocated repeal of the United Nations resolution that asserted, "Zionism is a form of racism and racial discrimination," which Quayle described as "a modern version of the blood libel."[7]

When the event ended, Lender boarded a chartered bus waiting to take participants to their hotels. He sat in the rear in the darkened bus as others boarded, his chin resting in his right hand, his elbow supported by his left hand. Deep in thought, he was oblivious to the exhaust fumes sifting through the open window next to him. Joel Tauber, who had been crisscrossing the country for more than a month to close senior level solicitations at Marvin's request, sat down next to him.

"That was good!" Tauber said, tilting his head toward the emptying auditorium.

"Is it enough?" Lender asked.

"Congress and the White House had to know the emigration is our burning issue," Tauber answered. "Not just UJA's but American Jewry's. I think they have the message."

"Is it enough?" Lender asked again. "The money I mean."

"We agreed not to solicit at this event," Tauber replied. "It was to set the table for federation fundraising." He thought for a moment. "Marvin, you just announced in there that in the past five weeks we have amassed $109 million!"

"It's not enough," Lender answered. "The goal I mean. It sounds crazy, but you know what? I have seen the daily emigration figures and I have been in Russia twice in recent weeks and I have seen the lines at the *Ovir* and I don't think $420 million is going to be enough."

UJA felt the wind at its back. The new angst was, had the goal been too low rather than too high? Still, the goal was far from being achieved.

While most donors to Operation Exodus were Jewish, many non-Jews gave

---

7 "Quayle Raps Zionism Resolution at Special Seder for Soviet Jews, *Jewish Telegraphic Agency*, April 5, 1990, p. 3.

as well. Most sent small checks accompanied by notes that said things such as, "I am not Jewish but I have great respect for what you are doing to take care of your own. I hope this helps." Or, "I am not Jewish, but I admire the Jews for your many contributions to the world. I hope this check helps Jews who can do more for mankind." There was also a letter stating this:

> "...Enclosed is a check for $100,000 on behalf of the Moral Majority for the United Jewish Appeal's Operation Exodus Campaign...."

> — (signed) (The Rev.) Jerry Falwell
> President

One of the characteristics of organized Jewish life is that is decentralized; there is no single "highest authority." Even in the religious sphere in Israel there are two Chief Rabbis. In the United States three major branches of Judaism have flourished, Orthodox, Conservative and Reform and there are divisions within them. It has long been so. For instance, two of the greatest Orthodox thinkers, the Vilna Gaon and the Baal Shem Tov, founder of Hasidim, were eighteenth century contemporaries but bitter ideological foes. "If you don't like what a rabbi tells you," a common joke goes, "ask another rabbi."

In organized American Jewish life in 1990, there were hundreds of organizations, each with its own mission, just on the national scene. Some promoted Judaism through a religious movement. Some sought to meet Jewish social or economic needs, or human needs in the general community believing that was a higher Jewish calling Some worked for health improvement, educational advancement, environmental preservation, political change, restitution of wrongs or cultural enrichment. American Jews were rarely unified behind a central priority but they came as close as they had in years in support for Operation Exodus.

This would seem remarkable since every Jewish organization was financially challenged by the unfolding aliyah. For example, among the national agencies raising funds for Israel, those aiding the great Israeli medical centers like Hadassah and Shaare Zedek knew those institutions would have many more patients requiring services and need more buildings, facilities and staff. Organizations supporting the great Israeli universities like the Technion: Israel Institute of Technology, the Weizmann Institute of Science, Hebrew University, Tel Aviv University, Bar-Ilan University, Ben Gurion University of the Negev and Haifa University knew those institutions would face rising applications, and would require more physical and human resources. Jewish National Fund expected more demand for land development through reforestation, and for building reservoirs and increasing the water supply. The American Jewish Committee, World Jewish Congress, American Jewish Congress, Anti-Defamation League — every organization knew it would be challenged.[8]

More particularly, since UJA sought to raise funds broadly in the Jewish community, such agencies' donors would likely be solicited for Operation Exodus and that could have been viewed as a funding threat. But it wasn't. Instead, organizations across the Jewish spectrum endorsed Operation Exodus. They pointed out to donors their institutions' added needs but made clear that Operation Exodus should be supported as well. Of course, these organizations' leaders knew that nothing could compete with the drama of Jews fleeing from the Soviet Union. But they had been leaders in the Soviet Jewry movement for years, providing and marshaling crucial financial, political and professional support. Even more important, these leaders wisely recognized that Jewish fundraising was not a zero sum game and that the donation pie could be expanded. They understood that their own institutional cause was only part of a nobler and more comprehensive mission, to better the lives of Jews everywhere. Happily, donors saw the larger picture too, and gave higher sums to such organizations even as they gave generously to Operation Exodus.

To combat the popular assumption that immigrants economically burden a country, UJA commissioned a monograph by Professor Julian L. Simon of the University of Maryland who had written books demonstrating that in Israel the opposite was the case. Studying Soviet Jews who arrived in Israel since the 1970s, Simon showed the immigrants were highly intelligent, deeply motivated and generally skilled. They became independent quickly and soon contributed to alleviating the Israeli taxpayer's heavy burden. The study, *"Economic Consequences of Immigration,"* was widely distributed by UJA, to its own and federation campaigners, to buttress solicitations and speeches.

Most Jews think about their Jewishness around Rosh Hashanah, Chanukah and Passover, and so most Jewish federations raise their main funds around those holidays. The major gifts season at UJA began in August with the Prime Minister's Mission, August 19 to 24, for which a commitment in advance of at least $100,000 was required. The Mission had been the annual kickoff for

---

8 The Development Corporation for Israel, better known as Israel Bonds, was not an American fundraising organization but an Israeli organization that enabled Jews and others to participate in building Israel by investing in bonds. Its response to Operation Exodus paralleled that of the American Jewish fundraising organizations.

years but had been abandoned in 1980 when the aging regulars found the eleven hour flight each way too difficult. When Alex Grass became National Chairman in 1984 he reinstituted it, promising travel aboard a chartered Concorde that reduced flight time to six and a half hours. Once Grass demonstrated that UJA could raise more than twice the $665,000 rental fee for the supersonic aircraft, the mission returned as the Campaign centerpiece.

Richard Pearlstone led the mission with donor heavyweights like New York builder Larry Silverstein joining Lender, Tauber, Arlene Zimmerman, Marty Stein and dozens of regulars for whom the mission was their main link to UJA. The Inaugural Mission Pearlstone had led to Russia and Israel five months earlier was not the prototype for the Prime Minister's Mission; it was the other way around: Prime Minister's Mission programming informed the March Inaugural trip.

In Israel, the 60 participants heard from, and had an opportunity to share their questions and thoughts with, Prime Minister Shamir, Defense Minister Rabin and Foreign Affairs Minister David Levy who encouraged them to give maximally to Operation Exodus. Participants met with immigrants in direct absorption in Ra'anana, and were inspired by its innovative mayor, Ze'ev Bielski, a direct-absorption leader. They then lunched at an absorption center for more exposure to the Campaign theme. They helicoptered to Misgav Am and Kfar Giladi, towns just south of the Lebanon border, where they grimly noted Israel's vulnerability but were impressed with Israeli courage. Elsewhere, they talked shop with industrialists and with Soviet immigrants hopeful of becoming Israeli entrepreneurs.

To drive home the point about the Biblical roots of Operation Exodus, UJA got Egypt into the act. It flew participants by chartered plane over the Sinai Desert and the Red Sea to Cairo where they met privately with President Hosni Mubarak, prayed at the ancient Ben Ezra Synagogue and dined at the Mena House, next to the Pyramids. All along, each participant was taken aside and asked to increase his or her gift. By the time the donors assembled before Finance Minister Peres in front of the Chagall Tapestries in the Knesset, they had been well primed by UJA's ministrations. They pledged $10,755,000 for Operation Exodus, an average of $179,250 per person.[9] UJA brought them home on the Concorde, which departed at 10 a.m. Israel time and arrived in New York, six time zones earlier, at 10:20 a.m. They enjoyed breakfast in Israel and UJA enabled many to be in their offices, with quite a story to tell,

---

9 UJA also continued to raise funds for the Annual Campaign throughout Operation Exodus. For example it raised $8,758,000 for it on the Prime Minister's Mission, a 15 percent increase of the sums participants had given to the previous year's Annual Campaign.

before lunch.

In other seasonal events, Joel Tauber led a contingent to the International Leadership Reunion in Geneva from September 9 to 12, the gathering of $250,000 donors that UJA conducted each fall with Keren Hayesod, its counterpart in other Diaspora countries. The Third Annual Emerald-Eye Lion of Judah Gathering in Washington on November 27 and 28, chaired by Lois Zoller, for women donating $25,000 in their own names, often in addition to their husbands' gifts, drew in more funds. The Ingathering Mission to Eastern Europe and Israel, chaired by Alan Crawford, was a $10,000 a person mission that brought participants to meet Soviet Jews in transit camps in Budapest and Bucharest as well as to Soviet Jews newly arrived in Israel. The Dor L'Dor (Generation to Generation) Mission, chaired by Richard Wexler for $50,000 donors around Chanukah, from December 23 to January 2, visited Soviet Jews in Bucharest and others already in Israel, raised more funds and rounded out the major gifts season.

In less dramatic times, UJA often discussed internally whether its ultimate responsibility was to "raise funds or raise Jews," giving lip service to the latter but functionally favoring the former. Indeed, its raison d'etre was to raise funds and it did that splendidly. But it also raised Jews. Not in the religious sense but in strengthening Jewish identity. Susan Stern, who was in the early stages of an up-and-coming career at UJA, took part in the Young Leadership Morasha (Heritage) Mission to Israel in the last weeks of 1990. Years later, as President of UJA-Federation of New York, she enthusiastically recalled what that mission and other UJA Operation Exodus missions meant to her:

> I'll never forget what it was like to be standing with the others on Morasha on the tarmac at Ben Gurion Airport waiting to see my first planeload of Soviet Jews. The tarmac was patched with tar and sticky and it was 3 a.m. because the Russians only let Jews fly out when they said they could fly out and that usually meant arrivals in Israel in the wee hours.

> We saw the plane land and taxi toward us and the ground crew move the staircase to it. Finally, the plane door swung open. They started to file down, one by one. An old man, an old woman, a woman my age, a father holding his daughter on his arm. I never saw any one of them before and--suddenly--it was my grandmother, my grandfather — *me!*

> One old man came down on crutches but the last step, onto the

tarmac, was hard and his wife moved to help him. He waved her away. She nodded. He struggled to get down that last step. Then he struggled to bend down onto the tarmac, where he kissed the ground. The ugly, schmutzy ground, he kissed it. Then he said something to his wife in Russian and closed his eyes tightly, restraining tears. Tears were on her cheeks. I don't speak a word of Russian but I sensed what he felt. He never dreamed he would get to Israel but he had. He was free. He was home.

Everyone on every Operation Exodus mission went onto the tarmac, if they didn't arrive on a pre-mission from Russia with immigrants on the plane. No one will ever forget the experience. The great voluntary migration of Jews in our time was happening. You saw it with your own eyes. Whatever the UJA said was true. And you had the chance, the privilege, to shape Jewish history. Sure you gave whatever they asked. You were thrilled to.

CHAPTER FOUR
The Local Campaigns

All Jews are responsible one for the other.

Talmud, Shevuot 39a.

Jews have long been known as a charitable people, yet there is no word in Hebrew for charity. When Jews speak of financial giving, they use the word "tzedakah," which means "righteousness." Charity evokes pity, but tzedakah focuses also on those with resources and denotes obligation. Charity implies that people who have and those who do not are on different levels; tzedakah implies that everyone is on the same level, that all worldly goods belong to God. Sharing with others is the right thing to do.

Tzedakah also means "justice." The famous Biblical injunction, "Justice, justice thou shalt pursue," is, in the original (Deut.16:20), "tzedek, tzedek tirdof," and it applies to giving. The precept that all Jews must give tzedakah is so encompassing that even the poor must do this, because there is always someone poorer. Furthermore, giving tzedakah is not an end, to meet an immediate need, but a means to a higher goal. And, when it is given, the circumstances, and even the donors' attitude and intentions, count.

Maimonides (1135-1204), the brilliant rabbi, scholar, philosopher and physician, identified a hierarchy of eight levels of tzedakah. From the lowest they are: giving grudgingly; giving amicably but insufficiently; giving directly to the person in need after being asked; giving directly to the person in need before being asked; giving where the recipient knows the donor but the donor does not know the recipient; giving where the donor knows the recipient but the recipient

---

1 Moses Maimonides (Rambam), *Code of the Law*, Book VII, 10:7-15.

does not know the donor. The highest levels are giving sufficiently and amicably where donor and recipient are unknown to each other; and, best of all, helping the recipient to achieve self-reliance. In Operation Exodus, American Jews gave on the highest levels of tzedakah.

The People of the Book have often been criticized for knowing little about the Book, and many in 1990 did not know about the hierarchal principles of tzedakah of Maimonides. But they understood innately their obligation to enable the historical aliyah to take place. And give they did, from nickels to millions. By doing so, they began, metaphorically, to write a great new chapter in Jewish history.

Passover 5750 began on the evening of April 9, 1990. For most local federations, the holiday marked the start of fundraising for Operation Exodus from donors of all giving abilities. The campaigns were locally organized and led, but inspired and enhanced by UJA, which offered proven fundraising missions and programs, experienced solicitors, motivational speakers, and meaningful marketing materials. At Passover, the Operation Exodus theme of redemption from tyranny and oppression could not have been more relevant and timely. Local Operation Exodus Campaigns were conducted in 189 federated communities and more than 400 smaller Jewish communities across the United States as Passover approached. Most began before Passover but some started later when federations thought additional planning and completion of their Annual Campaign would lead to better overall results. They were led by Jews of varying Jewish backgrounds but unified in a fervent belief that they had an obligation — which they yearned to fulfill — to help the Jews leave their bondage in the Soviet Union and emigrate to freedom and opportunity in Israel. Here are highlights of some of those local campaigns.[2]

New York

Cole Porter's famous refrain "You're the Top," could have been sung about New York in the constellation of American Jewish life. In population, wealth, fame or energy, it's *the top* -- the Coliseum, the Louvre Museum, the Tower of Pisa and the smile on the Mona Lisa. And when it speaks, as E. F. Hutton used to say, everybody listens. The million dollar New York donors at the Breakfast, Larry Tisch, Andrew Tisch, Ace Greenberg, Irving Schneider, Lew Rudin, Charles Bronfman, and Peter May, the New York Operation Exodus Chairman,

---

2 More than a million persons donated to Operation Exodus and there were thousands of events; names and events in these pages are illustrative, not exhaustive.

went on to solicit other senior level gifts, were listened to and obtained gifts. Standard bearers like Larry Silverstein, Harvey Schulweis, Alexander E. Fisher, Peggy Tishman, Morton Kornreich, Irwin Hochberg, David G. Sacks, Preston Tisch, James Tisch, Daniel Tisch and Thomas Tisch gave generously. They too were among those who solicited high level gifts, and recruited donors to fundraising events featuring authentic voices of Jews yearning for freedom, including Natan Sharansky.

Contributing at least a million dollars were the Louis and Ann Arons Foundation, the Baron De Hirsch Fund, the Forchheimer Foundation, Caroline and Joseph Gruss, Erica and Ludwig Jesselson, Ruth and Leonard Litwin, the Milstein Family Foundation, the Samuel I. Newhouse Foundation, Claudia and Nelson Peltz, Frederick and Daniel and Elihu Rose, the William Rosenwald family, the Scheuer Family Foundation, the Skirball Foundation, the firm of Wachtell, Lipton, Rose and Katz, and the Weiler and Arnow families.

Among those who contributed at least half a million dollars were Simon Bond, the Brookdale Foundation Group, Alfred and Gail Engelberg, Shirley and Milton Gralla, Maurice Greenberg and Family, Joseph Gurwin, Raphael Recanati, the Joseph and Norma Saul Foundation, Dianne and David Stern, the firm of Weil, Gotshal and Manges, and Elaine and James Wolfensohn. Michael Steinhardt, the hedge funds strategist, became a senior level donor to UJA-Federation for the first time in Operation Exodus.

Some 800 New Yorkers visited Jews in Uzbekistan and Ukraine seeking to emigrate, and then met with Soviet Jews newly arrived in Israel; they contributed a total of $3.6 million. UJA-Federation of New York was one of many federations that offered to name a flight to Israel filled with Soviet Jews in honor of groups that donated $250,000, the cost of the flight. Freedom Flights, as they were called, inspired country clubs and employees of large companies to pool their funds and stretch to a higher level. *The New York Jewish Week, Long Island Jewish World* and *Forward*, a national newspaper based in New York, provided excellent coverage.

Soviet Jews in Brighton Beach, Brooklyn, "Little Odessa by the Sea," who knew the meaning of Soviet oppression first hand, contributed $250,000. Campaigns in synagogues, professional associations, business organizations, housing cooperatives, colleges, day schools, yeshivas and among friends energized the New York Jewish community; their checks added to the millions collected, as did cash placed in 200,000 tzedakah boxes in Jewish-oriented stores and institutions. Seven thousand New Yorkers gave to UJA-Federation of New York for the first time, helping to ensure that the campaign would achieve its $75 million goal.

When thousands lined Fifth Avenue for the annual Salute to Israel Parade, a joyous celebration of Jewish freedom, the floats, placards and sidewalk chatter made obvious that the nascent emigration movement was a transcendent cause, uniting the often fractious New York Jewish community, and that Operation Exodus was its instrument. Operation Exodus was, to borrow from the name of The New Yorker column, the Talk of the Town.

The passion of donors at all levels was reflected in a simple note from a New York girl of about ten years old:

"Dear Operation Exodus,

Our Hebrew teacher has been telling us about the Jewish children in Russia and how much they want to escape to Israel. The Jewish children are sad in Russia. They will be happy in Israel. She told us you can help them get to Israel where they will have freedom. Our class has saved up $53.50 so far. Here it is. Please use it to help the Jewish children get out of Russia."

Love,

Alisa

The pent-up desire to deliver on the promise of years of endless strategy sessions, rallies, letter writing campaigns and prayers to open the gates for Soviet Jews overcame even experienced campaigners as captured in these vignettes from Adam Kahan, the New York UJA-Federation's Chief Operating Officer:

Alan Jaffe and I went to the home of a $10,000 donor to the [Annual] Campaign whom we thought had somewhat higher potential. Going in, we weren't sure how much play we would have with him. We laid out the case. He was deeply moved. He asked, 'How much do you want?' Alan and I looked at each other. Everything was so planned, but we went crazy. We said, '$100,000.'

He said, 'When do you want it?' We said, 'As soon as possible.' He said, 'OK.' Then he went into the next room and returned with his checkbook. He wrote a check and handed it to us for $100,000.

A few weeks later, Peter May and Al Einbinder led a mission to Israel for 40 to 60 participants. We brought them to dinner at Mishkenot Sha'ananim [a picturesque artist's colony overlooking the Old City in

Jerusalem]. We closed many gifts that evening. It was going very, very well. We all got excited about it.

Then we couldn't stop. We went to others in the restaurant. One guy was from the Midwest. He could feel the energy emanating from the mission group. We told him what was going on. Then we solicited him. He pledged thousands of dollars. We took his name and address and told him we would contact his local federation. He wasn't even in our community. I never heard of such a thing. We closed a gift of somebody we didn't even know.

Then we went over to a table of a man and woman and introduced ourselves. They looked well heeled. They said they were from South Africa but did not give to their local campaign. They felt the excitement and asked what was happening. We took them outside and solicited them successfully for $10,000. They were tourists from another country. Nobody even knew the name of their federation. We took their names and gave them to Keren Hayesod.

Chicago

The umbrella fundraising organization for the Chicago area, better known as the Jewish United Fund (JUF) /Jewish Federation of Metropolitan Chicago, was the second largest federation in the country, an indispensable source of potential funds, and a linchpin in UJA's effort to establish the Campaign in the Midwest.

Among Chicagoans, the Crown-Goodman family had already given $3 million at the Breakfast of Champions and immediately after it Lester Crown and Corky Goodman contacted Jay Pritzker, their fellow Chicagoan who had been abroad. Pritzker had purchased a Los Angeles hotel from a man named Hyatt von Dehn in 1967 and ran with the idea that hotels should have atriums and grand, open spaces rather than a penned-in feeling where every inch is appropriated. Pritzker replicated that idea, always providing state of the art conference and banquet facilities, and décor and restaurant cuisines that matched the local culture, and built a chain that crossed the country and reached around the world. By 1990 his Hyatt Regency, Grand Hyatt and Park Hyatt brands helped set the standard for hotelier quality. The family was also a main owner of Royal Caribbean Cruise Lines, prominent real estate, several mines and railroad cars. The Pritzkers were among Chicago's most generous philanthropists and a pillar of JUF campaigns. After Crown and Goodman informed Pritzker about the Campaign and its needs, Les Wexner and then Max Fisher visited. Pritzker said that his family would be pleased to contribute $5 million for Operation Exodus.

Knowing that his remarkable gift would influence others, Pritzker agreed to announce it at a UJA Midwest Regional Luncheon for Operation Exodus that Crown was organizing in his home for donors with a $250,000 potential. Crown's luncheon Co-Chairmen (and fellow solicitors) were Breakfast participants Wexner, Fisher and William Davidson as well as Albert B. Ratner of Cleveland's Forest City Ratner, the nation's largest publicly traded real estate corporation, who would also announce a multimillion dollar gift. The chance to break bread with these titans of business and industry, mingle with other movers and shakers, and have a private tour led by Crown of his spacious and well-appointed mansion and grounds, attracted 28 participants including six Chicagoans.

A UJA video set the luncheon's tone, with sound bites from menacing Russian anti-Semites, images of anti-Jewish graffiti, and testimony from Soviet Jews that they feared harm as the Soviet government weakened and lawlessness grew. Crown spoke of the importance of leaders leading and at that moment it meant giving large gifts. Simcha Dinitz of the Jewish Agency vividly described Soviet Jewish hardship and fear and documented sharp increases in the numbers of Jews waiting at all junctures in the complex Soviet process for aliyah. Crown, Wexner, Pritzker, Ratner, Fisher and Davidson each noted his gift and urged participants to stretch to give as much as possible. In essence the message was that $250,000 was enough to bring a plane filled with immigrants to Israel but, since thousands of flights needed to be financed, that should be viewed as a minimum.

At the card calling, the Chicagoans pledged $9.2 million. Each gave more than he had given to the 1990 Annual Campaign, as much as eight times more. Overall, the 28 participants pledged $24,125,000 for Operation Exodus, equal to 210 percent of their 1990 Annual Campaign gifts. In the mix, 13 gifts totaling $8,685,000 were closed just before, and in time to be announced at, the luncheon. Nobody wanted to single himself out as a "low" donor in front of Crown, Wexner, Pritzker, Ratner, Fisher and Davidson. The dinner solidified the start of Chicago's Operation Exodus Campaign and, by serving as a regional hub for the megagift event, the JUF boosted the national totals and helped ignite several Midwest campaigns.

Chicago continued its major gifts program with parlor meetings, which combined the sense of exclusivity of the Midwest Regional Luncheon with the intimacy of a mission caucus and achieved significant gifts at the $50,000, $25,000 and $10,000 levels. The federation coalesced groups that stretched to reach $250,000 with the promise that a Freedom Flight, a specific flight filled with new immigrants, would be named for them.

The JUF fostered Operation Exodus fundraising at local agencies -- which normally looked to the JUF for funds. The JUF convened agency leaders and asked them for a moratorium on their own fundraising until after the summer, to open a corridor for Operation Exodus. Then it asked them to pencil in a date when the JUF could solicit them and caucus with their board members. The agency heads believed in the cause too and readily agreed. They and their agencies helped carry the ball locally for Operation Exodus.

In early June, soon after Country Club Day strengthened the major gifts program, the JUF distributed a special edition of its newspaper, *JUF News*, that reached 70,000 of the 107,000 Jewish households in metropolitan Chicago. This laid the basis for broad-based fundraising. In conjunction, the Chicago Board of Rabbis was engaged and its members made pulpit appeals.

The 14,000 Soviet Jews in the Chicago area, including 6,500 who had arrived from 1987 to 1989, were reached through the Russian language media and many gave individually. More than $50,000 was raised in one day at a bilingual program in Skokie. The International Fellowship of Christians and Jews, founded and led by Rabbi Yechiel Eckstein of Chicago, raised more than $70,000.

The JUF wrote to the 1,000 Chicagoans who had rallied at Freedom Sunday in Washington on December 6, 1987 and asked them to redeem their efforts by contributing to the emigration they had helped make possible. Federation-sponsored rallies, and speakers at events open to the general public, further focused public attention on giving. A Chanukah telethon with the theme, "Miracle in Our Time," and a year-end direct mail campaign, enabled JUF to exceed its formidable $28.6 million Operation Exodus goal.

Organizationally, like most major federations, Chicago utilized its existing structure but established separate leadership teams for Operation Exodus to provide it with the attention it deserved. All its divisions were engaged including Major Gifts, Women's, Young Leadership, Trades, and Congregations and Community Campaigns. Important roles were played by scores of Chicagoans such as UJA National Vice Chairmen Richard Wexler, Larry Hochberg and Lois Zoller, tireless crusaders for Operation Exodus, who injected their speeches and solicitations with compelling accounts from their personal experiences meeting with Jews in the Soviet Union.

The professional quarterback was Dr. Steven B. Nasatir whose leadership skills, and deep knowledge of Chicago Jewry and fundraising, were instrumental in positioning the JUF for transcendent results. "We were thrilled to help,"

Nasatir declared years later in an interview for this book. "Operation Exodus showed that there was an extensive network of Jews who cared about other Jews. It brought out the best of who we are as a people. Operation Exodus gave us, and all American Jews, a way to play a role in one of the great Jewish triumphs of the century."

Los Angeles

The third largest Jewish community in the nation, Los Angeles had raised $49.2 million in its 1989 Annual Campaign, a distance from New York's $125.4 million but very close to Chicago's $51.4 million. But Los Angeles had problems New York and Chicago never had to think of. Whereas those two cities had bedrock second, third and fourth generation American Jewish communities, with roots stretching back a century to Lower East Side tenements, most Jews in Los Angeles began life someplace else. They or their parents arrived once jet planes made air travel fast and convenient in the late 1950s and people began to pay more attention to sunshine, mobility, and the perceived opportunities that an automobile and a new job could bring.

What this meant for the Jewish Council of Greater Los Angeles, as the Federation was known, was that Los Angeles Jews were not rooted in Jewish community activity. Few were active in synagogues and temples, and most showed little interest in local Jewish life, let alone Jewish life thousands of miles away in the Soviet Union or Israel. The "Who is a Jew" issue hit hard in Los Angeles, where most were alienated by the strength of Israel's Orthodox Jewish establishment. As a Los Angeles woman said to me at a dinner just before Operation Exodus began, "Shabbat isn't important here like it is in New York."

Preliminary data from the Council of Jewish Federations' National Jewish Population Study of 1990, the most comprehensive Jewish census in American history, disclosed the terrifying finding that 52 percent of Jews were marrying out of their religion, and that the figure was even higher in Los Angeles. Affiliation with Jewish houses of worship, organizations, and causes was dropping nationally, but it was low to begin with and dropping even faster in Los Angeles. Exactly how was the Los Angeles Federation going to get local Jews out of their cars and into solicitation settings, where they could be shown and told the immigration story and persuaded to buy into it?

When the private solicitation phase began, campaign veterans Irwin Field (the first UJA National Chairman from the West), Bram Goldsmith and Stanley Hirsh each gave a million dollars. Others followed with gifts of a million or several hundred thousand dollars. As pledges above donor ratings were made at parlor meetings for the $50,000 to $1,000 levels, it was clear that the commitment to Operation Exodus was stronger than expected.

Since few Los Angeles Jews had visited Israel, and virtually none had seen the Soviet Union, campaign leaders brought in a steady stream of Soviet Jewish heroes via the UJA Speakers Bureau to parlor meetings in major donors' homes. Chief among these was Natan Sharansky, the most heroic fixture in Jewish life since Yosef Tekoah was repackaged as Ari Ben Canaan and played by Paul Newman in the screen version of Leon Uris' *Exodus*. As David Sacks, the Major Gifts Director, remembers, "Sharansky's presence was electrifying. People who had read about him for years, and were thrilled by his heroism, were now seated in a circle with him, hearing that they had to give money to Operation Exodus. Of course they did. How could they not?" In one week, Sharansky spoke at five events and raised $2 million.

Prisoners of Zion Vladimir Slepak, Iosef Begun and Anna and Vassily Paukov followed. They told about the dissident movement and their personal struggles, how they were beaten and imprisoned but persevered to bring the movement to the portal of freedom. Marina Furman, who had electrified the UJA Young Leadership Conference, told her story at several gatherings in Los Angeles as part of a broader tour of the West. Others were riveted by Ella Tsveyer, the woman who had spurred UJA National Officers to start the Operation Exodus Campaign with her description of how the KGB threatened to kill her children if she did not end her dissent.

The experience wasn't so distant after all. Richard Gunther, the federation's Operation Exodus Chairman and one of several of Los Angeles campaigners interviewed for this book, said, "In each parlor meeting I would ask for a show of hands from those with an Eastern European heritage. Eighty percent would raise their hands and I would say, 'If it hadn't been for your grandparents, you would be waiting for Operation Exodus to bring you out.'" Nor were the leaders untraveled. "I was with a mission on a plane from Russia to Israel and walked down the aisle," Gunther told them. "There was a couple, both doctors, from Leningrad. They were fearful of leaving for Israel but their daughter had experienced anti-Semitism. A woman from Baku (in Azerbaijan) was studying Hebrew at four in the morning. A man with a chest full of medals said none of them did him any good as a Jew in Russia. The donors understood that this could have been them, would have been them if their grandparents had not left when they did. Everyone at every parlor meeting understood that." In all, more than 50 parlor meetings were held. Locally planned, organized and administered, and enhanced by solicitations from Tauber, Pearlstone, Lender,

Zimmerman and Stein, they raised millions.

A major gifts dinner was held for hundreds at the downtown Music Centre. It featured a performance of "Soul of a Jew," a Haifa Municipal Theater play, preceded by the first catered kosher dinner ever held at the Music Centre, and followed by an appeal from federation leadership to those who had not yet given to Operation Exodus to do so immediately.

Los Angeles opened the public campaign just before Passover with a lively rally featuring Sharansky that drew thousands. They cheered wildly. Visibly moved, Sharansky thanked them for their past activism and challenged them to help achieve the goal they had fought for: escape to Israel. Normally dispassionate and not religious, he said emotionally, "You must look at it as if you went forth from Egypt, as if you were in the Soviet Union needing to leave for the Jewish land." The crowd was like steeds that could not wait to get out of the gate.

Dr. Stephen Windmueller, Director of the local Jewish Community Relations Council, reflected, "The wall-to-wall giving occurred because of the credibility of the Operation Exodus leadership in town; the continuity from our prior activism for Soviet Jewry; and our shame at our failure as a community to deal with the rise of Hitler. Operation Exodus was a chance to redeem ourselves too, as an American Jewish community. We could not undo the apathy of some 50 years earlier but we could see to it that it wouldn't happen again."

Unlike New York Jews, who often wore their Jewishness publicly like a badge, Los Angeles Jews were more discreet. But this time signs of the Operation Exodus campaign were everywhere. The campaign was advertised on radio and television, in the *Los Angeles Times* and on bus shelters, and huge banners for Operation Exodus hung in front of the federation, local agency offices and synagogues.

The federation raised $17 million by June 30; the total reached $26.3 million after the Chanukah direct mail and telephone appeals. Operation Exodus showed that despite assimilation, intermarriage, nonaffiliation and cultural distance from Jerusalem, New York and Moscow, Los Angeles Jews were Jews in their hearts. They were inspired by a special moment in Jewish history, committed to Jewish potential, confident in their ability to institute change and, perhaps, still feeling vulnerable after 3,300 years. As Field recalled, "Operation Exodus was a proud moment in Jewish history, in which we felt privileged to participate. It inspired us throughout 1990 and we kept on going."

Fredi Rembaum, Director of the Community Campaign, found that Operation Exodus touched a raw nerve in Los Angeles Jewry:

> The campaign went better than expected in that we raised more money at events we planned, but what I keep remembering was how money

came in from where we did not expect it....

The Iranian Jewish Federation was not a major donor to our campaign but they invited us to their annual gala to receive a check. We were shocked when they presented us with $500,000. They said that, as new immigrants, they wanted to help newer Jewish refugees flee oppression.

The Orthodox Union presented us with a check for $50,000. The Hancock Park Orthodox community, with the official support of the head of Agudah [Agudath Israel] in New York, organized a parlor meeting. So did other Orthodox groups.

The 39 Club, a Holocaust survivors' organization, dedicated their proceeds to Operation Exodus. They said, 'If only we had a strong Jewish community to rescue us from Europe, and a State of Israel to go to, six million would not have perished.'

The Association of Soviet Jewish Émigrés and War Veterans each sponsored campaigns and invited us to events to receive the checks...

The Israeli community here organized an art auction from which came a generous contribution from donors who do not contribute to the community campaign.

Many people brought their contributions in personally. Young teens came in with Bar Mitzvah or Bat Mitzvah gifts, and their parents often had tears of pride in their eyes when their children described how they wanted to help and be part of such a noble cause. Sometimes it was elderly men and women, accompanied by a young relative or companion caretaker, who came in.

One time I came back 20 minutes late from a meeting and found an elderly couple waiting for me. They berated me for coming late, but I sat and listened. They said they did not do enough, no Jews outside Europe did enough, to save Jewish lives in the Holocaust, and that should never happen again. Then the woman said to him, "Give her the check." She said to me, "It's for a hundred." When I looked down, I was shocked to see that the hundred was $100,000."

Cleveland

The Jewish Community Federation of Cleveland had always been a bellwether for United Jewish Appeal, a federation that UJA looked to for an indication whether its campaigns would be viable out in the country, beyond UJA headquarters in its glass-walled high-rise in New York. As Marshall Jacobson (the UJA Senior Assistant Vice President who had previously been the Cleveland Campaign Director) was fond of saying, "If it won't fly in Cleveland, it won't fly anywhere."

Cleveland was a bellwether because it had an extraordinary group of lay leaders who not only gave, but also were reliable for giving; who not only were reliable but raised funds from others; who not only raised funds from others but actively led the Campaign. In some other communities, the federation Campaign Chairmanship would go to whomever wanted it most, or to whomever was willing to accept it; but in Cleveland the leadership would meet and decide who from among the many qualified prospects in that community was best to lead the campaign, whether the person wanted the position or not. Thus, to be selected was a matter of significant prestige. "Leaders" is a noun oft used in Jewish life, sometimes as a euphemism for "major donors;" among Cleveland's Jews the word was used in its true sense.

These leaders approached the Campaign as they did their businesses, hands-on and with a feeling of proprietary interest. They visited the federation often, worked closely with professionals in designing and executing plans, and knew the importance of their presence at events where donors were giving small sums, to emphasize that every gift, and every federation activity, was important. They ran the Campaign so much like their businesses that sometimes the lines were blurred. As Jacobson recalled, "Some were known to say to their company's suppliers, where millions of dollars were involved, they could have the account after they donated such-and-such amount to the Cleveland federation. Pure and simple, tax deductible, but quid pro quo."

Cleveland's professional leader was Stephen H. Hoffman, one of Jewish life's outstanding professionals and a man long active in the cause of Soviet Jewry. So it was cause for some concern on a conference call of the Top 19 Federation Executive Directors in early 1990, when Hoffman informed his Cleveland predecessor, UJA President Stanley Horowitz, that Cleveland would not campaign full throttle until June, even though most other Top 19s would be in full swing by Passover. Furthermore, while New York, Chicago and Los Angeles had guaranteed they would raise their proportional shares of the $420 million goal even if they had to borrow from the bank, Hoffman said that Cleveland would not provide any formal guarantee.

Horowitz admonished his successor, but could not argue with his reasons. After all, it was Horowitz himself who had established the processes that governed Cleveland's methodical decision making that lay behind Hoffman's decision to plan fully and shore up the Annual Campaign first. Although successors often feign that they are aghast at the mess they were left, and predecessors damn their successors with faint praise or purport to be astounded by their naiveté, Hoffman and Horowitz never criticized each other. Both had built their careers at the federation and rose to CEO on outstanding management skills and an intimate knowledge of the Cleveland Jewish community. Horowitz knew that Cleveland *looked* easy to manage, but he also knew that if you wanted to harness the community's highly independent self-made individualists, weld them into a focused team and keep all the horses pulling in the same direction, you had to be good, very good. Hoffman was, and when he said Cleveland would surpass the $14.1 million UJA said it needed and would reach $16 million, that was enough for UJA.

Cleveland's senior donors and veteran activists stepped up to the plate as soon as the Cleveland campaign began and some earlier: brothers like Albert and Charles Ratner and Peter and Fred Rzepka and others including Morton Mandel, Morry Weiss, Robert Goldberg, Victor Gelb, Samuel Miller, Lawrence Goldberg, Michael Siegel, Robert Silverman, Maury Saltzman, Julius Kravitz, Al Demb and Max Freedman.

But then, Cleveland had roots in the Soviet Jewry movement as deep as 1964, when the Cleveland Council on Soviet Anti-Semitism was formed, in part with federation funding. The Council was a forerunner of the National Conference on Soviet Jewry and the Union of Councils for Soviet Jews that carried the ball nationally in the 1970s and '80s. Cleveland Jews made frequent clandestine visits to Soviet Jews, beginning in 1966, to exchange information, encourage the Jews and bring in material goods and religious articles. In 1975 Donna and Bennett Yanowitz led a fact-finding mission to Russia that broadened Clevelanders' awareness and deepened support. In the early 1980s the federation urged Louis Stokes, a popular African American Representative, to chair the new Congressional Coalition on Soviet Jewry that broadened American government support and helped make Soviet Jewry a national issue. In the mid-1980s an activist named Anita Gray, returning from a mission, was strip-searched at Leningrad International Airport in a vain hunt for state secrets. When she came home and told her story the whole city was galvanized. Thousands of Clevelanders boarded buses at 2 a.m. on December 6, 1987, to demonstrate at the massive Freedom Sunday for Soviet Jews rally in Washington that pried open the gates of freedom. Whereas Passage to Freedom in 1989 failed to achieve its $75 million national goal, reaching only $49 million, Clevelanders raised $2.5 million, their full proportional share.

Peter Rzepka, a strong campaigner, was named Cleveland Operation Exodus Chairman. Rzepka was born in Poland and, like Joe Wilf, a Breakfast of Champions donor, had escaped with his family into the Soviet Union ahead of the Nazis. He wound up in Siberia, where he worked as a slave laborer in exchange for food, shelter and Soviet *protectsia*. After the war Rzepka made it to Shanghai, then Austria, obtained a United States visa, moved to Cleveland and, with only a little money to lose, invested aggressively to become a real estate powerhouse. When Rzepka described his own wartime yearning to be free, and his recent meetings with Jews in the Soviet Union, the quest to help win Jewish freedom could not be denied.

Cleveland conducted a textbook campaign, engaging and guiding leadership in all federation departments and following a meticulously crafted local plan enhanced by national services such as solicitors, speakers, events and communications materials. Charles Bronfman, the Seagram's leader who was a Breakfast of Champions participant, was among the UJA resources, keynoting a parlor meeting for $40,000 donors at the home of Sarah and Edwin Roth. Mayor Edward I. Koch of New York delivered the message at a $10,000 a plate dinner at Landerhaven. Mark Talisman of the Council of Jewish Federations, who as a young Congressional aide drafted the landmark Jackson-Vanik Amendment in the 1970s that made U.S. wheat sales to the Soviet Union dependent on increased Soviet Jewish emigration, presented the case at a gathering of hundreds of $1,500 donors at Fairmount Temple.

Although Cleveland did not begin its public phase at Passover, Rzepka led a delegation of Clevelanders on Pearlstone and Lender's Inaugural Operation Exodus Mission to Russia and Israel in March. Hoffman's staff arranged for the Mission's participants to be solicitation resources and parlor meeting speakers beginning in April. Meanwhile, Jeff Rzepka, Peter's son, led the Cleveland delegation to the UJA Young Leadership Conference in March, reunited the delegates at David Shifrin's home, briefed them, fired them up and sent them off to solicit other Young Leaders. Cleveland showed UJA videos, distributed its leadership briefings and fact sheets and, when the campaign was public, published its advertisements with a tear-off box for direct donor response. The *Cleveland Jewish News*, like most of the 151 American Jewish newspapers, published a stream of feature and news stories from UJA complemented by accounts of local campaign achievements.

Hoffman negotiated with the local Israel Bonds office for a joint appeal, then arranged for the federation to have an open corridor for a comprehensive High Holidays synagogue campaign. Rallies, direct mail, telephone requests and a 1.5 mile Freedom March broadened results.

On September 10 the federation offered "An Evening with Yitzhak Rabin," a champagne and dessert reception at B'nai Jeshurun Congregation for $1,000 donors. The event pushed Cleveland up to the goal requested by the UJA. The federation kept going, reaching $15.3 million by year's end, when it added $1 million from its endowments to exceed even its own more formidable challenge to itself of $16 million.

Detroit

The Jewish Federation of Metropolitan Detroit, in and around a city with one of the country's largest Arab American communities, was best known to Jewish insiders for having cultivated an extraordinarily large number of national Jewish leaders. These included Max Fisher; Joel Tauber; David Hermelin; Jane Sherman; Mandell Berman, the CJF President; Dr. Conrad Giles, an ophthalmologist and future CJF President; and Martin Kraar, the CJF Executive Vice President. William Davidson, the automobile glass manufacturer who participated at the Breakfast of Champions, and A. Alfred Taubman, the luxury shopping malls builder, were early top donors from Detroit.

The Detroit federation's challenge from UJA was to raise $14.9 million for Operation Exodus. On February 6, the day CJF endorsed the Campaign, Detroit Executive Vice President Robert P. Aronson told Morris Sherman, the UJA Vice President for Campaign, that Detroit would guarantee $15 million, raise at least $16.4 million, and set a $19 million goal. Preliminary discussions with pacesetters had indicated this was feasible.

The Annual Campaign was closed early, on March 22, at $25.4 million, a Detroit record. David S. Mondry, the Detroit Operation Exodus Chairman, along with Lawrence Jackier, Mark Schlussel and Joseph Orley lined up donors, and private solicitations and parlor meetings quickly began. Joel Tauber and David Hermelin returned from solicitations in the West, South and New England to close solicitations and address groups in their home town. "We met Jew after Jew in Moscow and Kiev who told of losing their job because they were Jewish, having their children beaten in schools, and other violence against Jews," Tauber said at one parlor meeting, drawing on several of his trips to the USSR. "The climate of hate is out in the open and spreading. We can't be indecisive as American Jews were during the Holocaust." Hermelin told another group, "In all those meetings in the Soviet Union I kept thinking, the difference between the Holocaust era and now is that now Jews have a place to go, Israel, and a people, us, to get them there."

Shoshana Cardin, the National Conference on Soviet Jewry Chairman, addressed a parlor meeting for $25,000 donors at the home of Marlene and Paul Borman on May 14. "I have met hundreds of Jews on these trips to the USSR," she said. "Some have been hounded, beaten, terrorized for years. Others suffer simple but blatant discrimination, like a graduating university student I met last week who finished first in his class but was denied a job that was given to a woman who finished last in the same class. When he inquired, he was told, 'You know why that happened: you are a Jew.' That evening his wife said, 'We must go to Israel. That is our home'."

Mondry dealt bluntly with potential donors who complained to solicitors that they disagreed with Shamir on issues like "Who is a Jew?" and building West Bank settlements. Mondry asserted, "I hear, 'I don't like Shamir.' 'I don't like Peres.' 'I don't like Israel's Shas Party.' 'I don't like Israel's Orthodox parties.' Well, I don't like them either. But what does that have to do with freedom for Soviet Jews?" Four million dollars was raised at the Bormans' home.

Leon Uris, whose novel *Exodus* (1958) inspired Jews and others worldwide with its story of the birth of Israel, addressed 403 donors at a $5,000 cocktail party at the Knollwood Country Club on June 4. He was introduced with an energizing UJA video including a narrative he wrote for Operation Exodus. Uris said, "The Soviet Union is a house about to collapse. I saw a Pamyat rally in the USSR last fall. The old Soviet anti-Semitism is bubbling to the surface." He added, "Every generation of Jews since the fall of the Second Temple has been blessed and burdened with saving our people. Operation Exodus is a wonderful opportunity for the Jews. You should support it as much as you can." More than $2.8 million was raised.

Vladimir Slepak, a Prisoner of Zion, told a gathering on June 20, "What Operation Exodus is doing can be heard by Soviet Jews struggling to get out. By Gorbachev. By Bush. Money speaks. You can speak up for the Soviet Jews tonight." They pledged $4 million.

A mission to Russia and Israel for Detroit area residents resulted in another $1 million. Women's Division raised $650,000. Young Adults Division contributed $77,768 after hearing Joel Tauber speak at a reception at Shelley and Joel Tauber's home. Helen and Arthur Braverman canceled their 40th anniversary party, sent the funds they had set aside to Operation Exodus and asked the disinvited guests to support the Campaign. Unsolicited checks arrived by mail including one for $25,000 from a woman not on any federation lists. An attorney who gave $500 to the Annual Campaign gave $10,000 for Operation Exodus. A young bakery deliveryman gave $500. Soviet immigrants in Detroit contributed. Schoolchildren collected from schoolmates; many gave their allowances. A 3.3 mile Solidarity Walk drew 7,000, energized the community, and brought in thousands of small but important gifts.

Detroit raised $19 million by June 22, and $20.8 million by December 31. "We received more than 6,000 pledges," Allan Gelfond, the Campaign Director said. "It was the largest response to a special appeal we ever had."

Philadelphia

The Jewish federation of Greater Philadelphia was so successful at the start of the Operation Exodus Campaign, it worried UJA. When Walter Annenberg told Max Fisher he would donate $15 million in February, Operation Exodus had not yet officially begun. Even the private phase was only a few days old. When Annenberg said yes to Fisher's $15 million request after he had been rated as $750,000 by the federation, the former Ambassador to the Court of Saint James and Nixon confidante completed 87 percent of Philadelphia's UJA-requested $17.2 million campaign goal on the spot.

While joyous, Lender telephoned Miriam Schneirov, a UJA National Vice Chairman from Philadelphia, and asked that the federation ignore the Annenberg bonanza, or count it as a $750,000 campaign jump start, and raise funds as if most of the goal was still unmet. Philadelphia went UJA one better. It said it would count the gift as it was, achieve the UJA goal without it and keep on going.

Philadelphia felt confident. For while it was the only large federation never to receive a million dollar Annual Campaign gift, it sensed the community excitement about the unfolding exodus. Philadelphia had deep roots in the Soviet Jewry movement. Philadelphians were early activists, working with the fledgling Cleveland group, and as part of early national efforts led by Malcolm Hoenlein, Yaacov Birnbaum, Rabbi Israel Miller, Rabbi Haskel Lookstein, Albert Chernin and others. They placed articles in local newspapers, sponsored letter writing campaigns and rallies, and sent thousands to Washington for Freedom Sunday. Moreover, as a city of choice for Soviet Jews who were able to leave in 1989 for the United States, the issue was already topical.

Philadelphia surprised UJA, but not itself. As Annenberg cut his first $5 million check in March, and the federation dispatched it quickly to UJA for use in Moscow, other solicitations were opened. Appointments with prospects were set, presentations made, sums floated, needs detailed, objections overcome and solicitations closed faster than you could say Benjamin Franklin. The philanthropy rule of thumb that 80 percent of a campaign is raised from 20 percent of the donors, and 90 from 10 percent in UJA life, was rendered

a low profile 50 years earlier. The *Baltimore Jewish Times* published illuminating, substantive news and feature stories, and Gary Rosenblatt, the editor-in-chief, wrote persuasive editorials that captured the idiom of a moment in history. Darryl Friedman, then the federation CEO, recalled in an interview, "More than 5,000 came to a rally at Temple Oheb Shalom to hear Leon Uris and a Soviet Jewish family that spoke about their hardships and discrimination. The crowd was so large it spilled out onto the street. People discovered that a chord had been struck, in themselves, in the community. For months we received checks from people who had not yet been asked to give." A High Holidays synagogue campaign, campus and school fundraising, and Chanukah appeals enabled Baltimore to finish the year at a very impressive $19.3 million.

Miami

Like most large federations, the Greater Miami Jewish Federation felt the community's enthusiasm and challenged itself to exceed UJA's goal, $11.6 million. It declared a higher one of $16.5 million. Fundraising began on March 21 with a parlor meeting at the home of Ted Arison, founder of Carnival Cruise Lines, that raised $4.5 million. Norman Braman, Michael Adler, Norman Lipoff, Aaron Podhurst, Michael Scheck and David Schaecter contributed.

A week later the federation took 800 donors of $5,000 and more on a UJA-organized mission to Russia and Israel that raised $4 million. The mission provided an additional treasure: a passionate, informed cadre of volunteers who returned to solicit their business associates and friends; and presented eyewitness accounts of the contemporary Jewish struggle that were broadcast on Miami television, and published in the *Miami Herald* and *Miami Jewish Tribune*. They set the table for the mass campaign that opened a week after Miami's Jews set the table for the first Seder on April 9.

On April 25, federation President Donald E. Lefton summoned heads of the 75 federation-funded agencies and told the packed conference room, "Every Jew in Greater Miami must learn, through us and our agencies, about our responsibilities to assist our fellow Jews at this historic time." Those agencies conducted campaigns among their boards, supporters and clients and deepened overall results.

The federation's Women's, Young Leadership and Trades and Professions departments sponsored events. The Rabbinic department coordinated synagogue appeals, aided by sample sermons for Passover, Rosh Hashanah and Chanukah from the UJA Rabbinic Cabinet that established historical perspective on the contemporary issue. The federation published advertisements and packaged

UJA briefings and photographs into local newsletters that warmed prospects for giving. A comprehensive condominium campaign was mounted, engaging retired Jews who remembered Jewish weakness during the Holocaust and Israel's struggles for survival: it raised a million dollars. The federation, quarterbacked by Jacob Solomon, a talented and dedicated CEO, finished the year with $16.6 million for Operation Exodus.

St. Louis

Deep in the American heartland and distant culturally and geographically from frenetic UJA headquarters in New York, the Jewish Federation of St. Louis was Marvin Lender's first stop after the Council of Jewish Federations ratified the Operation Exodus Campaign on February 6. He wanted to demonstrate that every American Jewish community, and every American Jew, was important to Operation Exodus. He left town on February 9 with pledges of $100,000 from Marlyn and Alyn Essman, Bud Levin, Samuel Goldstein, Thomas Greene, Al Siteman, Lester Miller and Jack Deutsch.

St. Louis opened the public phase with a rally on a sunny Sunday morning after Passover at the baseball diamonds of the Jewish Community Centers Association. There Marlyn Essman, the local Operation Exodus Chairman, testified to the anguish and hope she had seen on UJA's Inaugural Operation Exodus Mission to Russia and Israel. "I am tormented by the faces of Jews I met in the Soviet Union; they are fearful and have reason to be afraid," she said. "I saw the faces of Soviet Jews as they landed in Israel, faces of relief, streaming with tears of joy. We will not be silent."

Mary Travers of the folk trio Peter, Paul and Mary, on a federation tour of the country sponsored by UJA, opened with Bob Dylan's song, "The times they are a'changin'. "The pragmatism of the 1990s combined with the idealism of the 1960's as 3,500 St. Louisans turned out last Sunday for a mass rally in support of Operation Exodus," Robert A. Cohn, editor of the *St. Louis Jewish Light* and President of the American Jewish Press Association, wrote. "Travers closed the concert and the rally with a stirring rendition of, "Blowin' in the Wind," in which she was joined by the entire audience who rose as one to lock arms and sing the anthem of freedom of the 1960s to meet the challenges of the 1990s." The rally raised $200,000.

Passion permeated the campaign. Elissa Udell, 12, donated all her Bat Mitzvah gifts to Operation Exodus. The 95 members of the Mamroth family, which came from Lomze, Russia during the pogroms, pooled their resources to help other families escape. Samuel Wise, who came from Minsk, Belarus as a small child, gave the $640 he had just received in honor of his 90th birthday. Wise stated:

> My uncles told me stories about the pogroms. The Cossack soldiers would come into the Jewish section of Minsk, shooting in the air and breaking windows. The captain would sit down with the rabbi and say, 'This is how much it will cost your people for us to leave you alone.' It has always taken money. We've always had to pay for our safety. My family escaped 90 years ago because relatives sent money. Until recently that was the only way for Jews to get out of the Soviet Union. Today, Operation Exodus is working to get all the Jews out. But it still takes money.

St. Louis funded one of the campaign's first Freedom Flights, which led Marlyn Essman to state:

> In 1939, a ship named the St. Louis left Europe filled with Jews fleeing the growing Nazi oppression, but the Jews were denied entry into Cuba, Canada and the United States. With nowhere for Jews to go, the ship returned to Europe where the Nazis awaited. The name 'St. Louis' evokes memories of those who lost their lives because good people did nothing. This time there is a place for all Jews in danger to go, and transports bearing the name St. Louis will not be turned away.

Other Campaigns

The Campaign was successfully pursued in other cities and towns too, including San Francisco, home to some of the most generous philanthropists, including the Swig, Haas and Koret families. There, Melvin Swig's generosity earned him the nickname, "the fastest checkbook in the West," and the rest of his family was the same. The Haas family included siblings Walter Haas, Jr., Peter Haas and Rhoda Haas Goldman, philanthropists whose great granduncle was Levi Strauss, the nineteenth century pioneer who had produced and marketed jeans. The Korets, women's clothing manufacturers, had built their Foundation into one of the largest in the country. Koret and Koret Foundation gifts of from $1 million to $4 million inspired giving at all levels and propelled the Jewish Community Federation of San Francisco, Peninsula, Marin and Sonoma Counties to $20 million, double the sum UJA requested.

At the Jewish Federation of Greater Washington, Herschel Blumberg, who had been UJA National Chairman from 1980 to 1982 and had played tennis weekly with Yitzhak Rabin when Rabin was Israel's Ambassador to

Washington, was one of many local longtime supporters of Soviet Jewish emigration. Thousands of others joined the cause at the Freedom Sunday for Soviet Jews rally in 1987. Veterans and newcomers, they gave at federation events, rallies, synagogue campaigns and Super Sunday, a fundraising idea that had been developed at the Washington federation. Greater Washington raised $15 million.

Henry Taub, a Breakfast of Champions participant, past president of United Israel Appeal and a JDC and UJA trustee, was the rainmaker at the United Jewish Appeal of Bergen County and North Hudson in New Jersey. In addition to giving, and raising funds nationally, Taub hosted a parlor meeting in his home in May that raised $2 million. Close to New York City and its inundation of news, Bergen Jews were well aware of the need and gave generously. Bergen became the first federation to achieve its goal, $5.5 million, and continued on to $9 million.

At the United Jewish Federation of Pittsburgh, a gifted administrator and fundraiser, Howard Rieger, the Executive Vice President, engaged his strong lay leadership and able staff behind an ambitious, but carefully crafted, campaign plan. Pittsburgh was out of the gate early with a $1.5 million gift from Abraham Shapira in March and it effectively utilized this pace setting example to set the stage for an effective and comprehensive major gifts program. The federation broadened the campaign in the former mill town, which had become home to a young and growing Jewish community; and through Women's, Young Leadership, Super Sunday and other events reached out to everyone. UJF's campaign excellence, and a willing and motivated local Jewish community, resulted in $8.2 million for Operation Exodus.

At the Combined Jewish Philanthropies of Greater Boston, a spring mission to Russia and Israel initiated the campaign and established a corps of energetic, informed solicitors. A major gifts luncheon featuring Simcha Dinitz broadened results. Paul Fireman's $500,000 gift and $300,000 each from Steve Grossman, Frank Resnek and the Kline Foundation were among the first gifts to come in. An engaged leadership, years of activism for Soviet Jews and CEO Barry Shrage's solid planning and management contributed to an $8 million achievement.

United Jewish Federation of MetroWest (New Jersey) entered the campaign with leaders knowledgeable from UJA missions to Israel and Russia. and years of activism on behalf of Soviet Jewry. UJA National Vice Chairmen Sanford Hollander, a persuasive solicitor, and Joel Leibowitz, a solicitation trainer, both local residents, enhanced the major gifts program. MetroWest made good use of a panoply of UJA products, especially marketing materials. Howard Charish, the Executive Vice President, contributed solid professional management. Outstanding coverage by the *Jewish News*, which published articles and editorials frequently on the plight of Soviet Jews, showed the campaign's continuing urgency. MetroWest, based in two populous counties in the metropolitan area west of New York City, added $8 million to the national pot.

In Atlanta, the names sounded as Jewish as turn of the century Lower East Side tailors, Sidney Feldman, Gerald Cohen and Milton Weinstein, but the persons who bore them were American-born big businessmen with Southern accents. When Irwin Zaban, who had convened major gift gatherings for the Jewish Federation of Greater Atlanta for years, gathered Feldman, Cohen, Weinstein and others at the Standard Club before Passover, the name that counted most was Operation Exodus and the accent was on giving. More than $2 million was raised. Atlanta's activism in the Soviet Jewry movement in the 1980s, when it chartered planes and buses for Freedom Sunday, held local rallies and letter-writing projects, and mounted missions to the Soviet Union, had built a broad fundraising base. Atlanta registered a $7 million achievement.

Aided by the efforts of UJA National Vice Chairmen from Minneapolis Arnold Lifson, Richard Spiegel and Stephen Lieberman, solicitations by Lender, Tauber and Pearlstone, and yet another UJA motivational speaker, *New York Times* columnist A. M. Rosenthal, the Minneapolis Federation for Jewish Service raised $6.4 million.

Herbert Solomon, Shearn Platt, Lawrence Sherman, Rod Stone and Stephen Abramson of the United Jewish Federation of San Diego participated in the UJA Inaugural Mission and summoned a news conference upon their return. They described the Jewish quest for freedom and announced the inception of the San Diego campaign. Their leadership, mass giving and UJA speakers including Marina Furman generated $6.2 million.

North of Miami, the Jewish Federation of Palm Beach raised $4.2 million; the Jewish Federation of Fort Lauderdale, $3.9 million; the Jewish Federation of South Broward, $3.1 million; and the Jewish Federation of South Palm Beach, $2.6 million. Edgar Bronfman spoke in each community, beginning with a parlor meeting in South Broward that raised $1.1 million. UJA leaders who were year-round residents such as H. Irwin Levy and Alan Shulman, and winter residents such as Max Fisher and Sylvia Hassenfeld, opened their homes for parlor meetings and personally closed major gifts. The campaigns attracted broad support from older residents, who remembered decades of Jewish struggle abroad and, in the case of Holocaust survivors, had suffered themselves. The growing younger population gave too, enthralled by the breathtaking drama of Jewish freedom. Winter residents gave both in Florida and in the north.

Jews in Milwaukee, home of Marty Stein and Alan Crawford, contributed $5.7 million. Houston's Jews gave $5.5 million and Dallas', $5.3 million. Those in Columbus, in addition to Wexner, gave $4.7 million. Jews in Cincinnati, where Stanley Chesley and Richard Shenk spearheaded efforts, gave $4.2 million. Jews in Phoenix gave $3.7 million; in Rhode Island, $3.6 million; in Seattle, $3 million; and in Oakland, $3.1 million.

In Birmingham Donald and Ronne Hess, Martin and Heidi Damsky, Steven and Susan Greene and Steven Brickman and Richard Friedman participated on the UJA Inaugural Mission. They returned with firsthand accounts that filled the media, meeting rooms and public gatherings, then filled deep coffers as the Deep South town raised $1.8 million.

Memphis Jews weren't singing the blues. They responded to solicitations by Arlene Zimmerman, Andrew Groveman, Jan Belz Groveman, Joel Tauber and Radio Shack co-founder Bernard Appel. Former Prisoner of Zion Iosef Begun told them Russia was no Graceland. Memphis Jews gave $1.6 million for Soviet Jewish emigration.

Jews gave from $1 million to $3 million in checks of thousands and coins of pennies to federation campaigns in Buffalo, Denver, Hartford, Indianapolis, Kansas City, New Haven, and Rochester; in Tidewater, Toledo, Tucson and Tulsa; on the North Shore of Massachusetts and in Central, Middlesex, Northern and Southern New Jersey; and from Allentown to Youngstown. The Jews in Orlando showed they weren't in Disney World and gave $1 million. Chattanooga Jews were on the right track with $491,000. The old ladies and others in Peoria chipped in $182,500.

"There's no doubt about it," Lender wrote to UJA National Officers as the year's totals were tallied. "This is a mass campaign." And that was the understatement of the year.

CHAPTER FIVE
Operation Exodus Finishes
But It Doesn't End

We are like fiddlers on the roof.

Tevye the Milkman, Fiddler on the Roof.

When 1990 began, few thought that the United Jewish Appeal could raise $420 million in a year for Operation Exodus. When it ended, $503.6 million had been raised. More than 1.1 million American Jews gave of their hard earned money to realize that staggering achievement. For them, decent, selfless, spectacularly generous men, women and children, it was a chance to bring about a miracle in Jewish destiny in their own time.

Historians could write whatever they wanted about any other generation but those American Jews stood up and were counted. They had strong motivations, including guilt and vulnerability. Guilt that their parents' generation did not do enough to save Jews in the Holocaust even though they themselves had no reason to feel guilt. Vulnerability in that they identified with Jews in danger even though they themselves were not in danger. But they acted as surely in hope, in selfless idealism that the good things they enjoyed, like religious freedom, should be shared. Operation Exodus was a crowning achievement in human selflessness, spectacular even by Jewish, even by UJA, standards. Half a billion dollars in gifts; we're talking about real money.

Yet it was more than money. They felt privileged, not only to live in freedom but to be able to play a lasting role in shaping Jewish destiny. They gave in order to realize the contemporary aspirations of their ancient people. They gave freely, willingly, happily. They gave in love and support for a distant branch of the Jewish family. They gave to redeem Jews still not free after the suffering in ancient Egypt, the Crusades, the Inquisition, the pogroms and the Holocaust. They gave to let all Jews know, all tyrants know, that someday every

Jew would be free. Nothing material in America could hold a candle to the overwhelming satisfaction that came from that.

Thanks to them, the Israelis, and Jews in 45 other countries who contributed $85.6 million to Keren Hayesod, 184,681 Jews who had awakened to religious oppression in the disintegrating Soviet monstrosity when the year began, soon called Israel home. A place where the new immigrants were not victimized but welcomed. *Their country. Their language. Their people.* Their dream had come true. Every immigrant child was enrolled in a school immune to anti-Semitic vitriol. Every worker felt secure that no one would bar his or her advancement because of religion. Every mother laughed in joy, as Sarah did in ancient days when the impossible dream was coming true. Every one of the 184,681 Jews had come home. And their lives were just beginning.

Nearly one in four was a professional or creative artist. They included 6,101 physicians who were amazed by Israeli medical standards; 1,648 scientists awed by laboratory equipment; 10,453 teachers inspired by a curriculum that promoted democracy; 24,913 engineers impressed by Israeli technical knowledge; and 5,153 artists, writers and musicians ecstatic over creative freedom. So many musicians arrived that symphony orchestras sprouted in cities and towns. Beersheba had none when the year began, three when it ended. Israelis joked that Soviet Jews needed to play a musical instrument to obtain a visa. "If you see an immigrant getting off the plane and not carrying a violin," they laughed, "he must be a pianist." It was the laugh of Sarah too. The immigration was sweet music to the Israeli branch of the world Jewish family.

Sixty percent of immigrants chose direct absorption and moved into their own apartments upon arrival, their rent and other expenses paid by the Jewish Agency and Israeli taxpayers. Most who chose absorption centers moved into their own apartments within months. So many arrived that cities like Haifa and Ashdod took on a Russian cultural flavor. They found Russian added, just for them, to street signs everywhere. They were wide-eyed as storekeepers in supermarkets, butcher shops, bakeries and cafés scurried to include Russian fare and eagerly learned the Russian words for fruit, meat and bread. They lived in freedom with a touch of their former home.

For the Israelis, their society was changing more rapidly than since the country's founding. The population increase, 5.3 percent, was like bringing the entire population of Beijing and Tokyo to the United States in a year. Inflation rose from the new immigrants' buying power, and so did unemployment, and taxes in the most heavily taxed democracy. Lines grew in shops and government offices. Streets clogged with pedestrians and motorists. And still the Israelis (the earlier Israelis, as the newcomers were Israelis too) welcomed the Soviet Jews.

During the year, xenophobic riots broke out in England, France and Belgium over miniscule increases in foreigners, but not in Israel. Not one demonstration took place in Israel against the immigration. Although the Jews already in Israel were inconvenienced, irritated and challenged by the waves of immigration, they still embraced the aliyah. After all, most Israelis, or their parents, had been immigrants themselves. And the ingathering of the exiles was their dream too, the Zionist dream.

The Israeli response enraptured American Jews, some of whom gave two and three times during the year. Thousands of Jews gave to UJA for the first time, enthralled by the immigrants' escape to freedom, the Israelis' warm welcome and their own opportunity to shape modern Jewish history. Scenes of arriving immigrants stepping from the airplanes onto the tarmac at Ben Gurion Airport, greeted with songs and flowers, were played and replayed on American television and featured in American newspapers. No one could doubt that the greatest voluntary movement of Jews since the Exodus from Egypt, a magnificent ingathering thousands of years in the making, was truly underway. Fears that the immigrants would settle on the West Bank proved unfounded as 99.6 percent chose to remain within Israel's pre-1967 borders. Operation Exodus was a Soviet Jew's dream. It was an Israeli Jew's dream. It was an American Jew's dream. It was a fundraiser's dream.

Operation Exodus raised enough for federations to provide eight percent of its funds to aid Soviet Jewish resettlement in the United States. Overall, by the end of 1990, Operation Exodus and the Annual Campaign raised an astonishing $1.105 billion. That's more than a billion dollars from a base of six million Jews. Few charities ever achieve that level; the indispensable United Way raised $3 billion from a base of 248 million people. UJA and federations raised an average of $3 million dollars a day. Moreover, UJA increased its annual budget by only $2.3 million to conduct Operation Exodus, a mere ten percent, squeezing out every cent it could to bring immigrants to Israel.

Sobering the euphoria, instability in the Soviet Union grew throughout the year. Despite fierce American pressure for Gorbachev to permit direct flights to Israel, he procrastinated under countervailing Arab and Palestinian threats of violence. The aliyah still depended upon much that was beyond Jewish control. European countries might decide to stop permitting tens of thousands of Jewish transients to fly into their capitals, and live in camps on their soil for weeks, a crucial passageway in the absence of direct flights. The Dutch Embassy in Moscow that represented Israeli interests in the void of diplomatic recognition might be coerced to end its role. The exasperating and mercurial Soviet bureaucracy could vitiate diplomatic advances.

Jews fled from everywhere, from large Republics like Russia and Ukraine and small ones like Uzbekistan, where the 20,969 who got out in 1990 represented a fifth of the local Jewish population.[1] They emptied out of cities where Jews had lived for a thousand years, like Vilnius, Riga, Minsk, Kishinev and Odessa. They eclipsed the scope of the legendary year-long ingatherings of 20,703 after the Six-Day War and 31,979 after the Yom Kippur War. A bunch of liberal arts majors, the fundraisers could hardly compute the percentage increase that 184,681 represented compared to the 220 that emigrated to Israel in all of 1986 (83,846 percent). Most breathtaking of all, the rate of aliyah soared higher and higher as the year progressed:[2]

1990	Number of immigrants
January	4,796
February	5,683
March	7,090
April	11,004
May	10,261
June	11,037
July	15,378
August	17,527
September	18,776
October	21,988
November	25,582
December	35,569

Despite everything, hundreds of thousands of Jews were still trapped in the Soviet Union. Operation Exodus had succeeded beyond anyone's wildest imagination, but as the year ended it looked as if it still was not enough. Open rebellions were underway in Soviet cities and *Pamyat* was flexing its muscle in the countryside. As the empire collapsed around them, the predicament of the Jews worsened. As the dissident Alexander Bronstein warned upon his

---

1 Baruch Gur-Gurevitz, *After Gorbachev History in the Making: Its Effects on the Jews in the Former Soviet Union 1989-94*, Jerusalem: Jewish Agency, 1995, p. 132.

2 Gur-Gurevitz, p. 191.

arrival on the last aliyah flight of the year, "The gates may close at any time. They may not reopen for years, if ever." No Jew wanted to be left behind. Operation Exodus had finished; it had achieved its goal. But it did not end. In some ways it was just beginning.

"Ha!" Lender said to a small group of insiders with a nervous laugh. "This is great. Now how, exactly, do we keep this campaign going?"

CHAPTER SIX
Neither Rain, Nor Snow,
Nor Missiles of Night

In war, only one thing is certain: no one knows what
will happen.

Dwight D. Eisenhower

On the night of November 9 and 10, 1938, mobs that were organized, incited and led by the National Socialist Party rampaged through Jewish sections of Austria and Germany. Thirty thousand Jews were arrested for the crime of being Jewish; most were sent to camps and eventually killed. Hundreds were injured and at least 36 died.[1] Orchestrated by Hermann Goering after ominous warnings that the Nazis would deal harshly with interference, the mobs destroyed 815 Jewish-owned shops, set afire 191 synagogues and demolished 76 others, and decimated 171 homes and 29 warehouses. The Holocaust had begun.

Amid the horrific sights of the disaster was an indelible sound throughout the night, the sound of broken glass. The pogrom was named Kristallnacht, the Night of Broken Glass. It riveted American Jews, complacent and assimilationist, 4,000 miles away.

In the United States, the three main American Jewish fundraising organizations, the National Coordinating Committee for Aid to Refugees that assisted Jews in the United States, the United Palestine Appeal that provided for Jews in the Middle East and the American Jewish Joint Distribution Committee that helped Jews in Europe, had feuded for years. An attempt to merge their campaigns in 1935 had failed, but now they knew they had to unite to confront the ghastly peril. William Rosenwald of NCCAR, Rabbi Abba Hillel Silver of UPA and Rabbi Jonah B. Wise of JDC signed the founding

---

1 *Encyclopedia Judaica*, Jerusalem: Keter, 1972, X, p. 1,263.

document on January 10, 1939. They named the new organization the United Jewish Appeal.[2]

The fledgling group doubled and quadrupled the forerunners' combined 1938 fundraising total of $7 million, raising $15 million in 1939 and $28.4 million in 1940. Results rose steadily throughout the war, reaching $57.3 million in 1945. Through the UJA, American Jews rescued 162,000 Jews and sustained life for hundreds of thousands of others during the Holocaust, whomever its field teams could reach.

After the war, Rosenwald laid down an unprecedented challenge: raise $100 million for refugee relief in 1946. Many scoffed. He gave one of philanthropy's first million dollar gifts, and hundreds of thousands of others gave what they could. UJA raised an astounding $131 million in 1946 and $157 million in 1947. UJA had clearly become the central address in American Jewish philanthropy and one of the most successful philanthropies in the world.

With an opportunity to help establish Israel, a Jewish haven from wandering and persecution sorely missing for 2,000 years, UJA raised $201 million in 1948. Golda Meir, then Golda Myerson, a Jewish Agency department head, personally raised $50 million in the first three months of the year. In Israel's early years, UJA funds constituted the equivalent of 25 percent of the national budget. As Chaim Weizmann, the country's first President said, "On the basis of what has been created in the past by the United Jewish Appeal, we now have obtained the status of national independence."[3]

From 1948 to 1951, UJA financed Operation Ezra and Nehemiah, an airlift of 120,000 Jews from Iraq; Operation Magic Carpet, an air and sea evacuation of 50,000 Jews from Yemen; and the aliyahs of hundreds of thousands of Holocaust survivors from Europe, 40,000 Jews from Turkey, 18,000 from Iran, the entire Bulgarian Jewish community; and half the Jews of Yugoslavia.

UJA was viewed in Washington as the representative of American Jews, now no longer quiet. "I can personally testify," wrote Abba Eban, Israel's first Ambassador to Washington and the United Nations, "that the decision of the United States Congress and of successive presidents to include Israel in their foreign aid programs from 1951 onward was largely influenced by the example of private and voluntary agencies among which the United Jewish Appeal stood head and shoulders above all others."[4] When Secretary of State John Foster Dulles

---

2 See *The Whole UJA Catalog 50 Years of Service 1939-89*, pp. 3-12, and *Keeping the Promise The First Fifty Years at the United Jewish Appeal*, pp. 5-15, both distributed by UJA in 1989; and Abraham J. Karp, *To Give Life: The UJA in the Shaping of the American Jewish Community*, New York: Schocken Books, 1980, for more on UJA and its campaigns.

3 *Keeping the Promise*, p. 11.

4 *Keeping the Promise*, p. 8.

wanted to relieve pressure on himself from American Jews in the Suez Crisis in 1956, he threatened that the government would disallow tax deductibility of gifts to UJA; American Jews gave even more.

On June 5, 1967 Israel found itself in a war for survival against 22 Arab armies but within six days it achieved an astounding military triumph. American Jews were horrified, then thrilled. They were enraptured daily by Eban's eloquence at the United Nations. They exulted publicly in their Jewishness, in workplaces and schools. They began to believe that the fate of Jews worldwide was linked to the future of the Jewish State. Within the context of their love for America, they joyfully embraced Israel. A sure sign of their euphoria was the UJA campaign: they gave $317 million in 1967, up from $137 million in 1966. The campaign reached $660 million after Israel was hunkered down in the Yom Kippur War of October 1973. The UJA slogan, conceived in that war, became its mantra and articulated the enduring ideal in the fractious Jewish community: "We Are One."

Even as UJA conducted annual and emergency campaigns, whose results were always impressive, it conducted multi-year campaigns. In 1978 UJA introduced Project Renewal to make life easier for 300,000 disadvantaged Israelis in 97 towns and cities. By 1989 Project Renewal raised $193 million that built recreation centers, improved transportation and communications, trained Israelis for jobs and provided for cultural enrichment. Even more far reaching, Project Renewal established a system of designating particular Israeli towns for help by specific American Jewish communities, thereby giving American Jews a direct stake in Israel's future and exposing many Israelis to American Jews for the first time. Thousands of American Jews visited their "twin" community and brought leaders of those towns to be guests in their homes in the United States. Project Renewal built a bridge of understanding across the huge cultural and informational chasm that had long separated American Jews and Israelis, and blazed the path for hundreds of similar programs that followed.

In other special campaigns, Operation Moses, a clandestine rescue of Ethiopian Jews in 1984 and 1985, raised $64 million--amazingly in secret (please see Chapter 7). And Passage to Freedom raised $49 million in 1989 to aid Soviet Jewish emigration to the United States, the only UJA campaign not focused on aid abroad.

In its first 50 years UJA, in partnership with the federations, raised $6 billion dollars. It spent nearly all of it immediately on human needs. UJA helped bring 1.9 million Jews to Israel from 131 countries. It established 593 rural communities within Israel's pre-1967 borders where bronze-skinned pioneers, aided by Israeli engineering ingenuity, grew crops in the Negev desert in the south and brave souls tilled in the lonely reaches of the north near hostile neighbors. It nurtured 275,000 Israeli orphans and children from broken homes, and cared for 150,000 aging Israelis.

By providing 99 percent of the annual budgets of the gallant Joint Distribution Committee, UJA sustained life for poor Jews around the globe with food, clothing, shelter, eyeglasses, hearing aids and medical care; and kept Jewish life alive with Passover packages, prayer books and Jewish culture in Poland, Romania, Hungary, Morocco, Tunisia, Chile, India and dozens of other countries.

UJA's priceless reputation helped federations to secure billions for human needs in the United States, especially in the earlier decades when donors gave mainly for Israel.

Yet by UJA's golden anniversary it was receiving only 44 percent of UJA-Federation Campaign funds, which were always remitted by donors to federations. This was down from 50 percent on UJA's silver anniversary and 90 percent in its early years. The Campaign was still one of the largest of any philanthropy, totaling over $700 million a year, but it did not keep pace with inflation or rising needs at home or budgets abroad. From Israel's perspective UJA gifts, which once funded the equivalent of 25 percent of the national budget, provided the equivalent of only about two percent in 1989. Many donors were alienated by Shamir's policies on "Who is a Jew?" and West Bank settlements. Fewer Jews felt Israel was important in their life at all. UJA and federations were in persistent conflict over how to divide the stagnant campaign pie. This writer even composed a confidential internal document titled, "Is UJA Dying?"

Operation Exodus rescued Jews but in 1990 it also rescued the UJA. Yet by the end of that banner year, donors seemed spent, as was their money. "What could sustain Operation Exodus in 1991?" Lender wondered. Tragedy and triumph had propelled UJA campaigns in the past. Tragedy and triumph were in store for 1991.

The winds of war had blown over Iraq from the day Saddam Hussein became President on July 17, 1979. After brutally suppressing resistance at home, Saddam invaded his eastern neighbor Iran on September 22, 1980, hoping to seize its oil-rich Khuzestan region. He expected early victory, believing Iran was militarily weak and distracted by its nettlesome ten-month hostage crisis with the United States. But Ayatollah Ruhollah Khomeini's forces beat back Iraqi advances. With Saddam conscripting teenagers and promising them eternity with 72 virgins if they died as martyrs, and Khomeini drafting 12-year-olds and sending them into battle with the Key to Heaven around their necks, the war raged until 1988. The United Nations finally secured a ceasefire but only after as many as 1.5 million people had been killed.[5]

Not that that dissuaded Saddam from foreign military adventures. On February 24, 1990, as Israelis focused on the nascent Soviet emigration and UJA leaders made their final Breakfast of Champions preparations, Saddam made a threat to attack Israel. His immediate target, however, was his southern neighbor Kuwait and its rich oil resources. Despite diplomatic rumblings concerning his troop movements toward the Kuwait border, formidable international opposition did not congeal and by July 25, 35,000 Iraqi troops stood there poised to invade.

That day, as Saddam was meeting with April Glaspie, the United States Ambassador to Baghdad, he stepped out to take a call from President Hosni Mubarak of Egypt. He told Mubarak, but not Glaspie, that he would not invade Kuwait, information Mubarak happily shared with other Arab leaders. Cables released months later to the Senate Foreign Relations Committee disclosed that Glaspie told Saddam the United States advocated a peaceful settlement but stated, "We have no opinion on the Arab-Arab conflicts, like your border disagreement with Kuwait."[6] Eight days later, on August 2, 140,000 Iraqi troops and 1,800 tanks invaded and quickly conquered Kuwait. Iraq established a puppet government and annexed the country within the week.

Diplomatic efforts to persuade Iraq to withdraw failed. President George H.W. Bush, working through the United Nations, secured a Security Council resolution authorizing the use of force, and put together a military coalition to dislodge Iraq from Kuwait. Saddam seized Westerners as hostages on August 13 and detained them until December 6, but the action radiated none of the drama that Iran's did during the last 444 days of the Carter Administration. Bush's focus was on securing Arab support for the Coalition, which he viewed as an alliance to help establish a new world order for peace. He won the participation of Egypt and of Saudi Arabia, Iraq's southwestern neighbor that shared an even longer border with Iraq than did Iran or Kuwait. To secure the Coalition, Bush barred Israel's participation and pressured it not to respond even if attacked by Iraq. On November 29, 1990 Bush set January 15, 1991 as Saddam's final deadline to begin withdrawal. Wars often begin with a surprise attack; this was a war by appointment.[7]

With war days away, Iraqi Foreign Minister Tariq Aziz was asked if Iraq

---

5 *Columbia Encyclopedia*, New York: Columbia University Press, 6th ed., 2001.

6 U. S. News and World Report, *Triumph Without Victory*, New York: Random House, 1992, pp. 24–25.

7 Lawrence Freedman and Efraim Karsh, *The Gulf Conflict 1990–91*, Princeton, N.J.: Princeton University Press, 1993.

would strike Israel if attacked by Coalition forces. "Yes," he said. "Absolutely. Yes." Saddam, who some believed to possess biological, chemical and nuclear weapons, ratcheted up the public relations war, threatening to destroy Israel and send 30,000 Americans home in body bags.

The final diplomatic effort, a flight by Secretary of State James Baker to meet with Aziz in Geneva on January 9, failed. The United States Senate voted by 52 to 47 and the House of Representatives voted by 250 to 183 on January 12 to authorize the President to wage war. Bush signed a National Security Directive on January 15 authorizing Defense Secretary Richard B. Cheney to institute military action. General Colin L. Powell, Chairman of the Joint Chiefs of Staff, ordered General H. Norman Schwarzkopf, Jr., Commander of Operations, to initiate hostilities.

Operation Desert Storm, as the war was named, began on Wednesday, January 16 at 7 p.m. Washington time, as the Coalition of 32 countries struck with 400 planes and 160 tankers and command aircraft, spearheaded by special forces in Apache helicopters. It issued staggering blows from the air that quickly eliminated eight radar stations, caused substantial troop disarray and forced Scud launchers from destroyed installations into the field. The war by appointment was a public war, broadcast live to television viewers worldwide. The young Cable News Network brought the explosions of bombs, flashes of light and screams of sirens into millions of homes and offices in real time, accompanying the coverage with on-site reportage of journalists and in-studio explanations by military experts.[8]

Within 24 hours, Iraq attacked Israel with eight Scud missiles that landed in civilian neighborhoods in and near Tel Aviv. The Israeli military remained on highest alert, its pilots strapped in their cockpits 24 hours a day, as missiles rained on Israeli civilians, but Shamir acceded to Bush's pressure not to respond. Saddam fought defensively against Coalition forces, but turned his offensive weapons on Israel and Saudi Arabia. This reminded older Israelis of how Hitler devoted scarce resources to pursuing the Holocaust in the east rather than deploying those resources against Allied forces attacking from the west. Saddam's strategy was to push Israel into the war, to discourage Egypt and Saudi Arabia from fighting on the same side as Israel.

It was difficult for Israel to show restraint. The country prized its reputation of responding to all attacks as a deterrent measure. After days of assaults Defense Minister Moshe Arens warned Cheney on a secure line, "Israel's patience is

---

8 Viewers mainly observed nighttime battles illuminated by Coalition bombs and night vision technology. It was difficult for most to understand the images and context of the action without the expert explanations.

wearing thin." Cheney refused Arens' request to open a four-hour air corridor for Israel and share the electronic identification codes that would enable it to distinguish between Coalition and Iraqi aircraft. What Shamir and Arens did not know was that the United States had developed contingency plans to immediately ground all Coalition planes in the area in case Israel defied American pressure and moved to attack Iraq.[9]

The United States gave priority to preempting attacks on Israel by finding and destroying Scud launchers in what became known among war planners as the Great Scud Hunt.[10] The Coalition destroyed many Scud launchers and forced others into the field, which limited their ability to target Israel's population centers. Iraqis were forced to improvise so as not to bomb Palestinian towns on the West Bank. The efficacy of the Patriot interceptors, which the United States had stationed in and around Israeli population centers, was lauded in wartime interviews but inadequate in practice. Israelis were protected by the Scuds' inaccuracy and then the Iraqi defeat.[11]

The Coalition secured control of the air in mid-February. Bush warned of a ground war if Iraq did not withdraw from Kuwait. Saddam rallied his troops with bloodcurdling threats of massive Coalition deaths in "the mother of all battles."[12] The ground war began on February 24; four days later Iraq was defeated, Saddam acceded to Bush's demand and Bush declared a ceasefire.[13]

In battle, 240 Coalition fighters were killed including 148 Americans. There were 776 Coalition personnel wounded including 458 Americans. Iraqi losses were estimated as at least 20,000 killed and 60,000 wounded.[14]

Throughout the war life in Israel, as portrayed by television networks around the world, consisted of fear of attack, safe rooms, gas masks, and special cribs with protective coverings in safe rooms for infants too small to wear gas masks. Forty Scuds reached Israel, killing two civilians directly and leading to 18 deaths from heart attacks or gas mask malfunctions. Hundreds were injured, and most of the country lived in anxiety if not shock. Four thousand buildings were damaged. In Saudi Arabia, 46 Scuds killed 31 and injured 400. Throughout the 45 days of war no one in Israel knew what was in store, whether Scuds would arrive carrying weapons of mass destruction, whether the Patriots would

---

9 Friedman and Karsh, p. 335.

10 Friedman and Karsh, p. 309.

11 Friedman and Karsh, p. 311.

12 Steve A. Yetiv, *The Persian Gulf Crisis*, Westport, CT: Greenwood Press, 1997, p. 177.

13 *Columbia Encyclopedia*.

14 Friedman and Karsh, p. 408.

intercept them, whether Israel would enter the war and whether the Coalition would collapse.

Every night Soviet television showed footage of missiles landing near Israel's only international airport and families hunkered down in sealed rooms in gas masks. Did that stop the Soviet Jews from coming? Not much.

The war may have begun at 3 a.m. Jerusalem time on January 17, 1991, but four El Al jets landed at Ben Gurion International Airport the same day, as 740 Soviet Jews kept to their plans and moved to Israel. Scud missiles may have landed in nearby Tel Aviv the next day, but 127 Soviet Jews landed too, to begin their new lives in Israel. Another 247 arrived on January 19, and 605 on January 20. In January, 12,730 Soviet Jews arrived in Israel, a family of five for every couple a year earlier. In February 1991, 7,134 arrived, compared to 5,706 a year earlier. Among them, on February 10, 1991 was the 200,000[th] Soviet Jewish immigrant since January 1, 1990. The immigration might have been higher were it not for the war. On the other hand, 19,864 arrived in those two war months, nearly double the 10,479 who had arrived in the comparatively peaceful corresponding period in 1990.

As Simon Griver wrote in "Caught in the Crossfire:"[15]

> The Frefeld family's flight touched down in Israel just one hour before the United Nations deadline for Saddam Hussein to leave Kuwait expired. As the fateful ultimatum came into effect the Frefelds were being processed by immigration officials at Ben-Gurion International Airport.
>
> On the morning of January 16, Alexander and Ella Frefeld, their 15-year-old daughter Lena, and 9-year-old son Dima gave up their Soviet citizenship and became Israelis. They headed straight to their new apartment in Tel Aviv, the city targeted by Iraq's Scud missiles.
>
> 'Of course in the present, tense international climate we have mixed feelings about coming to Israel,' Alexander said, 'but we decided that the dangers were much greater in the Soviet Union.'

Simcha Dinitz of the Jewish Agency was reminded of, and remembered, an experience in an interview for this book:

> Yes, I remember it. I was on a flight to Israel with *olim* [immigrants] aboard. Departure was delayed because of missile attacks near Ben Gurion. The crew opened the doors to allow passengers to wait in the terminal.

---

15 Feature story released by the Jewish Agency on Jan. 17, 1991.

There were four empty seats on the plane. After a few hours, the Scuds stopped falling and the passengers reboarded. All the new immigrants returned, and the four seats were filled by immigrants who had come early for the next flight and they wanted to get to Israel faster.

UJA's role was to continue to fund the aliyah through Operation Exodus, and aid hundreds of thousands of others through the Annual Campaign. It kept donors and campaign workers informed and motivated, in part by *Israel in Crisis,* a daily faxed newsletter. The excerpts from it below give a sense of the information flowing from UJA to enhance solicitations, speeches and federation as well as UJA marketing materials:

> If a state of emergency is declared Israel Radio and TV will broadcast messages in Hebrew, English, Russian, Amharic, French, Spanish, Georgian, Bukharan and Arabic. Nevertheless, immigrants are learning the phrases for 'war,' 'attack,' 'safe room' and 'gas mask' that they may hear first on the street. Immigrants will be briefed on arrival. [January 16, 1991.]

> Everyone breathed a sigh of relief at early war reports that the Coalition had destroyed bases in Iraq that had missiles aimed at Israel. But the nation remains on alert, gas masks nearby. Many Israelis have not gone to work. The streets are practically deserted. [January 17.]

> The war has not made an appreciable dent in aliyah. Since hostilities began on Thursday 1,719 Soviet *olim* have arrived on nine flights. Shabbat flights are permitted by the rabbis because they save Jews in danger abroad. Two more planesful are expected today... The Jewish Agency is finalizing plans to open four new absorption centers. [January 21.]

> In the past four months, 1,800 Soviet scientists have arrived in Israel. Last week, the Jewish Agency held a conference to match them with jobs. [January 21.]

> The City of Tel Aviv has placed in hotels the 660 persons whose apartments were damaged in last week's missile attacks. [January 21.]

> Today 394 immigrants arrived; 700 are expected tomorrow. [January 22.]

> The Chief Rabbis have announced that Jews may keep their radios on softly on Shabbat to hear emergency announcements. [January 22.]

Shock waves rolled through the country following last night's third missile attack in Ramat Gan. The relief at the initial allied strikes at Scud installations has been eliminated. [January 23.]

Former Ambassador Naphtali Lavie, UJA's Director-General in Israel, reports that, everyone in the country has a 'sealed room' story. 'Here's mine. Last night we had friends visiting when the sirens sounded. All of us grabbed our gas masks and moved into our sealed room — the bedroom. A lot of people put wireless phones, televisions and coffee pots there, for information and a sense of normalcy. I know of a Rabbi Shulsinger in B'nei B'rak. He has eleven children to get into gas masks and a three-month-old grandchild to settle in a protective crib. He and his wife have to work fast. Once in their sealed room the family prays together for survival.' [January 23.]

Lavie adds: My brother [Israel's Chief Ashkenazic Rabbi, Rabbi Israel Meir Lau, the youngest survivor of Birkenau] said, 'This is the second time I faced gas in my life. But only once did someone give me a mask.' [January 23.]

Israel Television and Radio reported last night in Hebrew, Russian and English about the UJA's Operation Exodus Campaign. Since then, Israelis are calling UJA in Israel to express gratitude. [January 25.]

The country was virtually shut down from January 17 to 20. Finance Minister Yitzhak Moda'i said it cost $1 billion. [January 25.]

The euphoria following the initial Allied victories has been succeeded by intense anxiety after the missile attacks. A Patriot missile intercepted a Scud directed at Haifa last night, but damage is evident and there is fear of more, including chemical attacks. [January 25.]

Barry Shrage, Michael Bohnen, Lawrence Green and Robert Beal of the Combined Jewish Philanthropies of Greater Boston visited in solidarity with Israel, as Marvin Lender and a national delegation did on a mission several days ago. The Bostonians met with recent immigrants, one of whom said, 'I escaped the turmoil in Baku [USSR]. A Scud fell near my home and the traumas of Baku seemed close again. Nevertheless, here at least we don't fear anti-Semitism or being beaten or killed by a neighbor for no reason.' A 20-year-old immigrant who had just arrived told them, 'I have dreamed of coming to Israel all my life. Saddam Hussein can't keep me away.' Missions are very helpful to Israeli morale. [January 28.]

The Hebrew press is filled with news and opinion about everything. Many letters express outrage that Israel is not responding to attacks, but a poll of 650 in Tel Aviv and Haifa showed 80 percent support for restraint. [January 29.]

Maariv printed the names of 205 Western companies that equipped the Iraqi war machine. It blamed Germany, Austria, United States, England, France, Italy, Spain, the Netherlands, Switzerland, Belgium, Japan and Monaco for allowing this to happen. Gunter Grass, the German writer, called for the Chancellor Helmut Kohl to resign over this. 'For the second time in this century Jews find themselves under the threat of German gas,' Grass noted. [January 29.]

The frequent Iraqi missile attacks have placed a particular strain on Israel's handicapped and senior citizens. At Shikma, a recipient of UJA-Federation funding through JDC, the 300 mentally handicapped patients are unaware of the need to help themselves when sirens sound. They resist the rapid movement into sealed rooms and dislike the gas masks. Moments are crucial, though. All public rooms at Shikma have been sealed and most staff members are here 12 to 24 hours a day. [January 29.]

Three thousand Israelis are homeless from Scud attack damage and 518 have been treated for anxiety or shock. Fourteen deaths have been reported. But life goes on in Israel, however surreal. At Sha'are Zedek Hospital in Jerusalem, 100 babies were born during the first week of the war. Healthy twins were delivered to a mother in a gas mask by a medical team also wearing gas masks. [January 31.]

Amos Oz, A. B. Yehoshua, Yael Dayan and Yoram Kaniuk, novelists on the left, warned Palestinians that glee over Iraqi missile attacks on Israel was destroying support in Israel for a Palestinian State. Palestinians were on rooftops in West Bank towns cheering as Israeli sirens sounded and shouting, 'Saddam, Saddam, our friend,' and 'Come on, come on, hit Tel Aviv.' [February 5.]

Lebanon Radio quotes a Palestinian Liberation Organization spokesman as saying the PLO utilized Israel's distraction to carry out attacks on Israeli towns in the Galilee. He said it was a good opportunity to escalate the armed struggle. [February 6.]

Natan Sharansky said Saddam's missiles have given new immigrants something else in common with other Israelis: a war... Now all the languages in Israel melt into one phrase: 'Put on your gas mask.' Are the new Soviet immigrants frightened? Of course, like everyone. But it is not the fear they knew in the Soviet Union. Their pasts are past. They have a common future with all Jews... The missiles have turned the new immigrants into genuine Israelis. [February 7.]

Soviet Jews continue to seek to emigrate. Placards in Moscow reading, 'Don't go to Jew [sic] doctors. They poison their patients,' show what Soviet Jews are fleeing into a war zone from... More than 60,000 wait in transit stations in Bucharest, Budapest and Warsaw. Bulgaria has announced it would become a transit station as well. Direct flights would speed even this spectacular aliyah. [February 14.]

The Israel Museum presented an exhibition of young artists. The drawings of demolished homes, wild animals, gas masks and skylines featuring missiles reminded some of the drawings of the children of Terezin before the children were killed by the Nazis. [February 15.]

The Hebrew press quoted David, age 65, who came here from the Soviet Union seven months ago and was almost killed by a Scud that destroyed his apartment building yesterday. Tears streaming down his face, David said, 'With or without missiles, Israel is better than Russia.' Also yesterday, seven Jews were murdered in Tajikistan, USSR, by Islamic fundamentalists enraged that Israel is still standing a month into the war. [February 19.]

Menachem Perlmutter, a Holocaust survivor and a Negev pioneer who helped make the desert bloom, said, 'It is horrible to sit with my grandchildren in a sealed room, but at least they have Israel to protect them. That's everything compared to what we had in trying to survive Hitler. Some neighborhoods look like war zones, but so little human life here has been lost it is a miracle. Another miracle is that we are still growing fresh vegetables and fruits every day. Despite the Scuds, we are building a stronger nation.' [February 22.]

The violinist Isaac Stern performed in a solo concert at the Jerusalem Theater when the sirens went off. Everyone in the audience sat with gas masks on their laps and put them on. Stern kept playing. Then there was an all clear. Surreal is real in Israel. [February 25.]

A popular Soviet news program showed footage of destruction in Baghdad. Unfortunately, it was reported as Tel Aviv. That may have been to discourage Soviet Jews from leaving. Nothing else has worked. That won't either. [February 25.]

Israel's expenditure for immigrant absorption exceeded its defense expenditure for the first time in decades, the Israeli media reported. [February 27.]

Humor, always humor by Jews as an escape:

A cartoon in *Haaretz* showed a split frame, a helmeted soldier in one, speaking to his parents and small siblings in the other in gas masks in their safe room. *'Shalom, Ima? Ma hadash b'hazit?'* ('Hello, Ma? What's new on the front?') [January 24.]

Tel Avivans jokingly renamed their city—Scudinavia. [February 14.]

A T-shirt popular with teenagers reads, 'My Graduation Class,' and features 30 look-alikes in gas masks. [February 18.]

Symbolically, the war ended on Purim, the holiday that marks the deliverance of Jews from physical destruction in ancient Persia, next door to modern Iraq. The Israelis celebrated with relief, flocking into the streets again and eating three-cornered prune and cheese Danish they named Saddamtashen. The next evening Shabbat began and Israelis took a deep breath and tried to relax.

The war was tragic for the loss of life on all sides. But Israel also suffered in the way it viewed itself and in the way others viewed it. The tiny country that defied all odds and established itself after 2,000 years of dispersion, that defeated 22 Arab armies and that survived surprise attack during the Yom Kippur War, did not defend its citizens from attack in their own homes. In some ways, Israel came to be perceived as a client state of the United States. On the other hand, the war against Israel made American Jews identify more closely with the Jewish state and not take its future for granted. Suddenly, the Six-Day War victory became ancient history and Israel's future looked decidedly uncertain.

American Jews were able to pray and hope, follow the news closely and express their opinions. The hardiest visited Israel during the war. They could also affirm their support for Israel and particularly for aliyah, Israel's raison d'être and its future. That meant giving to Operation Exodus. The mood of campaigners as well as donors was somber during the Gulf War, but Operation Exodus provided a meaningful way in which American Jews expressed their support. Jewish fundraising often takes a holiday in January and February, after the Chanukah appeals and the end of the of the tax year on December 31, but in 1991 UJA roared forward with Operation Exodus. It did not try to capitalize on Israel's plight; donors were aware that the effort to bomb Israel into oblivion was on a continuum of enduring quests to drive the Jews into the sea. Previously scheduled UJA conferences, seminars, retreats and missions were held, although the war dominated all of them. UJA speakers traveled across the country and videos, advertisements, direct mail and other materials were created and marketed. The UJA Campaign Executive Committee (Marvin Lender, Joel Tauber, Richard Pearlstone, Arlene Zimmerman, Martin Stein, Morton Kornreich, Alan Shulman, David Hermelin and Alan Crawford) continued to meet monthly, speak on conference calls weekly, make decisions and conduct solicitations across the country. The UJA National Officers increased their engagements and financial commitments. Federation board members did the same. Federations brought the Campaign message to local constituents on all levels, including with extensive Super Sunday telemarketing in January. The weather was inclement in much of the United States, in Russia and in Jerusalem, where it rained intensively and even briefly snowed. But the immigrants kept coming even though the missiles kept falling, and American Jews responded by coming up with more money for Operation Exodus.

UJA and federations raised $36 million for Operation Exodus in the first two months of the year to realize a total of $539.6 million. They were pleased with the results but mainly relieved that greater tragedy had been averted, for Coalition forces and Israel. But it would take a miracle, something like a whole new exodus, to sustain Operation Exodus any longer. That was coming up next.

CHAPTER SEVEN
Operation Solomon

There is no greater commandment than the ransom of captives.
Maimonides

There is no Zionism except the rescue of Jews.
Golda Meir

They were called Falashas and they disliked the name. It meant "stranger" in their native Amharic and they were not strangers at all. They had lived in Ethiopia for thousands of years and that is the opposite of being a stranger. But they were different.

Like many tribes they kept to themselves and maintained their own traditions, and they were unnoticed by outsiders for centuries. Then, in the early 1700s, European missionaries returning from the Horn of Africa said they heard of them. In 1769 a Scottish explorer named James Bruce accidentally met them. In 1867 a representative of a European philanthropic group, Joseph Halevy, went to look for them. And in 1904, Jacques Faitlovitch, a student of Halevy's, went to help them. They were like everyone around them except for their religion. They were Jews.

No one knows how Jews came to be in Ethiopia. The prophet Isaiah spoke of the return of the Jews from Cush, now mainly northern Ethiopia. Many historians, as well as the Ethiopian Jews, believed they descended from the tribe of Dan that fled from a war in Jerusalem at the time of King Solomon three thousand years ago.

They told Faitlovitch, who lived among them and observed them for months, that they traced their roots to the ancient Hebrews. They said their ancestors were slaves in Egypt who crossed the parted Red Sea and stood at the foot of Mount Sinai to receive the Torah brought down by Moses. They observed the Sabbath, celebrated Passover, kept kosher and maintained mikvahs, bathing areas for ritual purity, as required by the Torah. But they knew nothing whatsoever of the Oral Law that other Jews believed God had communicated to Moses on Sinai and that was recorded by the rabbis in the years 150 to 400 of the Common Era, in the Mishnah and Talmud. They consumed only cold Sabbath meals in observance of the Torah prohibition against kindling lights on the Sabbath, unaware that the Talmud allowed reheating on a fire kindled before the Sabbath. They slaughtered an animal in the hours before Passover, uninformed that the Talmud said this was only symbolic. They never heard of Chanukah and Purim, which commemorated events that took place centuries after the Written Law was given, and which were described in later Scripture.

Occasionally, in the dozens of centuries that they lived in the region, they achieved military and economic power, but more often they suffered abuse from hostile neighbors and wished to be left alone. When Faitlovitch found them in northern Ethiopia they lived mainly in Gondar Province, although disputes in about the year 1850 led some to move to Tigre Province nearby. Like Jews elsewhere, those in Gondar and Tigre hardly spoke to each other.

Faitlovitch's reports were the talk of the Jewish world. By 1908 the chief rabbis in 44 countries recognized the tribe as Jewish. In 1921, the revered Chief Rabbi in Jerusalem, Isaac Kook, declared that they were Jewish. The Sephardic Chief Rabbi, Ovadia Yosef, recognized them in 1973; and the Ashkenazic Chief Rabbi, Shlomo Goren, did so in 1977. In 1975, the Israeli Government recognized them as Jewish, which qualified them to become Israeli citizens under the Law of Return. Over these decades the Ethiopian Jews came to accept all those others as Jewish too. That wasn't the assumption earlier on, when the European visitors had begun to come to Ethiopia. After all, the Ethiopian Jews had asked themselves, who ever heard of a white Jew before?

They called themselves Beta Israel, the House of Israel. And every day they dreamed of returning to Jerusalem.

In the 1970s, some Ethiopian Jews attempted a perilous trek to Israel, from Tigre and Gondar via Sudan, with the help of the Mossad, Israel's intelligence agency. The Ethiopian Jews yearned to live in Israel, which they now knew existed, and they feared starvation if they remained in Ethiopia. But the escape to Sudan was treacherous. The terrain was formidable, including steep mountains, deep rivers, dense forests and parched deserts that had to be crossed by foot. Some Jews were killed by government agents for illegally trying to leave Ethiopia, or by bandits en route, or by Sudanese if they made it to Sudan. The few hundred Jews who had made it to Israel sent messages home to Gondar and Tigre that life was much better in Israel than in Africa. But none made it through to Israel in 1978, only 32 in 1979, 679 in 1980 and 598 in 1981[1]. Two thousand died trying.

In those years, as the Ethiopian Jews mulled over their fate--where did life await, where did death await?--more Jews elsewhere became aware of their plight. An advocacy group, the American Association for Ethiopian Jewry, was founded in 1969, which gained visibility for the cause, especially in the late 1970s. However, it was widely viewed as a radical group for publicly advocating rescue, and it alienated other organizations and Israelis by pugnaciously denouncing them as apathetic and racist. AAEJ attempted small rescues on its own that it claimed were successful, but that the Mossad alleged, without proof, had caused deaths and endangered thousands. Nevertheless, when Menachem Begin was elected Prime Minister in 1977 as the choice of those who felt excluded from power in Israel, AAEJ persuaded him to support their cause. Their agitation forced Ethiopian Jewry onto the agenda of the General Assembly of the Council of Jewish Federations in 1979. With a famine beginning in Ethiopia, several Jewish federations went to the country to bring food, clothing and medical care, joining the trail-blazing Organization for Rehabilitation and Training that had been there since 1959, the Jewish Agency and the Joint Distribution Committee. The new groups included the World Jewish Congress, the Religious Action Center of Reform Jewry, the United Synagogue of Conservative Judaism, Emunah Women, Hadassah and the Hebrew Immigrant Aid Society. The AAEJ made Ethiopian Jewry a priority and made itself a pariah.

In August 1982, as a drought began and famine descended on the Horn of Africa the situation became acute. Then, an advocate named Barbara Ribakove Gordon founded the North American Conference on Ethiopian Jewry. While Ribakove Gordon and NACOEJ were initially viewed skeptically by Israel and American Jewish federations, which sometimes denounced them as know-nothings who made matters worse, she disarmed her opponents with a cooperative strategy, passionately but respectfully advocated the cause to government leaders in the United States and Israel, and spoke almost every night to American Jewish groups to raise visibility and dollars. Even her strongest critics could not challenge her manner, statistics and accounts of what she had seen and heard in Ethiopia. Her role was crucial in making the cause mainstream. At about the same time, Nate Shapiro, a Chicago businessman who also favored honey over vinegar, became AAEJ President. Shapiro lessened opposition to AAEJ by instituting a strategy of cooperation. He secured funding, prestige and visibility

---

1 See Mitchell G. Bard, *From Tragedy to Triumph: The Politics Behind the Rescue of Ethiopian Jewry*, Westport, CT: Praeger, 2002, a source for this section, p. 105 and elsewhere.

by gaining the active support of the Pritzker family of Chicago, whose family had built the Hyatt hotels chain. And he, Ribakove Gordon and the Pritzker family persuaded Members of Congress to address the issue of Ethiopian Jews at hearings on religious persecution.

In late 1983 the plight of Ethiopian Jews worsened. The famine deepened in Ethiopia, more Jews died en route, and the refugee camps in Sudan were beset by malaria, dysentery, kwashiorkor, marasmus, polluted water, starvation and fear of attack. The United Nations High Commissioner for Refugees was pressured to visit the camps. He reported that there was no food or medicine shortage and that the death rate was normal. In truth, the camp squalor was acute and deaths were mounting. By early 1984, 5,000 Ethiopian Jews had made it to Israel but as many as 3,000 died en route, at least 10,000 were in the camps in Sudan and 13,000 were believed to still be in Ethiopia[2].

In the summer of 1984, the United States, with the approval of President Ronald Reagan and participation of Vice President Bush, brokered a deal whereby Sudan permitted Israel's Mossad to evacuate and airlift thousands of Jews from Sudan to Israel. President Gaafar el-Numeiry of Sudan agreed in exchange for American military aid, food for his starving multitudes, and the chance to free his country of unwanted refugees. Israel's goal was to redeem an ancient tribe. The American interest was purely humanitarian; even years later no evidence has been presented that the American motive was anything other than to save lives. In the Holocaust, endangered Jews had no place to go; now, as famine swept across Africa, the Jews were the only sufferers with a country willing and eager to take them in.

To devise a plan that would shield the effort from discovery, Numeiry ordered his secret police to meet with the Mossad. The intelligence agencies determined that the safest route was along dirt roads from the refugee camps north to Khartoum. The Israelis asked Georges Gutelman, a Belgian Orthodox Jew who owned Trans European Airlines to provide the aircraft. He agreed and obtained Belgian Prime Minister Wilfried Martens' approval for stopovers in Brussels since Numeiry refused direct flights to Israel. After weeks of planning, during which some Jews died in the camps, the operation was ready for implementation.

---

2 Although UNHCR claimed to have inspected the camp in 1984, an American diplomat in Khartoum determined that no such visit had taken place. UNHCR provisions of flour, dried milk and other foodstuffs were half of the minimum necessary, contributing to deaths by starvation. UNHCR then denied the death rate was as high as it was (Louis Rapoport, *Redemption Song: The Story of Operation Moses*, New York: Harcourt Brace Jovanovich, 1986, pp. 112-113). Estimates vary for the number of Jews in Gondar, Tigre, Addis Ababa, Sudan and areas of transit throughout the 1980s and at other times. Numbers in this chapter reflect common estimates.

In early November, Naphtali Lavie, Israel's Consul General in New York, received a call from Prime Minister Shimon Peres who informed him that Yitzhak Shamir, Foreign Minister in Peres' coalition government, would visit New York shortly and must meet with major UJA donors to discuss Ethiopian Jews. Lavie telephoned UJA President Stanley Horowitz and they arranged the meeting at the Consulate. Joseph Gruss, Ludwig Jesselson, Jack Resnick, Jack Weiler, William Rosenwald, Alex Grass, Robert Loup, Herschel Blumberg, Shamir, Lavie and Horowitz were among those present.

"Shamir told them that an effort to rescue Ethiopian Jews was about to begin and that $60 million was needed from American Jews," Lavie recalled in an interview for this book. "He said payments needed to begin immediately and be completed by March 31. They all gave generously, pledging huge sums on the spot. Then he stipulated the fundraising had to be conducted in secret, to protect the operation. Someone asked, 'How can we raise $60 million in secret?' Shamir answered, 'That's your problem'."

Martin Stein was appointed as the effort's chairman. UJA Vice President Elton Kerness briefed UJA Executive Staff members on November 13, and instructed them to develop plans to raise the funds; if they came up with a name for the campaign, he added, they should bring it to the staff meeting the next week. On November 19 after UJA plans were honed, Kerness reflected, "This Thursday is Thanksgiving in America. Maybe it will be Thanksgiving for Ethiopian Jews." He added, "The campaign needs a name. I came up with one. If you like it, fine. If you have a better one, fine. I think we should call it Operation Moses." No one had anything better. "OK," he said. "The campaign is named Operation Moses."

After dark on November 21, the Mossad brought 200 ragged, hungry and frightened refugees by bus on a five hour journey from a refugee camp in Sudan to an airstrip near Khartoum. They were accompanied by Ethiopian Jews who had returned from Israel and explained in Amharic what to expect. At 4 a.m. on Thursday, November 22, a TEA 707 landed nearby, the engine's roar and the sight of the gigantic bird terrifying the Ethiopian Jews. Some tried to run but they were restrained and reminded they had been told to expect that thunderous sound and intimidating sight. They boarded and the cabin door closed behind them. Their eyes opened widely as the roar resumed, this time muffled as they were inside the aircraft, and the floor vibrated. They felt an odd feeling as their temporary home tilted backwards, then the few lights below receded, the aircraft leveled and soon there was black night. Four hours later, they discovered Brussels at dawn, from the air, on the ground, then from the air again and soon, most incredulously, the shores and skyline of Israel beneath them in the crisp afternoon sunshine. They descended the staircase to the tarmac and many fell to their knees to kiss the ground. They were greeted by Ethiopian Jews who had arrived previously and who accompanied them into the terminal where they gave their names. They declared their Jewishness to Israeli officials and were approved for citizenship under Israel's Law of Return. Some were taken to hospitals but most arrived at absorption centers where they were greeted with smiles by more Ethiopian Israelis. "When the Lord brought the exiles back to Zion we were as dreamers," the Psalmist wrote. Within a day they had gone from hostility and hardship in Africa to citizenship and comfort in the Jewish State. After 30 centuries, they had returned to Zion.

UJA informed federations of the planned mass rescue, and asked them to accept specific allotments of the $60 million goal. But following the usual modus operandi of UJA, by the time federation leaders convened on December 2 to seal the agreement major gifts fundraising was already underway. As two aircraft a week, then three, then four, climbed into the skies over Sudan and veered northwest high en route to Brussels and Israel, federations joined in, and campaigning intensified. Operation Moses broadened quickly to all giving levels; synagogue campaigns led by the Union of American Hebrew Congregations, the United Synagogue of Conservative Judaism and the Orthodox Union were especially helpful in raising funds. The magic number was six: $60 million was needed; $6,000 to bring each Ethiopian Jew to Israel. Many synagogues set $6,000 goals while others set goals in multiples of $6,000. Donors who had never given more than $1,000 gave $6,000. Others joined with friends and neighbors to reach $6,000 or $600. Thousands remitted $60. Within three weeks, $32 million was raised.

UJA placed nothing in writing except to insiders, and issued nothing publicly. But many knew of the rescue and campaign, including journalists. In light of that, to pressure for a news blackout, every week this writer briefed Robert Cohn, President of the American Jewish Press Association, on condition of a complete embargo. Cohn in turn informed his 151 member publications, cryptically, that the operation continued but that nothing should be published until the Jews were safe. No actual information was transmitted by Cohn, only that the lid needed to stay on. Numerous journalists from the general media, such as *The New York Times*, telephoned this writer seeking confirmation. Their information was correct and they knew it to be reliable. The truth was not denied but they understood that lives could be lost if they published it; they too honored the news embargo.

Despite all these efforts, the life saving operation was still prematurely disclosed -- ironically mainly by Jewish Agency officials. Arye Dulzin, Chairman and CEO of the Jewish Agency Executive, told a publicly covered session of the Council of Jewish Federations' General Assembly in Toronto on November 14 that a secret rescue of Jews was planned. The *Long Island Jewish World* reported what he had said, but this did not adversely affect the plans. Weeks later, the *Washington Jewish Week* planned to write about it and was besieged by furious Israeli diplomats in Jerusalem, Washington and New York, and by other insiders including this writer, all warning that disclosure could jeopardize the operation. Charles Fenyvesi, the managing editor, insisted to me that Dulzin's comment placed the story in the public realm. He doubted that his article would give the general media an excuse to cover the story, or that his actions would directly or indirectly cost lives.

When the *Washington Jewish Week* disclosed in its December 6 issue that "the rescue of a substantial number of Ethiopian Jews has begun," the general news media widely considered that the Jewish community had now placed the story in the public sphere. *The New York Times* ran a page one story on December 11 under the headline, "Airlift to Israel is Reported Taking Thousands of Jews From Ethiopia." The article spoke of the quest for secrecy and fear that Arab governments might try to end the rescue, but cited the *Washington Jewish Week* article and Dulzin's comment as justification. The next day the *Boston Globe* reported that the United States had brought Sudan and Israel together to organize "the complex logistics for the humanitarian mission."

Amazingly, Sudan and other Arab States appeared unaware of the articles, or perhaps they had not yet decided to intervene, and the airlift continued. However, several days later, Yehuda Dominitz, Director-General of the Jewish Agency's Immigration and Absorption Department, told a journalist for *Nekuda*, a small Jewish West Bank newspaper, that half the Ethiopian Jews were already in Israel. The comment enraged Israel's media; a minor periodical had been able to publish a story they were prohibited from publishing. The Military Censor did not block articles quoting Dominitz in *Nekuda* that were published on page one of *Yediot Achronot*, the largest circulating afternoon newspaper, and *Maariv*, the main evening newspaper, on January 3, 1985. The Associated Press and Reuters quoted them and amplified the news worldwide. Prime Minister Peres confirmed the facts on January 4. On January 5, after 35 flights, Operation Moses was shut down by Sudan.

Operation Moses was a stunning achievement. The world's television viewers who had watched agonizing images of helpless, starving Africans for weeks learned of the bold and heroic rescue of nearly 10,000 African Jews, plucked from famine and brought to Israel. Centuries earlier whites took blacks out of Africa in chains, to enslave them, but the Israelis rescued them from misery and brought them to lives of freedom. Thousands were transported in a few hours from an ancient existence to modern times. American Jews gave $62.5 million in six weeks, technically for absorption but freeing a like sum for ransom. Yet few rejoiced. Hundreds remained in the camps or near the airstrip, their fate uncertain.

The dictator Numeiry was desperate for economic aid to remain in power; he sent word that if aid would come the remaining Jews in Sudan could go. In an astounding example of zipped lips (in contrast to the loose lips of some in the Jewish community a few weeks earlier), Senators Alphonse D'Amato, Republican of New York, and Alan Cranston, Democrat of California obtained the signatures of every United States Senator on a letter to President Reagan; it was so confidential, their own aides did not know about the letter for weeks. It urged the President to provide economic aid and save the Jews.

Reagan received the letter privately and in advance of a previously scheduled visit by Vice President Bush to Khartoum. He and Bush met at the White House and agreed that Bush should tell Numeiry that if he let the Jews leave, $200 million of delayed American economic aid would be provided. Reagan stipulated that although the Mossad and Sudanese intelligence agency could participate, the operation must be conducted by the Central Intelligence Agency. He told Bush, "Be sure it is completed quickly.[3]"

Bush visited Numeiry in his palace on March 3 and obtained his approval. The CIA, aided by Ethiopian Jews brought from Israel, entered the refugee camps and found the 634 Jews known to be there. They also located 180 other Jews nearby. The 814 were airlifted to Israel via Europe on the night of March 28. The American mission was named Operation Sheba and, with Operation Moses, more than 10,000 Ethiopian Jews were saved and brought to Israel.

On April 4, Numeiry was overthrown. He was arrested, tried, convicted and executed for taking bribes to allow Operation Moses to take place and for collusion with "the Zionist enemy." His Vice President, Omar Tayeb, was arrested, tried, convicted and sentenced to two 32-year prison terms on the same charges. Hundreds of other Sudanese who cooperated with Operation Moses were hunted down, imprisoned for bribe taking and collusion or killed. Nearly 15,000 Ethiopian Jews were now in Israel, but at least 13,000 languished

---

3 Bard, pp. 162-65. Rapoport's information was that Reagan said he wanted the remaining Jews out of Sudan "regardless of the consequences."

in Ethiopia. No movement from Gondar would be possible for awhile. It would take six more years before the miracle could be completed.

Upon conclusion of the rescue, the United Jewish Appeal released a panoply of materials published in newspapers that illuminated the rescue, provided background information and described the immigrants' early days in Israel. Federations packaged them in newsletters, direct mail, brochures and advertisements. News media stories abounded about Ethiopian Jews introduced for the first time to electric lights, refrigeration, air conditioning, television, movies, indoor heating and plumbing. The Ethiopian Jews could not believe what they had seen, heard, smelled, touched and tasted. In absorption centers they were given access to ample food, clothing, shelter and medical care, an orientation to Israel and modern life, and opportunities for acculturation they could make use of at their own pace. Israeli writer Wendy Elliman looked in on the children in school and filed anecdotes including these for the UJA Press Service:

'This is a different kind of aliyah,' said a kindergarten teacher here in Beersheba in Israel's south. 'These children have never played with toys before. At first they were frightened of dolls. But they learned fast. It's always easier with the kids.' [*"In the Kindergarten."*]

The children's minds are like sponges. They are eager to know now about life after they leave the absorption center. We had a lesson yesterday about the post office, supermarket, bank, police station and so on, places they never saw before. I showed pictures. That night we sponsored a parents' evening. We had 100 percent attendance. We showed the parents around the school and explained in Amharic what we're teaching and why. They wanted to know, 'Is my child working?' "Is she doing well?' We answered wholeheartedly, 'Yes. Yes. And they are learning fast.' [*"Tales Out Of Elementary School."*]

'Their motivation is enormous,' said Oded who has taught immigrants for 20 years. 'They are very cooperative and hardworking.' [*"From Schooling to Supermarket."*]

'These are gentle, refined people, and courtesy is a key element in their culture,' said Mordechai, a volunteer in Safed. 'I am sometimes greeted with a double-handed handshake and five or six kisses. It can take ten minutes to say hello. We abrasive Israelis can learn from them.' [*"God Understands Amharic Too."*]

'Do you know what it's like to be without food, without water?'

asked Menashe. 'I do. I and others walked across the desert for many days. At last we came to water. But suddenly bandits came and they showed long knives. They took everything, even our clothes. After that, some went back to the villages. I stayed with the rest and we traveled on.' ["*God Understands Amharic too.*"]

Here at Hodayot, a Youth Aliyah village near Tiberias, the school's principal, Yaakov, said, 'They face huge cultural gaps, but they are easily motivated. They see themselves as their family's representative in Israel and are preparing themselves to help when their parents arrive.' ["*Tales Out Of High School.*"]

'I do not know where my parents are. I need them with me.' ["*The Children Speak.*"]

Makonnen, in his 20s, learned some English and visited America a year later on a UJA speaker's tour. He addressed dinners, luncheons and federation board meetings but was able to sightsee along the way. This writer had lunch with him before his return to Israel and asked what he had seen since leaving Ethiopia that most surprised him. To paraphrase his words:

In Ethiopia I had never seen an airplane or automobile or train, let alone refrigerators, indoor heating and stoves but, you know, I could have imagined them. When I was a boy I imagined flying through the air like a bird. And having delicious food to eat all day. And moving faster than I could run along the ground. I didn't imagine the inventions, but I could have imagined having what they provided. But there was one thing I never could have imagined, could not believe when I saw it, and still can't. It is so unbelievable, every day I can't get it out of my head. Disneyland.

Most new immigrants lived in absorption centers, some moving into private housing after a year, but 2,000 Ethiopians were children under 14 who arrived without parents. The Jewish Agency cared for them in Youth Aliyah villages, which provided comprehensive year-round services including food, clothing, shelter, medical care, education, recreation and social services. Eli Amir, Youth Aliyah's Director-General, told the UJA Press Service:

We refuse to repeat the errors of the 1950s. We want them to understand and appreciate Israel today but encourage them to remember their own roots and traditions. They need that for their own grounding.

This time around we are trying to help maintain pride in who they are, to build on what they have and not destroy it as we did with some earlier waves of immigrants. They are dazzled by Western culture, and we want to help them see how it can be good for them, not to lead them to abandon their own. While they are with us, we are listening to them and trying to help them prepare for the future. We have welcomed them with open arms and a full heart.

But the early euphoria gave way to profound sadness over separation from family left behind and fears for their safety. As the years passed, the opportunity to bring them to Israel did not appear. Nights were lonely for children without parents. The rescue of Ethiopian Jews was not complete. The tear within families was an open wound that needed to be healed.

The Soviet Jewish aliyah was historic by all measures but for sheer drama nothing could match what was in store for the Jews in Ethiopia. As the fifth anniversary of Operation Sheba approached, President Mengistu Haile Mariam, a Marxist dictator, was facing civil war as repression and deprivation grew across the country. Declining military support from his main sponsor, the Soviet Union (which had reduced its foreign adventures to concentrate on its own survival), led Mengistu to seek arms from Israel to quell the rebellions. He recognized Israel and allowed some Jews to make aliyah, which rose from 100 in January to 500 in May 1990. In Israel, Ethiopian Jews held rallies to pressure Prime Minister Shamir to supply Mengistu with arms if he let their family members leave, but the United States, Israel's main arms supplier, opposed that tactic.

Fearing that the Jews in Gondar were in growing danger, and recognizing that large scale emigration was only feasible from Addis Ababa, the AAEJ persuaded the Jews to undertake the perilous journey to that city. Susan Pollock, its representative in Ethiopia, hired trucks and buses; traveled with them at night on main roads, byroads, dirt roads, and no roads; and paid anyone along the way who posed a threat. The Israelis were angry, believing that the action put the Jews in increased danger in the capital. They may have been right but once the AAEJ centralized the Jews in the capital, rescue was necessary once and for all. By June, 6,000 were in Addis Ababa.

The capital housed 2.5 million people and teemed with refugees. Conditions were squalid, with limited sanitation, water and medicine; despair and disease spread quickly. AAEJ and NACOEJ agreed that the more formidable Joint Distribution Committee should be in overall charge of caring for the Jews. JDC provided food, clothing, blankets and medical supplies, with funds from the Annual Campaign of UJA and federations. JDC's on-site chief was Ami Bergman who knew the people and the country well. Its medical team was led by Dr. Richard Hodes, a short, slim, bespectacled Long Islander in his 30s who, like Dr. Albert Schweitzer in Gabon decades earlier, devoted his life to providing medical services in Africa. Michael Schneider, JDC's Executive Vice President, and his experienced senior administrators Steven Schwager and Amir Shaviv, Associate Executive Vice Presidents, and Gideon Taylor, Director of Operations, visited frequently and provided overall direction and support.

As Israel stalled on arms negotiations, Mengistu cut back emigration beginning in July. Squalor in the camps, and rebels marching toward the capital, threatened to make the Jews sitting ducks for disaster. In response, Shamir telephoned veteran diplomat Uri Lubrani in October and gave him his next assignment.

Born in Haifa in 1926, Lubrani had fought in the War for Independence, where he showed heroism and coolness under pressure and rose to captain. Israel's first Foreign Minister Moshe Sharett named him his personal secretary, and Israel's first two Prime Ministers, David Ben Gurion and Levi Eshkol, made him a political and security aide. He entered the foreign service, serving as Ambassador to Uganda, Rwanda and Burundi and, from 1967 to 1970, to Ethiopia. Stationed in Iran in the 1970s, he dispatched cables of increasing concern, warning that the Shah could be brought down by revolution and that a fundamentalist Islamic State could result. Tel Aviv shared his cables with the United States Defense Department, which dismissed Lubrani's conclusions as unlikely. In the 1980s he chaired peace talks with Lebanon and negotiated the release of Israeli hostages and prisoners of war. He made friends of leaders who appreciated his deep interest in local culture, his easy manner with them and, especially, his ability to find solutions to difficult problems.

"He put it to me that I had to go to Addis and get the Jews out," Lubrani said in the first of seven interviews for this book. "He said 200 or 300 coming out each month was not enough, he wanted the number increased to 2,000 or 3,000. I asked him about money to make it happen. He said, 'Go talk to the American Jewish federations in the United States to get the money'."

Lubrani flew to New York and met with Joel Tauber, Marvin Lender and Morton Kornreich of UJA; Charles Goodman of CJF; Norman Lipoff of United Israel Appeal; Sylvia Hassenfeld, Schneider and Taylor of JDC; and Shoshana Cardin and Malcolm Hoenlein of the Conference of Presidents of Major American Jewish Organizations. He asked the UJA federation system to provide the funds. "I told them what we wanted to do and said it was going to cost a lost of money," Lubrani recalled. "I said I couldn't give the exact sum; there was no way to know yet what it would be. They said to me go ahead and do it; you'll have it. Just like that." Hoenlein, whose organization was the main diplomatic and political representative of the American Jewish community, recalled, "Jewish lives were at stake. Everything rode on the outcome. The discussion was very emotional."

Asked why Shamir did not guarantee the funds from the Israeli treasury, Lubrani said Shamir believed it was the responsibility of Diaspora Jews to pay for the ingathering of the exiles, their task spelled out in Israel's Declaration of Independence. "That's why he wanted the American Jews to give the money years earlier for [Operation] Moses." Lubrani said. "That is what he saw as their role."

Lubrani flew to Addis Ababa, presented his credentials to Mengistu and inspected the refugee camps. "The conditions were worse than I had imagined," he said. "Living conditions were atrocious, so dismal the community was disintegrating. If the process of getting them out continued at the pace it was, there would be no community left. A hundred a month, a few thousand a month was not enough. We had to get them all out in months or it would be too late."

The Jews weren't the only ones suffering in Ethiopia, but in their case there was another country, with something to offer, that was eager to take them in. Ethiopia was one of the world's oldest civilizations, but its history was long marked by power struggles rather than efforts to improve peasant life. Some leaders in the nineteenth and early twentieth century tried to modernize, but they lost out to tribalism, famine and disease. Haile Selassie established a constitutional monarchy in 1931, soon after his accession, but he was overthrown when Italy invaded in 1935 and, although he was reinstated after World War II, he accomplished little. When he was ousted again in 1974, this time in a coup by Lieut. Col. Mengistu Haile Mariam, only four percent of his people could read or write; transportation, communication and food supply were poor; and corruption was widespread. Mengistu was worse than any of his predecessors in recent centuries. A Marxist Leninist, he used his access to Soviet arms to suppress rebellions and fight border wars that killed millions of his own people. He rounded out his bloody suppression of the latest coup attempt in 1989 by executing his own generals. But the people had had it with his tyranny and in 1990 two rebel armies, from Eritrea and Tigre, which had nothing in common except hatred of Mengistu, gained victories in the provinces and moved toward Addis. The Soviet Union reduced military aid to focus on its own problems and Mengistu thought that Israel, which wanted something he had, Jews, might fill the arms gap.

At their first negotiation session in October 1990 Mengistu spoke Amharic even though both he and Lubrani were fluent in English. Lubrani's Amharic was passable but not perfect and he requested a translator. That turned out to be Kasa Kabede, whose father was a friend of Lubrani's in the 1960s, and who won a scholarship to Hebrew University in the 1970s with Lubrani's help. "Mengistu spoke for hours," Lubrani recalled in one of the interviews, "about his strengths, why he was right, why he would win out. Eventually he came around to his need for arms. I told him we would not sell him anything that shoots. We had promised the Americans. He wanted to know what Israel could do for him and I said provide technological assistance."

He let Mengistu bring up the issue of Ethiopian Jews. "That's what you really want," he said. "Why do you care so much about them?" Lubrani answered, "They are Jewish and Israel is their home. They want to come home and we want to bring them there."

Lubrani continued:

> In my first discussion with him about money, I asked him how much would it take. He was poker faced, a tough cookie, inflexible, arrogant. You felt you were dealing with an uncouth, cruel person. I looked him in the eyes and his killer instinct radiated. He said $180 million. I told him we had computed if they all flew first class on commercial flights it wouldn't cost a third of that. We had not much time, but some time. I had an idea what I would hear from him, and did what I planned but I was very worried. I thought, 'Who am I to put a price on Jewish lives? Suppose I am wrong and we run out of time?' How did I know what could happen in that chaotic situation? But *I had to sound credible and not desperate so a deal could be struck.* I said $30 million. He rejected it.

Mengistu told Lubrani to prove he could deliver technological assistance. Lubrani flew to London where he met with two old friends, David Alliance and Samuel Shamu; he briefed them and asked them to visit Ethiopia. He asked them to indicate they were interested in investing but assured them they did not have to invest at all. Alliance and Shamu visited and expressed keen interest. Mengistu was pleased and permitted the emigration to increase to several hundred a month.

Mengistu also sought military and economic aid from the United States but the Congressional Black Caucus opposed negotiations with him. Simcha Dinitz, a former Ambassador to Washington during the Nixon, Ford and Carter Presidencies, said in an interview that he was called into the picture in late 1990 because he "had good contacts" with Caucus members and flew to Washington to meet with eleven of them. He said he had persuaded them that American negotiations could save lives, Jews and others, and bring long term improvements to Ethiopia. Dinitz said he also met with Brent Scowcroft, Bush's National Security Advisor, and urged that America pressure Mengistu to let the Jews leave.

American Assistant Secretary of State Herman Cohen arrived in Addis Ababa after Thanksgiving and joined Lubrani at his next meeting with Mengistu. Cohen wholeheartedly endorsed freedom for Ethiopian Jews. No one doubted his sincerity, but some Israelis believed his real role was to ensure that the Israelis did not weaken and provide Mengistu with arms, or cash to buy arms. Mengistu probably thought he could so persuade the Israelis; he also hoped for American aid and wanted to keep the United States from stepping up its aid for the rebels, whom he knew the Central Intelligence Agency was advising. He did not get arms or cash, but as his talks with Lubrani continued he allowed more Jews to leave, 1,007 in December alone. Lubrani recalled:

> During the months I negotiated with him I kept giving him reasons to keep at it. First there were the London investors which took many weeks. Then we discussed a desalinization plant and I even brought in heavy equipment.

> His demand dropped to $100 million, then $57 million where he stayed for awhile. My goal was to keep getting out as many as we could and find an opening to bring out the rest. He thought it was just the money; finally the stereotype about the Jews helped us. He didn't force my hand because I always gave him the feeling he would get the money, that the issue between us was just the price, the price of Jewish freedom. He didn't know that to us it had nothing to do with money.

Meanwhile, JDC took over life in the camps. It imported vaccines and antibiotics and built a medical team that curbed the health crisis; it even hired teachers and established classes to provide normalcy for children. But the rebels were closing in.

In March 1991, they advanced to within 60 miles of Addis Ababa. Lubrani returned to Jerusalem to brief the Prime Minister:

> I told Shamir that Mengistu's situation was beginning to unravel and I do not recommend waiting much longer. He agreed. He said he would tell [Defense Minister Moshe] Arens and the army to get ready.

Then he said he wanted to get Mengistu's permission to mount the rescue. He knew that during the Entebbe operation, Israel was criticized in Africa for 'violating Ugandan and Kenyan sovereignty,' for coming in militarily without their approval. To avoid these problems, Shamir wanted an official Ethiopian approval beforehand.

Lubrani met with General Dan Shomron, the Israel Defense Forces Chief of Staff, who had planned the brazen rescue in Entebbe, Uganda, with plane refueling in Kenya, that saved 102 Jewish hostages on July 4, 1976. They were joined by Deputy Chief of Staff General Amnon Shahak, who had led daring commando raids in 1973 into Beirut when the Palestine Liberation Organization was holed up there orchestrating attacks on northern Israel. Shahak traveled to Ethiopia with Lubrani to plan the operation.

Shahak discerned serious risks to a caravan of thousands of civilians moving through the capital, from government soldiers near the camps, at the airport, along any of the routes, and from maverick gunmen on rooftops or in bushes. He said the Ethiopian government's approval was needed for military reasons.

Lubrani met again with Mengistu:

I told him that time was running out. I needed to take with me the whole community. All of them. I said I would also need his help to get them out. He held at $57 million. I said $35 million and left.

Now, American pressure was needed. The American Jews whom Lubrani had met with weeks earlier had been kept informed. As Lender, Tauber, Pearlstone and the other UJA leaders planned to raise whatever funds Lubrani needed, the Conference of Presidents concluded that only the personal authority of President Bush could break the logjam. The President was riding high from his Gulf War victory but Saddam Hussein's moves against the Kurds and a faltering American economy had captured most of Bush's attention. The President wanted to bring peace and democracy to the Horn of Africa and the CIA was aiding the rebels, but the Jews could be caught in the pincers if the battle entered the streets of Addis Ababa. Cardin and Hoenlein were White House regulars but wanted to enhance their case to Bush. Hoenlein telephoned Rudy Boschwitz.

Boschwitz, who had just completed two terms as a Republican United States Senator from Minnesota, where he was Chairman of the Senate's Ethiopian Jewry Caucus, entered his home as the phone rang. "I told him that the civil war was still raging in Ethiopia and asked him if he would go there," Hoenlein recalled in an interview. "I didn't say what the idea was but he said, without hesitation, 'Yes'."

Boschwitz, a UJA major donor and former President of the Minneapolis Federation for Jewish Service, was a personal friend of Bush. He reached the President and suggested that a personal delegation from him was necessary to save the Jews. The President listened, then telephoned Boschwitz later in the day after consulting National Security Council and State Department experts. He agreed and asked Boschwitz to lead the delegation. After three weeks of intensive briefings in Washington, Boschwitz said in an interview for this book, he met with the President in the Oval Office for final instructions. The President handed Boschwitz a letter to Mengistu stating that he was willing to arrange a peace conference, a roundtable among all forces, but only upon release of the Jews. Boschwitz arrived in Addis Ababa in early May with a team of experts. Mengistu had little time left. The same for the Jews.

Boschwitz described his negotiations with the dictator:

Mengistu was very calm and cool. You couldn't decipher from his attitude or conversation that the rebels were at the gates and his regime was collapsing about him. He spoke as though everything was just fine.

He opened with a long peroration of about three hours on all that he accomplished for his people and all he was going to do for them. He insisted on speaking in Amharic even though his English was so perfect that when the translator paused to find the right word he suggested it. I remember once he helped the translator out with the word in English, 'ornithologist.'

After he finished, I read him the letter from President Bush. The President would arrange a peace conference but first the Jews had to be let go....

I was there for about five days and met with him three or four times. He was very difficult. A lot of time was consumed by his fascination with American military power that had just been demonstrated in the Gulf War. He was awed by the weaponry and the military strategies. He fought hard in his desire for arms but I told him we weren't going to give him any arms and wouldn't let the Israelis either...

After each session, we briefed Scowcroft; when we needed the President on some nuances he was on the phone within minutes... Our negotiations were triggered by the plight of the Falashas but he [Bush] saw in the wider picture a chance to end the protracted civil war that had raged for 15 years...

[Mengistu] wanted money and I told him he had to work that out with the Israelis... He was worried about publicity. He knew what had happened after Operation Moses to Numeiry. I assured him as much as I could... He saw the Falashas as his trump card but he didn't want to play it too soon.

He began our last meeting by speaking English. That let me know he was ready to close a deal. His conditions were: no publicity, no American aircraft, Israeli aircraft but without insignias. He agreed that the money would have to come from the Israelis. He could work the details out with them. Once the Jews were out, the President would personally arrange for the roundtable somewhere in Europe.

When Lubrani returned to seal the agreement, Mengistu balked. He refused to budge from his demand for $57 million and he was concerned about publicity, about the details so the cover would not be blown. After several excruciating sessions, he recognized he was almost out of time. "The rebels were moving in on him and if it was going to be done it had to be done quickly," Lubrani said. "Soon it was in his interest as well as ours." Late on May 20, Mengistu agreed to $35 million, with refinements in the arrangements to take place the next morning. The deal was struck.

Lubrani was awakened before dawn on May 21 by a telephone call from Kabede. Mengistu had abdicated. Political as well as military chaos now loomed as the stunned Vice President, Testafaye Gibre-Kidan, struggled to secure power. Robert Houdek, the American charge d'affaires, briefed Testafaye on Boschwitz's agreement with Mengistu and said Bush's offer stood. Lubrani confirmed his agreements with Testafaye. On May 23, Testafaye agreed to everything, the final piece being acceptance of the $35 million. The deal was re-struck.

Israeli Ambassador Asher Naim was informed and contacted Foreign Minister David Levy who informed Shamir. The Prime Minister authorized the rescue to begin. Arens delegated the decision on timing to Shahak. The Israeli newspaper editors, who were aware of the pending operation from their journalists in Addis but had not published anything, were briefed that the airlift was about to begin but warned that the embargo must be strictly observed until the Jews were safe. American diplomats, at Israel's request, contacted Arab States along the escape route and informed them they would soon see significant Israeli air activity on their radar screens but that it was unrelated to them and would pose no threat. In Addis Ababa, Bergman of JDC telephoned the bus companies in Addis Ababa and said he wanted to charter buses to take all the children to the city zoo.[4]

"The zoo? In the middle of civil war?" they asked incredulously.

"Yes," Bergman replied. "The children need a break from all this."

At the compound, thousands of gallons of drinking water, hundreds of medical kits and other supplies were loaded onto unmarked trucks. Testafaye informed his security forces and imposed a curfew to prevent other Ethiopians, mired in strife, famine and hardship, who had no country to rescue them, from harming their countrymen.

Throughout the day and into the early night, Jewish Agency representatives moved through the compound with lists containing the name of every Ethiopian Jew, the final accounting to ensure that no one was left behind. They pasted circles, two and a half inches in diameter, onto the foreheads of every one of them. Some had the number 1, others 2, others 3 and so on. Family members shared the same number. A truck drove into the compound with long, thick ropes and the Jews were cordoned into sections by forehead numbers. Most complied but some became hysterical and had to be restrained. After dark, they were escorted by numbers, within cordons, from the compound to the buses. They boarded and, under the escort of Israeli soldiers in plainclothes and Ethiopian security forces, sped away. Operation Solomon had begun.

It is a four-to-five hour flight from Tel Aviv to Addis Ababa depending on the aircraft. When he was twenty minutes away from Bole Airport in Addis Ababa, the pilot of the first aircraft, an empty and unmarked Israel Air Force Hercules C-130 cargo jet, radioed for permission to land. Another empty jet was 40 minutes behind him, and behind that was another 40 minutes away. It was nighttime and the buses in the first caravan had arrived.

"Approaching from the north at 3,800 meters," the pilot said. "Request landing instructions."

"Who are you and who authorized you to land?" the tower demanded.

"We have permission from the palace."

"We have no record of this," the tower answered.

Security was tight and everything was carefully calibrated but no one had notified the traffic controllers. Airport security telephoned the palace and the call was directed to Kabede, who was meeting with Lubrani and military

---

4 This section based on *Jerusalem Post* articles, Bard, contemporary accounts, author interviews.

officials. Permission was granted and the tower was instructed that dozens more planes would arrive in succession.

When the jet landed, buses pulled alongside, a staircase was positioned and the immigrants boarded. Inside they found no seats. They filled the plane until there was almost no room to move inside. Jewish Agency representatives boarded to address any issues that might arise in flight and to ensure a smooth transition in Israel. The C-130 returned to the clouds, half an hour after landing, as another unmarked Israel military air transport was in final descent. The second jet landed on a nearby air strip, hundreds more poured into its belly and it was airborne as the third was about to land.

However, a huge problem was in store for Lubrani at the palace. As the third flight landed, the Ethiopians demanded their $35 million in cash. Lubrani stated:

> I was in the outer office of the Vice President and I get a phone call that the new Prime Minister (he had been the Minister of Foreign Affairs under Mengistu) wanted to know where the money was. I told Kasa I needed a bank account number. He said they wanted to see the money. I said I was not going to bring it in a valise like James Bond. I said I needed a bank account number and we would wire the money to it. There was a lot of back and forth. The permissions for the planes to land began to take longer and longer and the empty planes were circling in flight. The operation started to back up. Every one [of the Ethiopian Jews] was at the airport. I was very worried.
>
> I did not know the new Prime Minister as well so I asked to see the Minister of Finance. I had dealings with him in the 1970s when I was Ambassador to Ethiopia and we had mutual trust. We had worked together to help Ethiopia with its agriculture. I said I needed Ethiopia's bank account number. He said he did not know the number. They were all new in their positions and did not know the number of the account we should send the money to. He said the governor of the bank knew but he was in Kinshasa.
>
> "I took a daring lunge. I said, 'Tell your Prime Minister the money is already in your country's bank account.' 'What?!' he screamed. 'It isn't.' I said, 'Look, you know me. We know each other. I give you my word of honor on this. As soon as you give me the bank number it will be in the account.' He hesitated. I said, 'Do you think the Jewish people will not honor their commitment and would deprive the Ethiopian people of this money that belongs to them for letting us do something like this [the airlift]?' He agreed and said he would telephone the Prime Minister. Then I said, 'I will still need to know the number.' He

said, 'You have such a good intelligence service. Find out the number yourself.' He meant this as a compliment.

I said I would. He telephoned his Prime Minister in my presence and said, 'We have the money.' I went outside and made some calls. Someone in Israel called the World Bank and asked, 'If we want to give money to Ethiopia, for scholarships and other things, what is the number of the account we should send our money to? We are all set to do this.' They told us the number. The money was transferred.

Lubrani leaned back in his chair, relaxed, satisfied, proud. In his final interview for this book, he reflected, "It was a well organized operation and, when it played out, it was like an air shuttle from Addis Ababa airport to Ben Gurion."

From Friday, May 24 to Saturday, May 25, the Israeli Chief Rabbis having suspended the restrictions on Sabbath travel for the mitzvah of *pidyon hashevuim*, the ransom of captives, and *pikuach nefesh*, the saving of souls, the airlift continued. The planes, which were fueled in Israel for the round trip, were on and off the ground in Addis Ababa in as few as 36 minutes. The Jews flew above the Red Sea, 30,000 feet higher than the route their ancestors took to Israel 3,300 years earlier and, this time, with no enemy in pursuit. The aircraft, nine Hercules C-130s, nine El Al jets and one Ethiopian Airlines plane, formed an elliptical aeronautical caravan. A total of 40 flights soared south and north in succession, first in the terror of night, later in the azure skies high above the clouds in bright sunshine. At one juncture, more than 20 planes were aloft simultaneously. "The skies were filled with our airplanes flying the same route, mostly over the Red Sea," Captain Nir Dagan, the pilot of the second flight and several other C-130 flights said in an interview for this book. "We could see Sudan, Egypt and Saudi Arabia. It was good to know these Jews would soon be in Israel. It was overwhelming."

The operation proceeded smoothly but uncertainty lingered in the first hours that it might be interrupted like Operation Moses. The Israelis crowded as many refugees as would fit into each aircraft and one, an El Al 747 built for 440, transported 1,087. It entered the Guinness Book of World Records for the most passengers on a flight. The journey was efficient, although not sanitary; no aircraft had enough lavatories to accommodate everyone. Not one person died in the entire operation. In 26 hours, every one of the 14,324 Jews in the refugee camps arrived in Israel.

Ten others arrived as well, nine born in flight, one on a school bus, with birth fluids on their bodies. The excitement over fulfillment of their dream, or vehicle motion, probably both, induced labor. Most were given names in

Hebrew, not Amharic, reminiscent of Sharansky who changed his name from Anatoly to Natan when he reached Israel.

The Prime Minister, Speaker of the Knesset, cabinet ministers, heads of the Israel Defense Forces and leaders of the Jewish Agency and Joint Distribution Committee were among hundreds who had gathered on the tarmac to greet arriving flights. As the cabin doors opened and the Ethiopians stepped onto the silver staircase and descended to the tarmac, the Israelis broke into song, *Heveinu Shalom Aleichem.* Many newcomers kissed the ground. They were hugged by their greeters. Many smiled, some laughed, others broke into tears of joy, a few appeared dazed by their experience. *"Baruch haba'ah l'Aretz,"* someone said to the first arrivals. *"Baruch haba'ah habayitah."* ["Welcome to Israel. Welcome home."]

Inside the terminal the new immigrants were offered refreshments, and doctors and nurses aided anyone weak or ill. They were given the opportunity to declare that they were Jews and wished to exercise their right to become Israeli citizens. Everyone did. The paperwork had been prepared; processing was rapid. Within two days it would become official: each of them would become a citizen of Israel. After 3,000 years they had returned to Zion. Their journey of the centuries was completed.

Every effort had been made beforehand to learn where their relatives were living in Israel. Matches were made and hundreds of new Israelis were whisked in buses not only to new towns and new homes but to their families they had not seen since Operation Moses and Operation Sheba. Others were escorted to absorption centers, hotels and guest houses where their immediate needs were met and where the effort to reunite them with their families in Israel continued.

The rescue was the opening news on CBS, NBC, ABC, CNN and most European television networks, and on local television and radio stations; it made banner headlines in newspapers around the world.

As Bob Schieffer reported on *"The CBS Evening News with Bob Schieffer:"*

The Ethiopian capital of Addis Ababa has been in chaos since Tuesday as the Government's Marxist dictator has fled and rebel forces are now closing in. It seems only a matter of time now before the regime collapses. With more violence possible, thousands are fleeing. And no part of the exodus is more dramatic than that of the Ethiopian Jews.

Bernard Shaw opened the international CNN broadcast with the story, "The Jews of Ethiopia. One of the ten lost tribes of Israel. And tonight Israel is engaged in a desperate operation to get them home."

Jackson Diehl reported in the *Washington Post:*

> The completion of the airlift ended an often dramatic, seven-year odyssey by Ethiopia's Jews, who first began to leave en masse to Israel in a secret airlift in 1984. The interruption of the operation in 1985 left hundreds of families separated, and many were finally reunited only today, as the entire country celebrated another feat of rescue by the Jewish State.

Barry Peterson, a CBS reporter broadcasting from Ben Gurion as Ethiopian Jews descended onto the tarmac in the background, reported, "There is euphoria in this country, that this is the only country that would launch such an effort. That it is the only country that could pull it off." Prime Minister Shamir declared, "Now they are here, and they are Israeli citizens. So no one will persecute them any more." Foreign Minister David Levy noted, "The United States played a crucial and decisive role in this. It is another wondrous chapter in the relations between our peoples."

Journalist after journalist broadcast or wrote about whites saving blacks, Israelis rescuing Africans, in a campaign to be paid for privately by American Jews. It was a story as current as breaking news; as enduring as the quest for religious freedom; as Biblical as redemption from bondage. It pierced all disputes among the fractious Jewish people and spoke to the essence of the Jewish State. Joel Tauber stood next to Shamir and Levy welcoming the Ethiopian Jews to Israel and stated this on the *ABC-TV World News Tonight With Peter Jennings:*

> This is why Israel was created: to bring the Jewish people home.

Tauber was on the tarmac as Chairman of the UJA Eyewitness Mission to Operation Solomon; he led a delegation that, as soon as the clamor subsided, would help raise the $35 million the Jewish Agency borrowed to advance the payment to the account number provided by the World Bank. Soon they would begin to do this, but first they had to express their jubilation. Mission participant Susan Stern exclaimed:

> Today, I visited the President's Hotel where many Ethiopians in Israel gathered. I saw people only hours out of the clutches of hardship and fear in Ethiopia reunited with their relatives after years of not knowing if they would ever see one another again. This was accomplished by Israel and I am so proud to be connected to it through UJA. No

one can rise to an impossible challenge like the Israelis. When they do something, they know how to do it right.

Stuart Rossman said, "I wish every American Jew could feel the emotions running through this country right now, could make a spiritual connection and feel the excitement and enthusiasm, the commitment of Jews to one another." "The Israelis brought over so many toys, they said on the radio not to bring any more," William Shure said. Yona Goldberg added, "Everyone is overjoyed that the tribe has been ingathered." Jerry Benjamin, Thomas Falik, Shearn Platt, Philip Margolius of Washington D.C., Norman Levy of St. Louis, and Alan Goldstein of Boston, said they were thrilled to observe the fruits of a breathtaking Jewish humanitarian triumph. Anita Gray kept a diary and made these entries:

Thirty-two hotels were used, the largest of which was the Diplomat, [housing] 1,300 people. Hot water was turned off because it was feared the newcomers might scald themselves. Knobs were removed from doors on upper floors so that if adults were distracted by all that was going on, children would not fall. Mayor Teddy Kollek of Jerusalem told me he was celebrating his 80th birthday and that this was his best birthday present ever. Two-thirds of the immigrants are children. As many as 3,000 immigrants in one hour. How many were there when I went to Russia in the '80s? A few hundred all year!

Some families got separated and were quickly reunited. They got those families out of Ethiopia in one piece and then they got separated here. Go figure. They are going to have to have their teeth checked, but they gave the children punch, cookies and candy. A kid's first taste of candy? Yummy to taste, yummier to see! On the plane they were given bottles of water and had to be shown how to remove the caps — what a cultural shock to move centuries ahead so quickly.

Everywhere they went there were Ethiopian Israelis ready to help. A Jewish Agency worker asked a Russian olah [female immigrant] how she felt about the newer newcomers to her absorption center. She replied, 'American Jews, Russian Jews, Ethiopian Jews, what does it matter from where? We are all one people.'

I spoke to some of them through a translator. They had so much going on but were so polite, so graceful. So eloquent! One told me, 'My grandfather, my grandfather's grandfather, my grandfather's grandfather's grandfather all dreamed of going to Israel. I made it today. I made it for me and my husband and my children. I made it for them. Our dream since forever has become a reality. And today is the day we spoke of for centuries."

Martin Stein, who had chaired Operation Moses, said this:

After thousands of years, we are still our brother's keeper. We are responsible for one another and we act on it. We are the chosen people not because we are better than others but because we demonstrate in deeds, not just words, what ethical, moral conduct is all about. You can't see it every day but you see it every so often, enough to know that we are a 'light unto the nations.' Rescuing Jews, bringing them here, making them citizens, black or white, Amharic or Hebrew speaking, it makes no difference. We are one. This was a miracle in our time. It will stand out forever as a beacon for the people of the world.

In Ethiopia, after 10,000 had left, General Shahak, not having slept for two days, drove back along the route and into the staging area in Addis Ababa to see for himself that all known Ethiopian Jews had left. They had. Dr. Rick Hodes reported that so did every Ethiopian Jew in local hospitals. With the airlift in progress, the United States arranged for Testafaye's and rebel forces to meet in London to negotiate a truce. Lubrani invited Kabede and his family to join him on the last flight and they accepted. They were aboard along with the last Jewish Agency, JDC, NACOEJ, AAEJ and Israeli military personnel.[5]

Operation Solomon was over. No time was wasted: Operation Solomon fundraising began. In his first hours in Israel Lubrani met with the Prime Minister and Cabinet, then with the UJA Eyewitness Mission. Back in the United States, Lender and his team commenced private solicitations, focusing on the Northeast while Pearlstone headed to the Midwest and Zimmerman and Shulman took to the South. Eyewitness Mission participants played the authenticating role in Operation Solomon fundraising that those on the Inaugural Mission to Russia and Israel had played in opening Operation Exodus. A week later, UJA convened federation Campaign Chairmen in Chicago and they were thrilled by Tauber's ecstatic report and a dramatic UJA video, "Ethiopian Jewish Airlift: Coming Home," that presented vivid footage of the refugees moving from the camps, on the journey, to their joyous reception in Israel. The video weaved in footage of Tauber, Stein, Stern and the others which would add authority to

5 Israel later established that the Falash Mura, descendants of Ethiopians who had converted from Judaism centuries ago, were Jewish. Many made aliyah and all others who wished to do so were expected by 2007.

their fundraising speeches and solicitations. UJA marketing resources enhanced federation materials and exultant stories filled the American Jewish press.

Fundraising for Operation Solomon was based on a $130 million projected need for rescue and initial absorption and was rolled by UJA into Operation Exodus. In the beginning fundraising was easy. Fundraisers could have taken a vacation for a couple of months; the funds came in anyway from people who decided on their own to give. It was brisk, even in the summer months. American Jews were jubilant, selfless idealists aspiring to help others live better, more secure, lives. Lubrani said it was his first main contact with them and he was impressed. He learned more about American Jews when he toured their communities for UJA the next year. He said:

> I did not know much about American Jews until after Operation Solomon. I knew when I was in Ethiopia that they wanted to help. After all, they were the ones paying the $35 million. But when I met them I could see how deeply they felt. They would have paid whatever it took to get them out. They wanted to save Jews. They wanted to build their relations with the black community in the USA. They wanted to show that Israel was colorblind. No other community could ever be so accommodating.

At the time of the funds transfer, it was widely reported, believed by American Jews and promoted as such by UJA officials who believed it too, that the $35 million was a personal bribe to Mengistu. For his part, Lubrani said the sum was never discussed with Mengistu as a bribe and, "I didn't negotiate it as a bribe." However Boschwitz and others interviewed said there was no other way to understand it, especially since Mengistu negotiated to within hours of his departure when it was too late to buy, import and use the arms.

What happened to the $35 million? Several months after Operation Solomon, internal auditors at Citibank discovered that a $35 million deposit had been wired from a Jewish Agency account at Bank Leumi to an Ethiopian government account on May 25, 1991 and never claimed. As an unusual financial transaction involving foreign entities, Citibank was obligated to report it to the State Department where it was brought to the attention of Secretary of State Lawrence S. Eagleburger. Eagleburger telephoned Dinitz, who stated in an interview in 2003:

> We talked about it for a little while. He knew I had been involved in the wiring of it and asked me what I made of it. I said that Mengistu had fled into the night before it was sent and his Vice President was driven

out before he could get his hands on it. I also said that the money was no longer ours. The sum had been raised in good faith and had bought the freedom of the Ethiopian Jews. I told him the money belonged to the government of Ethiopia. I said I hope they put it to good use to alleviate the suffering of their people.

The final use of the $35 million could not be absolutely determined, but Dinitz and others said they believed that the sum was probably used by Mengistu's successors to ease the misery of their people. If so, American Jewish generosity not only helped rescue Ethiopian Jews but also was an unexpected boon to struggling Ethiopians who remained, who had no such benevolent supporters and no country willing and eager to take them in.

CHAPTER EIGHT
Challenges Mount

There is no brighter chapter in the whole history of philanthropy
than that which could be written of the work of the American Jews.
Herbert Hoover

In the opening months of 1991, the Jews were flowing out of the evil empire.
Good triumphed over evil in wartime as the Jews were saved from a modern
day Haman, in time to celebrate Purim. And an ancient tribe of Israel was
brought home, soaring high above the clouds over the Red Sea. Could it get any
better for UJA fundraisers? Yes.

The entire Albanian Jewish community, which nobody outside Albania
even knew existed, was brought home in yet another secret rescue. Nestled on
the Adriatic Sea between Greece and Yugoslavia, Albania had been a Stalinist
dictatorship for decades. Completely cut off from the outside world except for
strictly limited contacts with Communist China, nothing went in or out of the
country except for occasional strictly-censored letters to family members. The
country, the size of Maryland, had three million people who grew their own food
and lived under a constitution that banned emigration, immigration, tourism
and all religious practices. It was the most isolated country in the world.

Risking imprisonment for years, the older Albanian Jews had transmitted
what they knew of Judaism to younger ones, even though intermarriage with
Muslims and Christians had become commonplace. Many Jews fasted in the
fall around what might have been Yom Kippur. Some families held seders in
the spring where the elders recited the story of the Exodus and described what
they remembered of the symbols on their imaginary seder plate. Then, in early
1991, as the world focused elsewhere, the Jewish Agency entered Tirana, the
capital, aided by the American Jewish Joint Distribution Committee and the
Israeli Foreign Ministry[1], and clandestinely rescued all 300 Albanian Jews.

---

1 Bill Hutman, "Last of Albania's Jews Arrive After Secret Escape," *Jerusalem Post*, April 20, 1991, p. 1.

Every Jewish family and every family containing a Jew was rescued[2]. For the Albanian Jews, the flame of Zionism burned in their hearts.

The New York Times interviewed some of the new Israelis[3].

'We have always told our children it [the Israeli flag] is our flag,' said Isak Matathia, a 40-year-old electrical engineer who worked in a nuclear research laboratory. 'We showed it to them whenever we saw it on Italian television. We all cried when we saw so many of them at the airport here when we arrived...

'We hope that Albania soon becomes a democracy but we'll never go back to live there,' said Dr. Zino Matathia, Isak's 50-year-old brother, a surgeon. 'I have felt Jewish since my childhood. We always said, 'Next year in Jerusalem.' . . .

[When] Dr. Renate Burci, a 46-year-old physician, who came with her husband, Mustafa, a Muslim . . . told her husband that she wanted to emigrate to Israel, she recalled his response was, 'Immediately, immediately, immediately.'

Within hours of the Albanian Jewish rescue, two planes of Soviet Jews arrived; it seemed that there were forever more planes of immigrants landing and more contingents of Operation Exodus mission participants to greet them on the tarmac. The aliyah was broadening and deepening. In cities, towns and kibbutzim from the Galilee to the Negev, Israelis continued to greet the thousands of new immigrants happily. In every town in Israel this writer visited, in every town in Israel anyone visited, in any town no one visited, there was a mayor, a city council and storekeepers, shoppers and neighbors saying something, doing something, to welcome the new Israelis. Israel's population was soaring, and taxes were raised to keep pace with absorption costs, but few grumbled; they complained only of government waste as the cause for higher taxes. Everyone steered clear of even a hint of resistance to the aliyah; this was the dream they had for years. The absorption proceeded smoothly and the welcome mat remained out for all Jews who wanted to come home.

Operation Exodus continued to rise to the challenge. In the first half of

---

2 Several others emigrated earlier to the United States but their commitment to Judaism also appeared strong. "One Albanian man, when asked by an Italian customs official about the large menorah he had in his bag, reportedly said, 'Why are you asking me about this? I had to keep it buried in my yard for years.'" Aliza Marcus, "Jews Allowed to Leave Albania in What May Become New Exodus," Jewish Telegraphic Agency, Jan. 1, 1991, p. 1.

3 Henry Kamm, "Joyful News from 'Another Planet' Called Albania," The New York Times, Apr. 11, 1991, p. 3.

1991, UJA mounted several successful programs under the general direction of Marvin Lender, the brilliant strategist atop the Operation Exodus pyramid. UJA established the King David Society, a club for $25,000 donors that motivated givers of $15,000 and $18,000 to reach that level. Shearn Platt of San Diego and Harold Grossman of Phoenix led the inaugural weekend of the King David Society, the conception of Russell Robinson, UJA West Coast Regional Director who later became Executive Vice President of the Jewish National Fund. Under a program named "Fly-In," UJA flew its most experienced fundraisers to federations, to help them close selected solicitations. The UJA Women's Campaign sponsored a mission to Israel, obtained gifts through its Business and Professional Women's Council, and broadened support through its Women of Distinction affinity group. Carole Solomon, Roberta Holland, Yona Goldberg, Robyn Loup, Barbara Ginsberg, Elaine Berke and Sherry Lansing led Women's Campaign events. Heidi Damsky, Thomas Falik, Stuart Rossman, Susan Stern, Andrew Groveman of Memphis, Skip Schrayer of Chicago, Lewis Norry of Rochester and Bruce Arbit and Jerry Benjamin of Milwaukee spearheaded Young Leadership missions, events and solicitations. Scores of UJA National Officers crossed the country to address audiences and close major gifts. Meanwhile, federations pursued a variety of events on their own[4].

By mid-August, Operation Exodus pierced the $600 million mark as the number of immigrants from the Soviet Union for the year exceeded 100,000 and the total of new Israelis from all countries passed 125,000.

UJA major gifts season opened with the Prime Minister's Mission from August 18 to 23 for sixty-one $100,000 Annual Campaign donors and 59 of their spouses or adult children. Larry Hochberg of Chicago, founder of the Midwestern retail chain SportMart and an experienced UJA campaigner, was Mission Chairman. Jerry Gumenick of Richmond and Jerome Stern of Portland, Oregon, as well as Donald Hess, Marlyn Essman, Lender, Tauber and Pearlstone were integral to Hochberg's solicitation team. General Thomas Kelly, a familiar face from television coverage of the recently concluded Gulf War, and former Governor Ann Richards of Texas were UJA guests. Former Senator Rudy Boschwitz was a participant at the $100,000 level.

---

4 By August 1991, 14 federations reached or exceeded the $10 million level for campaigning that began in early 1990: New York ($100 million), Philadelphia ($34 million), Los Angeles ($31 million), Chicago ($28 million), San Francisco, Peninsula, Marin and Sonoma ($22 million), Detroit ($21 million), Baltimore ($20 million), Miami ($18 million), Boston ($17 million), Washington, D.C. ($16 million), Cleveland ($15 million), Pittsburgh ($13 million), Columbus ($10 million) and MetroWest ($10 million). Leslie Wexner, Larry Tisch, Charles Bronfman and Max Fisher were among the highest level donors who closed major solicitations. Several UJA National Vice Chairmen organized national programs that raised funds. Others like Edgar Bronfman solicited on request. Peter May, who had led New York past UJA's requested $75 million, declared a $100 million goal and in the summer reset New York's sights on $200 million.

UJA chartered an El Al 747 and raffled the Business Class seats, since every participant wanted one. Moments after the plane landed near Tel Aviv, Hochberg informed the Mission that Soviet Premier Mikhail Gorbachev had been detained in a Soviet right wing coup. The news was an encompassing umbrella for the UJA theme of uncertainty for Soviet Jews, and new immigrants personalized the message when participants visited them in their apartments, community centers and work places in Israel and heard about their experiences back in the Soviet Union. Boschwitz, who negotiated the release of over 14,000 Ethiopian Jews weeks earlier, beamed as he visited some of them. His remarks to fellow participants made clear that the exciting flow of Jews into Israel could not be taken for granted. Like a good baseball team that has a formidable set-up pitcher for the eighth inning and a strong closer for the ninth, UJA arranged visits to Ethiopian Jews on the final day as it strived to persuade the last holdouts to close at the highest gift levels possible. That evening, the participants found themselves in the Knesset, in front of the majestic Chagall Tapestries, where they were photographed individually with Prime Minister Yitzhak Shamir, heard from him on the importance of giving maximally and then were asked to announce their gifts at the microphone. In the magic that seemed to accompany Operation Exodus fundraising, Gorbachev remained a prisoner in the Crimea for four days, from the time the Mission landed until the participants announced their gifts. This provided UJA fundraisers with all the time they needed to thrill participants with past triumphs and underscore the uncertainty of the Jewish future abroad. Participants pledged $12.1 million to Operation Exodus, ten percent more than the impressive sums they had given a year earlier.

Following the High Holidays, which fell mainly in September that year, UJA resumed fundraising with the President's Mission. The 800 participants met new immigrants, visited Joint Distribution Committee facilities, heard from diplomats and generals and enjoyed Jerusalem's nightspots. The central component was a private meeting with President Chaim Herzog at Beit Hanassi, where Herzog spoke of the potential of the aliyah to transform Israel, and encouraged donors to give generously.

The International Leadership Reunion, for $250,000 annual donors to UJA or Keren Hayesod, was held in New York. Participants included Irving Stone, Albert Ratner, Sheldon Adelson, Sam Halpern, Sumner Feldberg, Irwin Levy, Tauber, Pearlstone, Lender, Richard Goldman, Joseph Gurwin, Irving Schneider and Bud Meyerhoff; as well as Lynn and Charles Schusterman of Tulsa and Abraham, Rosy, Arlene, Loren, Martin, Ada, Paul, Solly and Rita Krok. Mendel Kaplan, the Jewish Agency Chairman, and Julia Koschitzky of

Ontario, a Keren Hayesod leader, participated along with Jewish entrepreneurs from abroad such as Philip Granovsky of Toronto, Trevor Chinn of London and Ernst Weil of Zurich.

The program included delectable dinners, private tours of the Metropolitan Museum of Art, box seats to the Metropolitan Opera; and briefings by prominent Americans and Israelis. A panel discussion featuring Peter Jennings of ABC-TV, Tom Brokaw of NBC-TV and Dan Rather of CBS-TV and moderated by Barbara Walters of ABC-TV enabled participants to express their views, especially to Jennings, that Israel's quest for peace, strategic importance to the United States and value as a democracy deserved better coverage. The Operation Exodus pitch took up only a limited part of the weekend's celebrations but was effective enough so that the 58 American donors pledged $16.4 million to Operation Exodus while millions were raised by Keren Hayesod.

In October, the Women's Campaign convened a Lion of Judah Conference that was to become a biannual event in Washington. Conceived by Carole Solomon, the Conference fulfilled her vision and was beyond what anyone else had anticipated. Twelve hundred women gathered under UJA auspices and each committed to give at least $5,000 to Operation Exodus in her own name. The Conference obtained many such gifts at the $5,000, $10,000, $18,000 and $25,000 levels and established the viability of women giving large gifts independently of any men in their lives. Moreover, Solomon and her team obtained several written agreements by women to bequeath significant funds to UJA. The Conference not only benefited Operation Exodus but also demonstrated the indispensability and reliability of the Women's Campaign and foreshadowed its even greater role in UJA Federation Campaigns in the years ahead.

Most impressively, UJA was able to continue to turn pledges into cash. This was secured by the UJA National Cash Team under Victor Gelb of Cleveland, which went into "cash season" in December. The Cash Team consisted of a score of UJA National Vice Chairmen and Honorary Vice Chairmen with strong financial backgrounds and skills in persuasion. Cash Team members were knowledgeable about aliyah costs, such as plane tickets and baggage transport, and the Jewish Agency budget, so they could respond to any concerns that the funds might not be well spent. They were major donors whose own pledges had been paid, which positioned them to ask others to be current too. They meant business.

The Cash Team mainly sought to obtain cash from federations and helped them obtain cash from their constituents. Armed with data printouts, the Cash

Team conducted almost a paramilitary operation of telephone calls, meetings and general arm-twisting with specific "go to" people in every federation. They reminded federations of how much was due to UJA, based of course on what UJA decided was due. They helped federations assess their progress and made suggestions for improving their collection processes or persuading specific donors.

When federations said they might not be able to achieve the goal because of local problems such as a hurricane in the south or crop failures in farm states, the Cash Team was very understanding. But it quickly suggested that federations could simply borrow what they couldn't collect, and repay the bank over however long a period they and the bank liked. Or maybe the federations should make more effective use of tools that UJA had provided, such as materials for mailings, advertisements for newspapers and newsletters, and talking points. Or Cash Team members would be happy to get at the necks of any local major contributors whose pledges had not yet been redeemed.

When a federation achieved its goal, Cash Team members said in effect, "Thank you very much, but other federations might fall short and the overall sum is what counts. So now collect on other unpaid pledges." They did not fool around. Federation leaders understood the importance of collections too. They strived to collect every possible dollar. They did not fool around either.

The pressure was excruciating. No one wanted to be the one to say to the immigrants, finally able to leave the Soviet Union after decades of hope and twenty years of American Jewish advocacy, that they would not have the funds to depart. The desired results were achieved[5]. By the time Gelb's team finished officially on December 31 (they continued unofficially into January), UJA had collected all it needed, with a flourish of $100 million in the final weeks of the year.

Despite these continued extraordinary achievements, there were indications within the campaign system in 1991 that Operation Exodus might have crested.

---

5 Many communities achieved UJA's cash goals not only for Operation Exodus but also for the Annual Campaign as well, such as Baltimore, Cleveland, Miami, New York, Palm Beach County, Philadelphia, Pittsburgh, San Francisco, South Broward and Washington. So did Albuquerque, Allentown, Ann Arbor, Austin, Bergen County, Brevard County, Canton, Chattanooga, Cincinnati, Columbia, Columbus, Corpus Christi, Des Moines, Dutchess County, El Paso, Fall River, Flint, Fort Wayne, Grand Rapids, Greensboro, Indianapolis, Knoxville, Lee County, Long Beach, Louisville, Madison, Manchester, Milwaukee, Mobile, Nashville, New Haven, North Jersey, Oakland, Ocean County, Orange County, Orlando, Peoria, Portland (Oregon and Maine), Princeton, Quad Cities, Reading, Rhode Island, Rochester, Rockford, Rockland County, San Diego, San Jose, Santa Barbara, Sarasota, Savannah, Scranton, Seattle, Sioux City, South Bend, Southern New Jersey, Stamford, Toledo, Tulsa, Virginia Peninsula, Waco and Westport.

Atlanta, Boston, Chicago, Detroit, Los Angeles, MetroWest, St. Louis and South Palm Beach County met one goal by December 31 and the other in the first days of 1992, as did Atlantic City, Birmingham, Bridgeport, Delaware, Elmira, Fresno, Greenwich, Kansas City, Las Vegas, Memphis, Mercer-Bucks, Middlesex County, New Orleans, Omaha, Sacramento, St. Paul, Syracuse, Tidewater, Tucson, and Youngstown. Scores of others from Harrisburg to Tampa to Houston and Honolulu quickly followed.

Most of these were behind the scenes, concealed from the public eye. For one thing, while the Campaign continued at record levels, many donors had given twice, three times, even four times in two years, besides giving to the Annual Campaign, and some were financially tapped out. For another, while mission participation levels were still high, some who traveled to meet Soviet immigrants in 1990 would not have gone again in 1991 were it not for the Ethiopian olim, and said they would not return in 1992. Then too, payment collections in 1991 were astounding by any yardstick except that they were below those in 1990. These internal indicators suggested Operation Exodus had peaked. For two years donors had been enthralled, inspired, ecstatic, jubilant and enraptured, proud of Israel, proud of the world's Jews and proud of themselves, but they were emotionally drained. By the summer, UJA planners grappled with how to respond to what they called "donor exhaustion."

UJA leaders knew that they had planned, organized and executed an extraordinarily successful Campaign; but they had also been aided by world events that gave them wonderful opportunities to focus donors' attention. The timing of the Gulf War and Operation Solomon in UJA's off season seemed divinely inspired. Yet world events could not be counted upon to continue to buoy the Campaign.

When UJA declared in June 1991 – over the objection of federations -- that it was folding Operation Solomon fundraising into Operation Exodus, it exposed a deepening fault line in its uneasy alliance with them. Federations had endorsed Operation Exodus and subscribed to its financial goals in Miami in February 1990, but in the months since they had seen a decline in revenues to the Annual Campaign, on which their local agencies depended. UJA maintained the decision was only logical, to fold one rescue campaign into another. But it knew that federations had been remitting to UJA 90 percent of Operation Exodus collections and only 47 percent from the Annual Campaign[6]. UJA's realpolitiks, by seeking to channel donor enthusiasm for Operation Solomon into the Campaign where it received nearly all the funds, angered the federations, which looked to Operation Solomon to boost the overshadowed Annual Campaign. UJA's decision widened a schism that was to profoundly harm the overall relationship of UJA to federations. For the moment, though, it was a sure sign that UJA knew Operation Exodus was beginning to run out of steam.

The dispute also showed that UJA and federations were focused on how to divide the pie, rather than on ways to bake a bigger pie. Indeed, the highest

6 Federations remitted 75 percent in 1974 after the Yom Kippur War, but allocations to UJA dropped steadily, falling below 50 percent a decade later and inching down each year.

echelons of UJA and the Council of Jewish Federations had been privately, and gingerly, discussing for months whether there was a limit to what American Jews might give. Keren Hayesod donors also had their limits as did the heavily taxed Israelis. Maybe others could help.

He was born Courtney Goodman and his name was changed in infancy to Charles, but he was known to everyone, from childhood friends to business and political titans as Corky. His grandfather had given him the appellation and no one knows why. Corky Goodman graduated from the Massachusetts Institute of Technology in 1954 and went to work for Col. Henry Crown, a World War I veteran who had built a tiny sand and gravel business into a major construction supply enterprise in Chicago. He impressed Crown with his business sense, and the young man came to play an increasingly important role in Crown's enterprises, including General Dynamics, which the family, led by Crown, built into an international powerhouse. After a few years, Corky married Suzanne Crown, daughter of Henry's brother Irving. Henry Crown and Company was a partner of Conrad Hilton in the building of the Hilton Hotels chain, and by 1990 Crown and Company owned major positions in railroad lines, coal mines, airlines and sugar and meatpacking companies.

The family loved Chicago, where they built some of the tallest skyscrapers in the City of Big Shoulders and owned a large share of the Chicago Bulls, although they also had been co-owners of the Empire State Building and were the second largest owners of the New York Yankees after George Steinbrenner.

They were major philanthropists in scores of Jewish and general community causes, with Corky particularly active in the federation system. In the 1980s Corky was elected President of the Jewish Federation of Metropolitan Chicago and General Chairman of its Jewish United Fund. In 1990 he rose to become President of the Council of Jewish Federations. Goodman had been crucial in enlisting federation support for Operation Exodus in 1990 and had represented the family at the Breakfast of Champions.

As early as summer 1990, when the soaring immigration rate indicated that the optimistic three-year projection of 200,000 immigrants would soon be exceeded, Goodman felt that the limits of what Diaspora Jews could give and what Israelis could contribute through taxation need not be tested so soon, if at all. He perceived that there was an overlooked source of income: some of the Soviet Jewish immigrants themselves. He proposed that those who would likely be gainfully employed in Israel be asked to borrow to finance some of their immigration costs. He recalled in a conversation with this writer:

A high percentage of immigrants were physicians, dentists, lawyers, professors, engineers and others likely to adapt quickly, find jobs and be able to support themselves and their families. It seemed reasonable for them to assume a modicum of debt. At the same time, we were very careful not to require anything of those unable to repay, or who might feel unduly burdened, the elderly, handicapped, ill and so on.

Goodman emphasized that this would be a financing complement, not a shift of responsibility from federations to immigrants. In fact, he proposed that federations use their influence to secure bank approval and then guarantee the loans. He shared his idea with Mandell Berman, Shoshana Cardin, Joel Tauber and other CJF leaders. Meanwhile, Martin Kraar, CJF Executive Vice President, and his senior staff including Harold Adler, Bernard Olshansky and Norbert Freuhoff, explored how to implement such a program and win acceptance for it. Goodman flew to New York to brief Lender, Kornreich and other UJA Officers and Trustees, and United Israel Appeal leaders. Then Goodman and Kraar took the idea on the road, visiting major federations and holding conference calls with others. Tauber, a leader at both CJF and UJA, played a key role in developing the loan program and gaining federation approval. Tauber did this even though, as he recalled years later, "Some at UJA criticized my involvement because they felt that loans were inappropriate and the help should be all gifts. However, the program offered hard cash and was voluntary for the immigrants." The process was vintage CJF: share an idea, discuss, build consensus. UJA was mainly unaffected; it viewed the policy as an issue between federations and their trade association. Nor were most UJA campaigners interested; their goal was to test donors' limits regardless of what CJF did.

After Operation Solomon brought a $35 million rescue bill and projections of huge Ethiopian Jewry absorption costs to the table, Goodman's idea gathered momentum. Over breakfast at the Four Seasons Hotel in Manhattan years later, Goodman recalled:

The federations in Chicago, Cleveland, Baltimore, Detroit and Pittsburgh were in favor of it from the very beginning. I remember visiting Atlanta, Kansas City, St. Louis, Los Angeles and San Francisco and they came on board. New York, which is usually good about these things, had a lot of problems with it but they came on board. After Operation Solomon I remember revisiting communities that refused to participate before, and one by one they changed their minds. In the end, they all agreed to it.[7]

Goodman found the immigrants receptive:

In the beginning, the olim were concerned but we explained that
debt is something commonly incurred in free economies like Israel's
and they should not be afraid of it. They understood nothing was due
until the fourth year and they had ten years to repay. They knew this
was for only part of their expenses. They appreciated what the Diaspora
and the Israelis had done for them and recognized this was part of their
independence. We were very careful not to pressure them or impose
anything unreasonable and there were no harsh penalties. There was no
enforcement provision.[8]

During 1991, CJF and federations were fixated on the loan guarantee
program while UJA emphasized fundraising; the partners were moving onto
separate tracks. When UJA raised the Operation Exodus goal to $870 million
during the year, an action that was completely logical based on Jewish Agency
projections, CJF and federations felt UJA's goals and actions had less and less
to do with them.

The growing fissure between UJA and federations was symbolized by the
most unlikely of vehicles, a modest UJA advertising program for Operation
Exodus. Believing that Jews who had not yet given could be motivated to do so,
Marvin Lender had turned to his older brother Murray, who had made Lender's
Bagels a household name, to suggest how. At a meeting at the Lenders' office
in Woodbridge, Connecticut back in 1990 among the brothers, this writer and
other marketing professionals, Murray proposed that UJA, which had built and
maintained its communications programs by unpaid media, try to reach and
persuade non-donors by a paid advertisement. He suggested convening focus
groups to conceive of an original theme since the leitmotifs of war, rescue and
hope had not motivated them. He advised that the advertisement be placed in
general newspapers since most non-donors probably did not read American
Jewish newspapers. He said "some kind of premium" might induce prospects
to respond. He recommended that UJA create a free standing insert, or FSI,

---

7 The plan included a fair share formula in which federations, based on their relative prior year fundraising results, guaranteed proportional sums
to Israeli lending agencies. The elderly, handicapped, young people arriving without parents and others were not asked to borrow.

8 Goodman informed UJA Trustees at their December 1991 meeting that the program was in place, that most federations were on board and
that the written agreements were being prepared for federation guarantees. In the interview he said most borrowings were repaid by the former
immigrants, including 70 percent within the first ten years.

an advertisement not published in one of the newspaper's pages but slipped in between sections, that readers might notice upon opening the newspaper[9].

Murray's idea was developed and approved over several months by the UJA Communications Committee, Campaign Planning Committee, Campaign Executive Committee, Campaign Cabinet, National Officers and Budget Committee. It also was discussed and approved at conferences of federations. In early 1991, UJA Trustees had allocated $1.1 million, a modest sum in the multibillion dollar advertisement market, for the first UJA national advertising program in decades. Since 90 percent of American Jews lived in or near nine cities, to be cost efficient the program called for placement in the cities' nine general newspapers, such as *The New York Times* and *Miami Herald*.[10] With advertising costs in American Jewish newspapers low, and nationally thousands of their readers not having given, the placement was extended to all 151 of them. The publication date selected was the Sunday before Rosh Hashanah, the beginning of campaign high season.

Throughout the months-long process, federations were full participants and helped shape the program. Accordingly, when an advance copy of the detailed plan was issued to them on May 10, none objected. But then, after Operation Solomon took place three weeks later, UJA rolled Operation Solomon fundraising into Operation Exodus, not the beleaguered Annual Campaign. When the same document was reissued as part of the overall UJA Campaign Plan on June 10, many objected, and vehemently.

Scores claimed that the advertisement would be a threat to their Annual Campaign. The South Florida federations north of Miami argued that the placement in suburban editions of the *Miami Herald* would lead their Annual Campaign donors to give annually to Miami. Midwestern and Northeastern federations opposed the *Miami Herald* placement, with the same claim about their donors vacationing in, or newly relocated to, South Florida. Suburban federations outside New York, Los Angeles, San Francisco, Chicago, Boston, Baltimore, Washington and Philadelphia complained that placements in those cities would cost them donors, especially commuters. Everyone, except UJA-Federation of New York, opposed *The New York Times* placement in the national edition for the same reason. Many charged UJA with favoritism, except the nine core cities of course. UJA had stepped on a beehive. A simmering competition

---

9 Marvin Lender wanted to maximize revenues and knew that that the mother lode was in soliciting major contributors. He viewed the FSI more broadly, as a way for all American Jews to connect to the cause of Soviet Jews and to Israel, and to take part in the transcendent Jewish saga of their time.

10 The general newspapers were *The New York Times, Washington Post, Boston Globe, Los Angeles Times, Chicago Tribune, Miami Herald, San Francisco Chronicle-Examiner, Philadelphia Inquirer* and *Baltimore Sun*.

among federations for the long-shrinking Annual Campaign donor base was out in the open.

Federations showed no interest in the creative strategy[11], only the packaging, which devolved on a draft of a four-page 8.5x11" booklet with motivational and informational content and a sewn-in, postage-paid response envelope addressed to Operation Exodus at UJA. Scores of federations insisted that the response envelope be addressed to them -- even though there were 189 of them and 189 press runs would be cost prohibitive. Several objected to donors remitting checks to UJA as changing policy. They did not want publication of a toll free telephone number that UJA would manage, saying readers must telephone them directly. They could not agree on charge card policy since some accepted all major cards and others just a few. They could not agree on a placement date, vitiating UJA plans to build a news media program around the ad. Some even insisted that the content be changed to urge donors to give to the Annual Campaign, even though the project had been funded for Operation Exodus. None of them wanted the name of the United Jewish Appeal to appear anywhere on the material. It became clear that federations did not want to begin another campaign season with Operation Exodus featured so prominently in their communities. They got their wish as infighting postponed the project's implementation.

UJA was forced to make numerous concessions, eventually printing 17 editions with 17 different response envelopes listing as many as 25 different federation names and addresses on the back of the envelope. Prospects who had not yet given not only had to be motivated but also were required to figure out where to send their check. One federation insisted on a completely separate printing and then refused to allow UJA to place it, causing tens of thousands of ads to be discarded[12]. There was no credit card payment mechanism, no single day placement, and no staff member assigned at most federations to coordinate with UJA and ensure fulfillment with certificates. Federations still cared about the immigrants but they simply did not want the United Jewish Appeal in their towns.

---

11 To develop a theme, Harry Heller of New York, a new-products advertising specialist, asked Jewish non-donors across the country to reflect on the immigration. They continually referred to their parents' and grandparents' dreams in coming to the United States. From this finding, an FSI was developed with the headline and theme:

Give Your Family a Place in History

Give Another Family a Place in Israel.

For each contribution of $100 UJA promised to issue two certificates in honor of a donor's immigrant relative, "who came to the United States in search of freedom and opportunity." One certificate would be presented to the donor and the other would be placed in a Book of Honor to be kept in Jerusalem.

Designed as a simple outreach marketing initiative within a comprehensive major-gifts oriented UJA Campaign Plan, the advertisement became a lightning rod that exposed the growing chasm between UJA and federations. Federations had begun to perceive UJA as a competitor and Operation Exodus as a threat to their Annual Campaigns. Federations contended that it was time to roll Operation Exodus into the Annual Campaign. However, UJA's mandate was to support the immigration and it was not ready or willing to do that. Yet.

As UJA continued to assert itself on behalf of Operation Exodus, which in turn was part of its broader battle for supremacy against federations, it discovered it was weaker than it had thought. After Stanley B. Horowitz submitted his resignation as President to the UJA Board of Trustees effective on July 1, 1991, UJA discovered that replacing him with a desirable professional was not so easy.

At a Board of Trustees Search Committee meeting with a retained international executive recruitment company, UJA said it wanted a person of vision with knowledge of the American Jewish community and a commitment to Israel and Jewish needs. The candidate would have to be a good fiscal and administrative manager who could stand up to enormous pressure and reconcile competing interests. The position, which required extensive travel, nights and weekends, would pay about $300,000 plus an array of fringe benefits. The Trustees gave as examples former Secretary of State Henry A. Kissinger, former Senator Rudy Boschwitz, former White House advisor Stuart Eizenstat and Senator Frank Lautenberg. Each was contacted; none was interested.

Malcolm Hoenlein of the Conference of Presidents, David A. Harris, Executive Director of the American Jewish Committee, and Abraham H. Foxman, National Director of the Anti-Defamation League, were invited to become candidates. However, each declined, preferring to remain in his position. Several federation executives in the Midwest were suggested, but each said his professional and family commitments precluded acceptance. Morris Sherman, UJA Vice President for Campaign who became Acting President on July 1, was approached. Sherman knew what many other candidates suspected, that the position entailed too little power against too many competing interests, and that he would have too many masters to serve. He declined. The search continued.

---

12 UJA printed 11.2 million FSIs based on signed federation agreements and most appeared in winter 1991-92. UJA had the right to place the advertisements but was concerned that some federations might retaliate, such as by reducing allocations, not participating in other UJA programs and not providing information about local donors.

The job went to Rabbi Brian L. Lurie, who had been Executive Director of the Jewish Community Federation of San Francisco, the Peninsula, Marin and Sonoma Counties since 1974. Lurie had been born in Cleveland in 1942 to a mother he said was an atheist and a father who was a Reform Jew. He once laughed that when his family held a Passover seder instead of searching for the matzah as *afikomen*, the children searched for bread. He said he was influenced to become a rabbi by the example of Abba Hillel Silver, his temple rabbi, not because of what Silver had said, which as a child Lurie did not understand, but because of Silver's brilliant oratory.

Lurie enrolled at Hebrew Union College and was visiting Israel in June 1967 when the Six Day War broke out. He was awed by the Israeli people's determination to have their country survive, and he began a lifelong devotion to Israel. He kept his sandals from that first visit, bronzed, in every office where he worked.

After ordination, he served as a rabbi at a Southern temple and then at the prestigious Congregation Emanuel-El in San Francisco. He then moved through a series of administrative posts at the San Francisco federation that led to the position of CEO. Lurie inspired the federation leadership with his eloquence, and initiated and completed many important projects. He related well to the leadership and was comfortable in the world of the wealthy, having obtained a modicum of wealth himself. He also had married into the Haas family, descendants and heirs to the Levi Strauss fortune; and at the time of his UJA interviews he was married to Caroline Fromm, whose family ran the Paul Masson vineyards and was the distributor of Christian Brothers wine and brandy. Tall, thin, well built, with blond highlights on his full head of light brown hair, he swam five miles a week to keep trim and healthy and was once described as handsome as a Greek god.

But what Lurie was best known for at the time of his UJA interview, what made his selection as President so surprising, was that he was a prominent critic of the Jewish Agency, the chief beneficiary of UJA funds. In the 1980s many federation leaders, not just Lurie, criticized the Jewish Agency for failure to fund programs donors favored, such as financing visits by American Jewish students to Israel. But Lurie went one step farther. On his recommendation, the San Francisco federation's Board of Trustees increased its allocation for overseas programs, but voted to deduct $100,000 from its remittance to UJA and forward the money instead to projects it favored in Israel. By increasing the allocation Lurie established that the deduction was not an excuse to provide more funding for domestic programs; by funding programs outside the Jewish

Agency he posed a threat to the UJA itself.

The decision rocked the UJA and, for the first time, obtained a meaningful response. Kornreich, Lender, Tauber, Stein, Pearlstone and Horowitz were among those who had tried to dissuade Lurie and his board from approving that resolution; they then endeavored to keep his idea from spreading. Shortly before he was hired, Lurie had been traveling the country, making brilliant speeches advocating that other federations divert funds from the UJA.

In announcing Lurie's appointment, UJA spoke about him as an Israelophile, a visionary and an experienced federation professional, but it did not say how the appointment reconciled Lurie as UJA critic and leader. Neither did Lurie. To the outside world, in choosing Lurie UJA appeared open minded, willing to change, eager to embrace new ideas. To insiders it implied that, in failing to attract its favored candidates to become CEO, UJA no longer possessed the prestige and influence it had enjoyed for decades.

Operation Exodus gained a boost in September 1991 from the most unlikely of developments: a political mistake by the President of the United States that unwittingly encouraged anti-Semitic expression in the United States[13]. Earlier in the year, after the Gulf War, Shamir asked Bush to endorse legislation under which the United States would guarantee repayment of $400 million Israel wanted to borrow to build housing and otherwise aid the absorption of Soviet Jews. The sum was not a grant or even a loan, only a guarantee to enable Israel to obtain a more competitive interest rate. Bush was keenly aware that Israel had suffered missile attacks from Saddam Hussein and did not respond so as to allow Bush to retain Arab countries in his military coalition. Besides, Israel had an unblemished record of repaying its debts. Bush readily agreed and the bill passed Congress easily. By mid-year Israel was faced with substantial military costs, a growing national debt, higher inflation and increasing unemployment. The projected overall cost of absorption rose to a highest-case scenario of $40 billion.

As September began, Shamir asked Bush to guarantee $10 billion in loans, but this time Bush was prepared to say no, or at least not yet. Bush's post-war Middle East strategy was to utilize America's much more formidable influence with Arab countries to achieve peace between Israel and its neighbors. In particular, Bush's goal was to convene an international conference in which

13 See J. J. Goldberg, *Jewish Power: Inside the American Jewish Establishment*, New York: Addison-Wesley, 1996, pp. xv-xxvi; Winston Pickett, "The Day Bush Shocked the Jewish Lobby," *Baltimore Jewish Times*, Sept. 25, 1992, p. 52; David Twersky, "When Jewish Leadership was Tested Under Stress," *Forward*, Nov. 18, 1994, p. 1; James G. Besser, "Bush's Anger Toward Israel," *New York Jewish Week*, Sept. 20, 1991, p. 7 and *Baltimore Jewish Times*, Sept. 20, 1991, p. 36; R. W. Apple, "Bush is Adamant in Demanding Delay on Backing for Israel Loans," *The New York Times*, Sept. 13, 1991, p.1; and Clyde Haberman, "Israel Loan Dispute Turns Ugly; Rightist Calls Bush 'Anti-Semite,'" *The New York Times*, Sept. 16, 1991, p. 1.

Arab countries and the Palestine Liberation Organization would meet publicly with Israel, for the first time, and develop a structure to achieve a just and lasting peace. This being the Middle East, it wasn't easy. Shamir felt that Bush's ground rules favored the Arabs and PLO. In particular, Bush wanted Israel to agree to halt settlement building on the West Bank -- where new immigrants rarely settled -- before any such conference could take place. Bush, who long viewed Israeli settlement activity as an obstacle to peace, viewed it also as an impediment to a peace conference.

Only a few weeks earlier, the United States considered loan guarantees and settlements as completely separate issues. On July 1 in Kennebunkport, Bush had expressed dismay that the Israelis had not yet accepted his proposals but said that a building freeze was not required for loan guarantees. "I don't think it should be a quid pro quo," he stated. On July 23, White House Press Secretary Marlin Fitzwater reiterated that position saying, "There is no direct linkage between guarantees and settlements." However, during the summer, Housing Minister Ariel Sharon increased housing starts on the West Bank from 250 to 750 a month and the Bush administration's position changed. Vice President Dan Quayle told Israeli Defense Minister Moshe Arens that loan guarantees might depend on a building freeze. Jewish leaders close to Bush and Secretary of State James Baker III warned Shamir that American dismay over settlement building jeopardized the loan guarantees. After Shamir agreed to participate in the peace conference to take place in Madrid later in the fall, Shamir included revenues from the guarantees in his budget projections, causing Shoshana Cardin, Chairman of the Presidents Conference, to admonish him, "The loan guarantees are not a sure thing." On September 4, Baker asked Congress to delay approval of the guarantees until after the peace conference.

In response, the Conference of Presidents, the American Israel Public Affairs Committee, and the National Jewish Community Relations Advisory Council held a rally at the Capitol and visits to legislators on September 12 to advocate for loan guarantees. Shortly after noon that day, Bush entered the White House briefing room, visibly angry. He pounded the podium and charged he was "up against some powerful political forces." He asserted, "I heard today there were something like a thousand lobbyists on the Hill working the other side of the question. We've got one lonely little guy down here doing it[14]."

The implication that the President of the United States was reduced to "one lonely little guy" by powerful Jews resulted in thousands of letters and telegrams

14 Goldberg astutely observed (p. xxvi), "(T)he Jews were indisputably a powerful political force. George Bush was not wrong in believing that when he convened his September 12 press conference. Bush's mistake was saying it aloud."

that poured into the White House--praising him for standing up to the Jews. Talk radio discussions lambasted the Jews for controlling the government, the banks, the news media and for not placing America first. Even American Jews who rarely paid attention to Jewish issues or Israel were shocked by the diatribes that filled offices, faculty lounges and factory lunchrooms.

The President was stunned by the response and shaken after Cardin told him bluntly to his face that regardless of his intentions his remarks gave comfort to anti-Semites. Bush apologized on September 17 for his poor word choice, in a then-famous letter that began, "Dear Shoshana," and said he meant no offense. Every major American Jewish leader who knew Bush recognized the sincerity of his letter and none doubted it was only poor word choice in a heated moment. After all, Bush had provided substantial aid to Israel, exceptional support for Soviet Jews and decisive intervention that saved thousands of imperiled Jews in Operation Moses and Operation Solomon. Nevertheless, his words remained imprinted on the minds of Jews and Bush, who had won only 27 percent of the Jewish vote when he was elected President, was en route to eleven percent in his reelection bid the next year. For American Jews there was little they could do other than vote and vent. And give to Operation Exodus.

The Peace Conference opened in Madrid on October 30 and directly led to the Oslo process and the Oslo Accords. A year after the Madrid Conference, Yitzhak Rabin defeated Shamir to become Prime Minister on a platform to end new settlements. The United States finally guaranteed the loans.

Meanwhile, American Jews at the time may have accomplished more than just winning support to lessen Israel's debt. This writer later asked President George H. W. Bush in writing whether, on reflection, the immigration of Soviet Jews through Operation Exodus helped pressure Arab countries and the PLO to agree to meet Israel publicly face-to-face in Madrid. "In particular," I wrote, "did fears that many would settle on the West Bank and create an insurmountable obstacle to a Palestinian State help you obtain their participation at the Madrid Conference?" President Bush answered:

> I believe this decision on their part was based largely on respect for the United States and confidence in the U.S. role in promoting peace. But it is also possible that Arab and Palestinian concern that increased Jewish immigration to Israel would translate over time into increased Israeli settlement activity might have contributed to their decision to attend Madrid and negotiate directly with Israel.

In 1991, Operation Exodus raised $155.4 million, bringing the two-year total to $658.8 million. Meanwhile, the aging 1991 Annual Campaign raised $712 million by year's end compared to $688 million a year earlier. The 1992 Annual Campaign, already underway, stood at $238 million compared to the previous Annual Campaign's $217 million at that point a year earlier. These were huge sums but neither Annual Campaign was expected to exceed the Annual Campaign record of $760 million set just before Operation Exodus, let alone cover inflation and increased costs. The federation drumbeat to roll Operation Exodus into the Annual Campaign grew louder.

In 1991, 147,673 Soviet Jewish immigrants arrived in Israel for a two-year total of 332,354 that brought about an 8.3 percent increase in the country's Jewish population. A third of a million had arrived and, while the rate per year declined since 1990, two thirds of a million more were expected in the remainder of the decade.

If Operation Exodus planners could have had their wish for the world at the end of 1991 when the Campaign began, as free men and women, Americans, democrats and idealists, it might have been this: the collapse of the Soviet Union. Better yet, the fall of the Soviet Union without war or the loss of American lives. Maybe Gorbachev just declaring the whole empire dead and the USSR quietly passing into history. They got what they would have wished for -- but not what they expected.

Gorbachev couldn't move fast enough, in 1991 as earlier, to get ahead of the independence movements. He signed the Strategic Arms Reduction Treaty (START) with the United States to mutually reduce nuclear weapons by 30 percent; this emphasized he had shifted from guns to butter. He dissolved the Warsaw Pact military alliance, which demonstrated the end of foreign entanglements, so he could devote attention to domestic improvements. He abolished censorship and approved private ownership of land to give immense credibility to glasnost and perestroika. The right wing coup against him in August failed but only because of public outrage and a lack of military support; it did not stop the Soviet Union from unraveling. Estonia and Latvia declared independence during Gorbachev's four-day incarceration; and Moldova, Azerbaijan and Uzbekistan did so the next week. Moving faster than Gorbachev, the Supreme Soviet suspended Communist Party activities, in effect dissolving the Party, and the State Council abolished the KGB in the fall. The last republics declared independence by November as Gorbachev had no legions willing to put the movements down. On December 25 Gorbachev resigned as President and the Soviet Union (1917-1991) ceased to exist.

The collapse and fall of the Soviet Union was a paradigm "devoutly to be wish'd" and rightfully applauded by freedom lovers the world over. UJA and federation leaders rejoiced with millions of others. But, it turned out, the death of the Soviet Union was a body blow to Operation Exodus. The removal of the awesome specter of Soviet repression stripped the immigrants of their aura as valiant symbols of Jewish survival. The destruction of the terrifying power of the evil empire eliminated fears of a Jewish catastrophe in the years after the horrors of the Holocaust. The incredible end of the Soviet Union robbed the movement of its critical sense of urgency and deprived the Campaign of an identifiable enemy from whom Jews needed rescue.

It looked, in a flash, as if the Jews seeking to leave the former Soviet Union were merely economic migrants whose needs, while valid, were no more compelling than those of other Jews at home or abroad. But that was not the case at all. New dangers lurked, unleashed by the obliteration of Soviet power. On December 31, 1991 Lender, Tauber and Pearlstone received a fax from Mendel Kaplan at the Jewish Agency that the year's last planeful of Jews touched down at Ben Gurion Airport with 127 Tajikistani Jews aboard. The Jews were happy to be out but warned that the remaining Tajikistani Jews were in harm's way. The Soviet Union was dead for less than a week but bands of thugs from Pamyat and other groups roamed the countryside. In the gap between the departure of Soviet troops and establishment of sufficient policing authority, they taunted and beat up Jews. Kaplan said that nearly all 11,600 Jews in Tajikistan had applied to leave and that no one knew how the vacuum would be filled after the fall of the Soviet colossus. He said Jews lived in fear in other rural republics too. UJA had no choice but to keep Operation Exodus going. The question was: could it persuade American Jews to keep giving?

CHAPTER NINE
The Orange Squeezers

So this thin, scrawny businessman traveling through town stops off for dinner at a tavern and takes a seat at the bar when this husky oaf sits down on the stool next to him.

The big guy takes out an orange, cuts a small opening on the top, places it on the bar and says, "I bet you $100 that I can squeeze more juice out of this orange than you can." Then he snarls menacingly, "And you better take my bet."

The strong man picks up the orange first and squeezes it, grinning, as the bar's patrons, drinks in hand, gather 'round. A few ounces drip into an empty pretzel bowl. He squeezes some more, getting a little red in the face. After nothing else oozes out, he drops the shriveled orange on the bar. "Your turn," he sneers.

The scrawny man picks up the orange and, with hardly a strain, squeezes out several ounces. Then he squeezes out even more.

"What the---? I can't believe it!" the cowed bully exclaims dumbfoundedly. What are you? A weightlifter? An athlete? A body builder?"

"None of the above," the businessman answers matter-of-factly. "I'm a fundraiser for the United Jewish Appeal."

Joel David Tauber was born in Detroit on June 28, 1935, as Congress debated whether to enact Social Security, Huey Long filibustered against New Deal socialism, and President Franklin D. Roosevelt moved ahead with plans to pack the Supreme Court. Joel's father Benjamin was a lawyer and able to support his family, as well as aid neighbors, during the Depression. "We weren't rich but we ate well," Joel remembered in one of several interviews for this book.

Joel's father was the soft one, from whom he learned compassion. His mother Anne was strong and instilled in him his sense of commitment, continually summoning him to make something of himself.

Joel attended Hebrew school in the afternoons ("I hated it, everybody hated it, everybody who ever attended Hebrew school hated it"). But somehow despite his daydreaming about playing ball with his friends instead of being in Hebrew school, he came to understand that he was Jewish and that he was connected to other Jews even if they had lived long ago or were far away.

His neighborhood was comprised mainly of Jewish immigrants who formed an extended family among themselves, helping and socializing with one another, a microcosm of the worldwide Jewish family he would someday serve. Joel's grandparents, Sylvia and Reuven Merliss and Eva and Chaim Tauber, lived nearby. Turn of the century immigrants, his grandparents regaled the boy in his earliest youth with stories of family closeness and joy in the old country. Someday his European relatives would come to Detroit too, he was told, where their lives would be easier. The Merlisses were from Kiev, Ukraine, not far from an obscure ravine that would become notorious decades later: Babi Yar. The Taubers were from Frishnaplalya, Poland, near the Russian border, soon to be overrun by the invading Nazis. Nary a word of concern was uttered in his presence when his grandparents stopped receiving letters from the European relatives as the Holocaust unfolded.

After the war, Joel's grandparents' mood changed. They would send him out of the room to talk heatedly in Yiddish, plaintively, angrily, disbelievingly, about what they were discovering had happened in Europe. When he went to the movies with them a hand would descend in front of his face as Movietone News preceded the feature film with concentration camp footage. His grandparents devoted every possible moment to finding relatives who had survived the Holocaust, and brought to Detroit the few who did. Half a century later, sipping a pina colada on a gorgeous afternoon in an outdoor café on Ocean Drive in Miami Beach, a few yards from his luxury condominium, tears came to his eyes when he recalled his grandparents' anguish.

Joel excelled in high school, where he won letters for his athletic prowess, and he obtained a bachelor's degree, a law degree and a Master's in Business Administration degree from the University of Michigan, all before he was 26. "My interest in those years was in making money," he recalled. "I learned from the respect my grandparents had for anyone who had sound academic credentials that that was a good way for me to proceed. I set out with five priorities: family first; business and career second; physical fitness, because my father died in his

50s, third; philanthropy, which I had learned from my family and neighbors, fourth; and social, fifth. Although the time I could give to each of them varied, I kept to those priorities all my life."

In 1960, Tauber married Shelby Keywell, a hometown girl whose father, Barney Keywell, was in the scrap metal business. Barney loved Joel like a son and asked him if he wanted to run another business he was thinking of buying. Joel discussed this with Shelby and they agreed it was a good idea. They also agreed, as did Barney, that any business relationships between Barney and Joel would be separate from family relationships. "My father-in-law had a harsh exterior," Tauber recalled. "He was a rough-and-tumble businessman in a rough-and-tumble business. I knew nothing about it. But he gave me my head. He let me see what I could do. He permitted me to make mistakes and learn. He gave me the guidance I needed."

The business earned a profit so together they bought others. Each newly-acquired company had been doing poorly but was in metals, a business they knew. Keywell and Tauber invited the best local managers to stay on and buy into the new company, which gave them loyal and competent on-site overseers and enabled them to expand as absentee owners. They grew rapidly across the country, into middle-sized and small towns, and abroad. "We bought weak companies related to our core scrap metal business and turned them around quickly," said Tauber, who later bought Barney's interests. "We branched out quickly but near the business we knew. Our strategy was acquisitions, leveraged buyouts and debt and it paid off beautifully."

In Detroit the company began by selling nuts and bolts to automobile manufacturers. Soon it was purchasing the steel shaved off as cars and trucks were produced, selling it as scrap to reprocessing mills. It became the world's largest supplier of stainless steel scrap and high-temperature-alloy scrap for jet airplane engines. Then it became the sole supplier of nuts and bolts to Sears and K-Mart, which retailed them in millions of tiny plastic packets.

Meanwhile, as government and consumers demanded lighter and more fuel efficient vehicles, Tauber heeded the notorious advice of Mr. Robinson to Benjamin Braddock in "The Graduate," and moved into plastics. He became a major automobile plastics supplier. Compaq and Cisco bought his plastics to make its computers, Nokia its cell phones, Sanford its pens and ChapStick its lip balm.

Yet, success did not buy happiness and as the business took off around 1980 Joel and Shelby divorced. "I was miserably unhappy," he recalled. "That was the worst period of my life." His confidence shaken, he went to the Jewish

Federation of Metropolitan Detroit, where he was Campaign Chairman, and said that if they did not want a divorced man in that position, he was willing to resign. Fundraisers through and through, they said, "No way. The campaign under you is up."

Tauber married Shelley Chicurel of Detroit in 1984 and turned 50 the next year, taking stock of where he had been at 25 and what he wanted at 75. "I could have kept putting zeroes after the numbers on the balance sheet, but I felt there was no end to that," he reflected. "I wanted time with Shelley and the children. I wanted to spend more time giving back. I felt I had enough money and had to focus more on helping others. My five priorities never changed, but it was time to deemphasize the business and let the others flourish."

He became Treasurer of CJF and a UJA trustee, the rare person who rose high at both organizations, which had opposite institutional personalities. He did so not only because he donated sizeable sums, but also because both organizations prized his ability to articulate solutions and build coalitions, not easy in boards comprised of movers and shakers. He was a natural at CJF, which valued his experience in achieving national results from an amalgam of far flung, independent operations; and at UJA, which appreciated his decisiveness and passion.

Marvin Lender was one of the greatest UJA National Chairmen of all time and a tough act to follow. Tauber welcomed the challenge. The UJA Board of Trustees unanimously elected Tauber as UJA National Chairman on December 16, 1991, to take office on May 19, 1992.

It was Joel Tauber's job to lead the team that would squeeze the shriveled orange dry.

In his office in Southfield, Michigan, Tauber looked back over the faxes he had been receiving from UJA and the Jewish Agency. It was January 1992, in the first days after the fall of the Soviet Union, but there was nothing of the jubilation he hoped to see. A week earlier, on January 1, 1992, the Russian Post Office instituted new regulations that forbade Russians from delivering packages received from Israel: more harrassment. More worrisome, there were sporadic reports that the absence of Soviet power in the republics was giving way to lawlessness. The people had thrown off the yoke of Communist oppression but did not have any more to eat; no one seemed to have a road map of where to go to solve the massive problems that undid the Soviet colossus. Well, almost no one. Vladimir Zhirinovsky, who said the Jews were responsible for all the problems, dominated the right wing and announced as the year began that he would run for President of Russia. The people were frustrated and no one was about to stop the search for scapegoats. Anti-Semitic incidents were scattered but they were occurring in every republic.

Tauber read a copy of a UJA news release, "JDC to Begin Emergency Food Shipments to Former USSR," that said in part:

New York, Jan. 6--The American Jewish Joint Distribution Committee will begin shipments in the next several days of the first of thousands of food packages to Jews in the former Soviet Union in an emergency effort to avoid Jewish starvation in the midst of growing economic disarray.

The action follows months of meticulous planning in three countries to avert a calamity.

The first shipments, ready for departure, consist of 20,000 food packages, most containing about 22 pounds of food and distilled food products from a variety of food groups and each able to feed a family for weeks. The other packages, also providing for the full range of nutritional needs, contain over five pounds each.

All the food is coming from Israel where it is being produced and where, upon payment, funds from JDC pass directly into the Jewish State.

The food will be brought to storage centers in Moscow, St. Petersburg, Odessa and Kiev, from which it will be distributed to Jews, and to others, in what is now known as the Commonwealth of Independent States. JDC has established an infrastructure to store food in those four cities, and dispatched 14 Israelis, who had experience in distribution systems in the Soviet Union, to oversee the operation.

JDC is pursuing plans to establish storage facilities quickly in Ekatarinburg and Tashkent, to provide for wider geographical distribution, and will expand its storage network further.

JDC pre-tested its distribution system by providing food package deliveries, including to 4,000 in Moscow and 3,000 in St. Petersburg, known as Leningrad during most of the Communist regime.

JDC will continue its policy of aiding neighbors of Jews, for humanitarian reasons and to give neighbors a vested interest so as not to be jealous of local Jews and harm them.

"We are doing everything we can, but the scope of the challenge is breathtaking," said Sylvia Hassenfeld, JDC President. "There are many thousands of Jews who depend on our help to survive the wretched winter."

Tauber felt like going to Russia and unloading the food packages himself, but he knew he would be more effective planning his National Chairmanship. Sometimes as incoming UJA National Chairman he felt very powerful, at times like this weak indeed. He needed a break.

Everyone was exhausted, the donors, the fundraisers in federations, even the UJA. That was nothing compared to what the immigrants and immigrant hope-to-be's were going through, of course, or even the Jewish Agency and Joint Distribution Committee agents spread across the former Soviet empire seeking to keep the aliyah going, seeking to keep the people fed and clothed. Or the Israelis who faced the daunting task of absorbing the third of a million who had arrived and the hundreds of thousands expected to arrive.

He took out his copy of the *Detroit Free Press*, which he had glanced at over his muffin and coffee an hour earlier, which spoke of continuing economic difficulty in his hometown. He knew the automobile industry and that a local economic recovery was not yet in sight. He glanced through the *Wall Street Journal*. A national economic recovery was not in sight either. Now he needed some emotional support.

He and Marvin Lender had grown close to each other in recent months, brought together by their commitment to the cause of Jewish destiny, and he punched Lender's number into his telephone speed system. Tauber shared his concerns and Lender said the right things. Then Tauber said with a laugh, "Let's trade places. I'll take the past two years. You keep the operation going until who knows when." Lender laughed too. "No deal," Lender replied. "You thought I was nuts to set the goal at $420 million. Now you keep it going. We spotted you 650."

Tauber returned to his faxes and found a copy of a memorandum from Harold Cohen, UJA Assistant Vice President overseeing UJA regions, to Morris Sherman, Campaign Vice President, that Sherman had sent him marked FYI. It said:

There is genuine question on the part of a number of federations whether UJA is serious about continuing OE. They feel it is over, or should be. Our regional people, lay and professional, are hearing this from all over, north, south, east and west, major, intermediate and small federations and even in the non-federated communities.

Tauber had been in consultation with others on whom to appoint to positions and telephoned Richard Pearlstone, whose rise at UJA during Operation Exodus would bring him the next open seat on the UJA Board of Trustees. "Richie, I need you to oversee the regions in the next two years," Tauber said. "The situation looks like it is going to be bad for the Jews in the Former Soviet Union. We have to get them out as you know. As you also know, we need to continue to build our regional operations to get federations and groups of federations on board for funding it."

"I also know a thankless job when I see it," Pearlstone said with a chuckle. "This will give me more opportunity to bring the UJA message to federations so that, when I get there, they can tell me the message they want me to bring back to UJA."

"We'll restructure the regions and build on what we have," Tauber said. "Are you in for it?"

"Of course," Pearlstone said. "When do I start?"

"Officially in May when I am installed. Unofficially, yesterday."

They discussed candidates for chairmen of the four UJA regions under Pearlstone and agreed to ask Rani Garfinkle for the Northeast, Richard Spiegel for the Midwest, Donald Hess for the South and Shearn Platt for the West. Tauber informed Pearlstone he was inviting those who had served on the Campaign Executive Committee under Lender to continue to do so and suggested that Garfinkle, Spiegel, Hess and Platt would be valuable members as well. Pearlstone agreed and Tauber added the four to the Committee. Tauber then telephoned Henry Taub, the Automatic Data Processing co-founder who participated at the Breakfast of Champions, and had served as President of United Israel Appeal, and invited him to join the Committee. Next he invited Richard Wexler of Chicago, a campaign veteran who had served as Chairman of the National Conference on Soviet Jewry, to join. All accepted.

In the months prior to his installation as National Chairman, Tauber continued to consult, invite people to serve in his administration and prepare to lead the national campaigns. He tried to keep his hand in with his business, but that was the first thing to go. His new business was fundraising. His main challenges as a figure in UJA history were to sustain a gallant campaign that had been lifted then dropped flat by world events, follow the wildly popular Marvin Lender and carve out his own administration after he had been closely associated with Lender's. Of course, the core challenge was to be effective in the programs and methods where UJA had long been legendary: the world events did not raise the funds, the fundraisers did, capitalizing on those events. But now many wanted the campaign to be over. It gave him pause. Unlike a brilliant military maneuver, or a third baseman's catch of a ball that seemed likely to go down the line, fundraising looked easy. But it wasn't, even for the UJA. UJA was in a class by itself, but the fundraising was not easy. Tauber faced a daunting challenge.

The early months of the calendar year were quiet in Jewish major gifts fundraising. Jews usually gave around Rosh Hashanah and Yom Kippur and again around Chanukah when they were also beseeched to pay any unfulfilled pledges before the tax year ended. Fundraisers allowed them to hibernate until Passover when they reminded them, whatever was happening in the world, that this year was just like the ancient quest for Jewish freedom all over again. The early months of the year were a time for broadening the donor base through general community fundraising, retaining and upgrading major gifts prospects who had not given within the year, and holding events that solidified support.

The main public program was Super Sunday, what most people thought of as "the campaign," but which UJA and federations viewed as the finish, after most donors of means had contributed. Super Sunday gifts mainly came in pledges of $10, $18, $25 and, if the campaign was lucky, $100. UJA provided federations with pithy, persuasive scripts that enabled neophyte solicitors to open and close and respond succinctly with carefully thought out answers to common questions. It produced colorful posters that federations displayed at JCCs and other centers, and newspaper advertisement designs that encouraged donors to give when telephoned. But UJA's mandate was national, to raise major gifts; Super Sunday was mainly a federation program.

Federations loved Super Sunday and approached it with gusto. Super Sunday made the federations the center of local Jewish attention, attracted volunteers who gave more themselves and often stayed on for additional volunteer activities, and was inexpensive to mount. Volunteers found fundraising refreshing, became passionate advocates of the cause and made news media coverage buoyant with testimonies of colorful support. The federations shined. Super Sunday raised $25 million overall that winter, including a few million dollars for Operation Exodus.

At UJA, which gave only perfunctory support to Super Sunday, these months were the season of assessment, planning, budgeting, staff personnel changes and lay transition. Lender was still in charge of the campaign and would remain so until May. In the norms of UJA, though, once a National Chairman was elected, nothing happened without his consent. This loss of influence and attention for the outgoing Chairman was always painful. UJA accompanied the transition by glorious paeans to him, including a video tribute and gala dinner in a huge hotel ballroom. These events eased him from the campaign epicenter. UJA had, seemingly effortlessly, focused the news media spotlight on him for two years and gingerly began to redirect it to his successor. It was a sensitive time for high powered volunteers at the apex. But Lender and Tauber had been through the campaign wars together and had become close personal friends. The transition from Lender to Tauber was smooth, like spreading butter on a freshly toasted bagel.

Federations played the main role in broadening the base in the opening months of the year, but UJA provided strategic enhancements. For example, UJA secured speakers who could attract more donors and higher gifts. When the Palm Beach federation thought it could attract no more than 50 prospects to a Young Business and Professionals cocktail hour for $1,000 donors to the Annual Campaign and $200 donors to Operation Exodus, it turned to UJA. UJA asked Norman Braman, owner of the Philadelphia Eagles, to make the campaign pitch and remain afterwards to "talk football." Braman agreed and 125 donors appeared, giving gifts averaging $4,000 for the Annual Campaign and $1,000 to Operation Exodus. Many donors were new to the campaigns and the federation would contact them for future gifts.

At UJA itself, Women's Campaign and Young Leadership were prominent sponsors of events. UJA Women's Division took on the name Women's Campaign during the course of Operation Exodus, to demonstrate its independent value and its focus on fundraising rather than holding teas, a caricature that never applied to UJA women anyway. It wasn't that the women were trying to seem independent and equally valuable -- *they were.* Increasingly infused with women who grew up in the feminist movement, built their own businesses and professional practices and were interested in benefiting Jews worldwide, Women's Campaign raised $200 million a year for Operation Exodus and the Annual Campaign. Women not only earned their own money. They also influenced where their husbands' gifts were given, and they stood to inherit (and dispense from) family fortunes. By all projections, billions of dollars would be in the hands of thousands of Jewish women before long. The UJA women knew better than did the UJA men how to attract women to events, how to persuade them to give generously and how to encourage them to be active.

Men mainly ran the UJA, like other organizations, but they weren't threatened by UJA women's power. They loved it. The more money Women's Campaign raised, the happier the men were.

UJA Women's Campaign held parlor meetings to build its Lion of Judah Sapphire ($18,000) and Ruby ($10,000) programs in Palm Beach, respectively on February 5 and March 11. After upscale programming, riveting accounts by Soviet and Ethiopian Jews of how they had been rescued, and a donation pitch by Yona Goldberg, UJA Women's Campaign Chairman, the women announced their pledges. Women's Campaign adhered to the honored tradition of Jewish life, that largest donations were announced first, to float and keep floating the highest possible sums in front of those on the borderline, say between $15,000 and $18,000, or $8,000 and $10,000. Many women spoke about how good they felt achieving a higher gifts level than they had planned. Ninety five Sapphire club members and 77 Ruby members gave a total of $671,500 to Operation Exodus in addition to a combined $4.6 million to the Annual Campaign.[1] Heidi Damsky, Yona Goldberg, Sylvia Hassenfeld, Doreen Hermelin, Ronne Hess, Roberta Holland, Bobi Klotz, Helaine Lender, Harriet Sloane, Carole Solomon, Susan Stern, Harriet Zimmerman and Lois Zoller recruited, pre-solicited and closed gifts. Many of them remained in Palm Beach to close gifts that built or renewed membership in the Emerald ($25,000) club and recruit others to general ($5,000) Lion of Judah membership. They presented new members with an attractive gold Lion of Judah pin and saw to it that those who gave $10,000, $18,000 and $25,000 sported a ruby, sapphire or emerald, respectively, in the Lion's eye. Lion of Judah was a wildly successful program that attracted thousands of women who cared deeply about Israel and Jewish life and who wanted to be with women like themselves and mingle with women they admired. Of course, this being the UJA, "membership" would expire if not renewed annually.

The Seventh Annual United Jewish Appeal Young Leadership Conference, held at the Washington Hilton from March 15 to 17, attracted 2,500 committed Jews in their 30s and early 40s eager to learn more about how to build Jewish life and willing to contribute financially. The participants were similar to those at previous Conferences except that fewer remembered or were old enough to appreciate Israel's struggles for survival in the Six Day War in 1967 and the Yom Kippur War in 1973, and almost all were born after the Holocaust and Israel's War of Independence in 1948. What brought them together was a shared sense

---

1 Sixteen women at the Sapphire event advanced to the $18,000 level and ten to $25,000 as donors gave a total of $280,000 more than they had given previously. Eighteen women reached Ruby status as donors gave $123,000 more than they did previously.

of Jewish destiny.

Plenaries introduced broad issues, like Israel's struggles, and small group sessions followed on how to help by activism, lobbying or fundraising. Shoshana Cardin delivered a rousing Opening Plenary keynote address, emphasizing the dangers that exist for Israel and Jews, and noting that funding the aliyah was an important demonstration of support. Malcolm Hoenlein gave a brilliant and prescient speech in which he meticulously documented that Islamic fundamentalism was gaining a foothold in the West, and warned that by the end of the decade it would pose a threat to Europe and America itself. Professor Deborah Lipstadt of Emory University spoke on persistent anti-Semitism, writer Letty Cottin Pogrebin on Jewish feminism, Rabbi Irwin Kula of the Center for Leadership and Learning (CLAL) on beginning adult Jewish learning, Rabbi Jacob Rubenstein of UJA's Rabbinic Cabinet on achieving harmony among Jews, journalist Yosef Abramowitz on the value of activism, Andrea Levin of Camera on improving Israel's image in the news media, photojournalist Edward Serotta on contemporary Jewish life in Eastern and Central Europe, Mark Talisman of CJF's Washington office on pending legislation, Rabbi David Saperstein of the Union of American Hebrew Congregations on repairing the world and, of course, Marvin Lender, Joel Tauber and Brian Lurie on the material benefit of giving to Operation Exodus and other campaigns. Young Leadership Cabinet Chairs Susan Stern and Stuart Rossman, Conference Chairs Elizabeth Schrayer and Dr. Joel Schindler, and incoming Cabinet Chairs Michelle Rosen and Jerry Benjamin played key roles.[2]

Whereas Marina Furman, the petite young Jewish wife and mother who struggled to leave the Soviet Union, had been the main Conference attraction in 1990, the star in 1992 was former Israeli Prime Minister Yitzhak Rabin, hoping to make a comeback.

Rabin's day began in Montreal when an aide awakened him at 5 a.m. on March 17 for the brief ride to Montreal International Airport. There he was greeted by Joel Schindler and they boarded a small private aircraft for the flight to Dulles International Airport. I greeted him at Dulles and the three of us, accompanied by a security guard and a photographer, left for nearby Washington as daylight unfolded in northern Virginia.

Rabin was in a good mood. In the limousine, he reached into his rear

---

2 Plenary and workshop Chairs included Robert Max (Skip) Schrayer of Chicago; Jodi Schwartz and Eric Zahler of New York; Dr. Robert Meth of Los Angeles; Joel Beren of Toledo; Emily Zimmern of Charlotte; Ralph Grunewald of Washington, D.C.; Dr. Owen Perlman of Ann Arbor; Attorney General Lee Fisher of Ohio; Judge Amy Dean of Miami; Judy Harris of Minneapolis; Stanford Solomon of Tampa; Michael Lebovitz of Chattanooga; Tom Falik and Lauren Friedman of Houston; Lewis Norry of Rochester and Heidi Damsky of Birmingham.

pants pocket for his wallet, couldn't find it immediately, became momentarily alarmed then quickly checked his other pockets and found it in his front pants pocket. "You must have learned that traveling on Metros in European cities," I said. "Never keep your wallet in your back pocket." Rabin laughed.

"The Democratic Presidential primaries in Illinois and Michigan take place tonight," I said. "Have you been following the primaries?"

"A little," answered Rabin. "And the man from Massachusetts?"

"Maybe his last chance," I said. "Paul Tsongas."

"Tsonnngas? Tsonnngas?" he asked impishly. "What kind of a name is *Tsongas?"*

"Greek," I answered. "Clinton could have the field to himself in a few hours."

"Cleenton? Cleenton?" he asked, chuckling at his own rhetorical flourish. "What kind of a name is *Cleenton?"*

There was a pause. As I looked at him seated next to me, and he looked out the window moving deeply into thought, I thought he hadn't changed from the thin, wiry figure he had been on July 4, 1976, when he was Prime Minister and announced that over 100 hostages had been rescued from Palestinian terrorists at Entebbe.

Then he said out of the blue, "You know, he has done nothing for peace as Prime Minister. Nothing. So many opportunities ignored. So many chances lost. How much longer can this fighting go on?" He launched into a critique of Shamir, faulting him for failing to take advantage of openings to the Palestine Liberation Organization when they appeared. The Israeli national elections were fewer than 100 days away but there was no Israeli voter within earshot except his security guard. He seemed pent up and delivered an impromptu brief campaign speech.

About 50 Conference participants greeted him with enthusiastic applause at the Washington Hilton's side entrance as the vehicle drew up and he emerged.

"That's nice," I said, stepping out too.

"Sure you think it's nice—you arranged it," he laughed, his mood jovial again.

The entrance was under a steel carport and looked as it did when President Reagan passed through from his speech to the Young Leadership Conference in 1984, but the carport had not been erected when Reagan emerged from another organization's event there in 1981 and was shot on the spot. Rabin's security consisted of one person; no one expected him to be shot.

Rabin spent the morning in his suite exercising, resting and reviewing his speech. The American Jews spent the morning on Capitol Hill, meeting with

Members of Congress to promote Israeli and American Jewish interests. No one complained any more about a thousand lobbyists on the Hill.

At 1:15 p.m., standing outside the entrance doors to the Grand Ballroom we could hear the excitement growing inside, and it burst forth as Jerry Benjamin of Milwaukee introduced Rabin as "the next Prime Minister of Israel." Rabin worked his way through the crowd as hundreds encircled him, reaching over one another to shake his hand. He smiled and seemed to enjoy it. He took his seat on stage, stood to acknowledge the continuing applause, sat down again, rose again, signaled that was enough, and was reintroduced by Benjamin.

Speaking from notes, Rabin delivered a 45 minute address that described opportunities for peace he said were lost by the Shamir government, criticized settlement building in the West Bank and Gaza and stated that land had to be ceded to Palestinians to achieve peace. The longtime general interlaced his speech with references to his military career and called for courage in pursuit of peace. The news media in the audience included the Washington-based Israeli journalists from Israel TV, Israel Radio, *Yediot Achronot*, *Maariv*, *Haaretz* and the *Jerusalem Post*, his news media links to voters back home.

Rabin emphasized that Operation Exodus was continuing. "We are still in that moment in history," he said. "You should feel it is a privilege to help pay for the aliyah. Four hundred thousand into Israel in two years. Maybe bring a million Jews to Israel," he declared, to thunderous applause.

"I don't remember how many thousands I gave," Jerry Benjamin beamed in an interview a decade later. "But I do remember feeling wonderful writing the check."

Joel Tauber was fundraising in Kansas City, Missouri when Elizabeth Schrayer, a Conference Co-Chair, telephoned him with the final day's report. "Good," Tauber said. "I could feel the enthusiasm in the ballroom when I spoke there two days ago. As far as I am concerned, Operation Exodus is just beginning."

Of course, he knew it wasn't. In fact, pre-registration was insufficient for the upcoming biannual UJA National Conference, where Tauber wanted to gather the far-flung leadership, rejuvenate them, and host meetings to assure effective implementation of fundraising programs. The leaders had been to a good number of conferences and gatherings already and were worn out. The main draw, albeit a good one, was that the torch would be passed from Lender to Tauber. Many wanted to be present to honor Lender and celebrate his and their two years of Operation Exodus achievement. Still, UJA was never satisfied unless every meeting room was filled. Registration planning took a hit when Lender telephoned Tauber later that week to say that Prime Minister Shamir had declined UJA's invitation to address the National Conference, citing domestic responsibilities; what Shamir meant was that the Israeli national elections were just five weeks later and that he and Likud were facing a stiff challenge from Rabin and Labor.[3] Tauber came up with the idea of honoring Max Fisher, who had given nearly $30 million to UJA and federation over the years. That secured the enrollment.

The UJA National Conference took place in the Grand Ballroom of the Grand Hyatt Hotel in New York City from May 17 to 19 with two social centerpieces. One was "A Gala Dinner Dance in Honor of Marvin Lender," an evening of tribute to a National Chairman who had achieved enormous popularity because of his vision and campaign leadership as well as his deep humility and arrestingly warm persona. A UJA video, "Marvin," featured Lender conferring with heads of state, visiting Jews in many countries and raising funds at events across America. Formal footage showed Lender as an informed, hands on and effective leader on the world Jewish stage, while family home-movie segments lightened the mood and snippets of cinema verité footage glimpsed him laughing at his own foibles. Viewing himself on the huge Grand Ballroom screens, Lender wept as he saw himself stimulating a caucus with the words, "We are going to be written in the history books as a generation of Jews who played a great role in Jewish redemption." Lender ascended the stage afterwards to thunderous applause. He credited others for the achievements. Then he looked up from his prepared script and said, "I do not expect ever again to have such an opportunity to help as many people. It was my moment in Jewish history too, and I will treasure it forever."

"A UJA Salute to Max Fisher," was more formal but equally warm as the evening's Co-Chairmen, Charles Bronfman, Lester Crown and Leslie Wexner, thanked Fisher for his enormous generosity and applauded his wisdom. President Bush praised Fisher in a video tribute, and laudatory letters were read from former President Gerald R. Ford and former Secretaries of State George P. Shultz and Henry A. Kissinger. Fisher and his wife Marjorie, no strangers to accolades, were deeply moved. Jane Sherman spoke and said her parents inspired their entire family to act with nobility.

In Conference business meetings, the Prime Minister's Council held a

---

3 This writer had proposed the previous fall that Mikhail Gorbachev, who was then Premier of the Soviet Union, be invited to address the Conference. The idea was that, if Gorbachev did this, it would fill the Conference to capacity; attract enormous, and free, news coverage; and likely lead to an important statement on the future of Soviet Jewry. Many UJA leaders embraced the idea enthusiastically but others fretted it was too bold.

luncheon at Tavern on the Green where H. Irwin Levy of Palm Beach, the event chairman, recruited participants to join him on the next Prime Minister's Mission. Sumner Feldberg of Boston, the TJX Chairman, led a session preparing for the International Leadership Reunion. Richard Wexler chaired the President's Mission planning session. Thomas Green chaired the Major Gifts Committee that sought to enhance upward mobility in giving. Yona Goldberg, Carole Solomon and Roberta Holland led the honing of Women's Campaign plans. Robyn Loup of Denver and Valerie Salambier of New York furthered development of the Women of Distinction. Elaine Berke of Encino, California and Sandra Cahn of New York pursued plans to attract new donors through the Business and Professional Women's Council. Rabbis Michael Zedek and Jacob Rubenstein of the UJA Rabbinic Cabinet showed how Jewish learning could add dimensions to and enhance UJA campaigns. Betty Kane of Cherry Hill, New Jersey and Sanford Hollander provided solicitation training. Federation Campaign Chairmen and Campaign Directors shared ideas. Regional planning took place under Richard Pearlstone. Robert Loup hosted an ideas session among past UJA National Chairmen Senator Frank Lautenberg, Irwin Field, Herschel Blumberg, Alex Grass, Martin Stein, Morton Kornreich and Marvin Lender.

In plenary sessions, Professor Alan Dershowitz of Harvard said Israeli Arabs enjoyed more rights and freedoms than Arabs did in Arab countries. Professor Ruth Wisse of McGill University said Jewish knowledge and Jewish activism were crucial to Jewish survival. Professor Gary Tobin of Brandeis University spoke on trends in American Jewish philanthropy. Tauber, Lender, Mendel Kaplan and Sylvia Hassenfeld emphasized the importance of giving. Alan Ades of New Bedford presented the Pinchas Sapir Awards for campaign achievement to the Chicago, Cincinnati, Tulsa and Fort Wayne and Quad Cities federations. Orot Hashchuna, an Israeli teenage song and dance troupe, entertained; it was so popular UJA brought it back weeks later on a fundraising tour.

At a joint convocation of the UJA Board of Trustees and National Officers Lender became UJA President and Tauber became National Chairman. In brief remarks, Tauber promised to do his best and encouraged others to do the same. UJA had saluted its leaders, strengthened its teams, advanced its programs, and reinforced its messages to the campaign faithful. Fundraising was not the main purpose but, since this was a UJA event, millions were raised.

In early June, while the world watched on television in horror as yet another war engulfed civilians, the Joint Distribution Committee rescued 500 Jews and their neighbors from chaos and gunfire in crumbling Sarajevo and brought them to safety in Israel. The break up of Yugoslavia seemed like a good idea at the time but in 1991 and 1992 there were warring factions everywhere. Viewers saw a bomb explode in a marketplace and bodies strewn across fruit stalls as bloodied survivors wailed in agony. They did not see, a few hundred yards away, eight rickety school buses filled with 500 Sarajevans pass by en route to the airport. A week later, 111 Sarajevan Jewish teenagers were rescued. A UJA-JDC video, "Rescue from Sarajevo," buttressed summer solicitations and events, and aired on television, showing the general public how Jews take care of their own.

Meanwhile, the Israelis learned that there were 2,000 Jews living in Quara, Ethiopia, a high, isolated mountaintop village in the remote north that was reachable only by foot. Contact with the Quaran Jews had been lost prior to Operation Solomon. The Israelis visited them in early June with food and water and learned they wanted to live in Israel. The Israelis led the Quaran Jews on a difficult three-day trek down the slopes and across a 200-mile plateau, to where the Joint Distribution Committee, including Dr. Rick Hodes, was waiting. Fluent in Amharic, Hodes interviewed them, inoculated them and treated any injuries or discomforts.

The next morning, the Quaran Jews boarded flatbed trucks for the ten-hour journey along dusty, rudimentary roads to Bole Airport in Addis Ababa. Their hearts were filled with joy, with no room for fear. Their waiting aircraft were not gutted of seats to fit in as many as possible but were regularly furnished and supplied El Al jets with seats, foods they were familiar with, and a welcome video featuring Ethiopian Israelis. It was a quantum leap from Quara to modern day Israel and it inspired Israelis and American Jews all over again.

When United Jewish Appeal National Officers and Federation Campaign Chairmen held their retreats in mid-June, the first official events in Tauber's administration, the rescues were the talk of the gatherings. Tauber's keynote address reminded participants that Jewish life is precarious in many parts of the world and that American Jews must aid those who can and wish to make aliyah. Briefing sessions on financial needs abroad and solicitation training techniques were especially helpful to those who were new. UJA closed many gifts. It stressed that participants should play a crucial role in bringing home the message to their communities that Operation Exodus must be supported.

Tauber wanted to go back to the main well for more. And he did not want to wait until the fall. Although the fundraising environment was different, he believed, and his advisers agreed, it was worth trying to mount a successor to the

Breakfast of Champions. Such an event might raise large sums, inspire Prime Minister's Mission participants and create a ripple effect in the King David Society and on the President's Mission and influence the mass campaign.

During the winter, Tauber and Lender had telephoned 20 top prospects to explore whether they would consider committing another seven-figure sum. The prospects said they had already given substantially to Operation Exodus, were under pressure from other philanthropies, were hampered by the weak economy and believed the world situation had improved for the Jews. Some wondered aloud when it would ever be enough for UJA. Tauber and Lender said they appreciated the previous gifts but that they were increasing their own gifts and maintaining their other giving, and hoped others would do the same. They cited data indicating economic recovery was underway. They agreed that the Soviet Union was destroyed but pointed to instability in the successor countries. They noted that television commentator Patrick Buchanan, whose statements William F. Buckley, Jr., said could be seen as anti-Semitic, obtained 41 percent of the vote in the New Hampshire Republican Primary against a sitting Republican President, George Bush, and that if he could be so popular in an American state, Jewish life abroad could be uncertain anywhere. The prospects were not enthusiastic, but they did not close the door.

Tauber asserted that such an event should take place but that it needed more than repackaging. "My sense was that it would take something like a private meeting with the Prime Minister, which the Breakfast of Champions had not required," he recalled in an interview. "Secondly, the federations asked us to invite prospects in the name of the event Chairmen, not UJA which a few claimed would turn donors off. It was a difficult decision not to recruit in the name of UJA but we agreed. Les [Wexner] and Charles [Bronfman] were asked to be Co-Chairmen and the invitation went out from them."

The Campaign Executive Committee, Major Gifts Committee and federation leaders urged UJA to be more flexible on the gift-qualification level. While the critical mass had to come from new million-dollar gifts, Tauber agreed to allow donors to attend if they gave close to a million dollars, provided the gift exceeded a previous substantial gift. That way, donors who previously gave Operation Exodus $750,000, for example, could participate if they pledged $900,000. He also agreed not to hold donors to a payment timetable as in the Breakfast motif. These concessions were signs of the weakness in the Operation Exodus campaign.

Tauber mailed contingency letters of invitation, one addressed to Shamir, one addressed to Rabin, both post-dated to June 22, the date of the election, to

Naphtali Lavie, UJA's Director-General in Israel. Within hours after Rabin's election, Lavie met with him and handed him the invitation. Rabin's aides later said Rabin thought he could be present on July 20. UJA wrote to and telephoned every donor of $500,000 and over, inviting each to be present on the tentative date.

In early July, Rabin's aides informed Tauber that the Prime Minister would not be in the United States until August. UJA telephoned prospects to inform them and found them in a good mood because many favored Rabin, whose plans to reach out to the Palestinian Liberation Organization and enhance the status of Reform and Conservative Jewry in Israel appealed to them. Nevertheless, some surmised that the situation for Jews abroad was no longer threatening, pointing out that Gorbachev had been welcomed on a recent visit to Israel. To counter that, UJA sent the doubters a report by the respected Russian Center for Public Opinion and Marketing Research that found that anti-Semitic sentiments were spreading in the Former Soviet Union.

"When Rabin's aides said he wouldn't be available until August things stopped," Michael Fischer, a UJA Assistant Vice President who played the key professional role at the event, recalled in an interview. "We had everything in place, waiting for Rabin to say when he would come. We had recruited fully. We kept in close contact with every prospect. We had the formal letter of invitation to prospects prepared. We were all dressed for the prom, waiting for a date." The phone rang on August 1. The date with Rabin would be on August 13. UJA went into overdrive.

This writer happened to be alone with Brian Lurie in his office when Charles Bronfman returned the UJA CEO's call. Ever unorthodox in his approach, Lurie solicited Bronfman, who was also in Manhattan, on the phone. Lurie said he did not have to tell Bronfman about the situation of Jews in the Former Soviet Union, then described it as dire. He said he did not have to tell him how the immigrants could create great intellectual, scientific and cultural achievements in Israel and make Israel a light unto the nations, then said just that. He said he did not have to tell Bronfman that gifts speak louder than words. Then these words, what fundraisers call "the ask:"

> Charles, you and Edgar gave $5 million each for Operation Exodus. We appreciate that. Your gifts alone brought over thousands of immigrants. You should take pride in that. Charles, the economy is doing poorly, the donors feel sacked around by us, and we need you to do more. If they see you go up, it will help get them up. I need you and Edgar both to move up to $6 million. I need you to make that

statement.

(Pause.)

"Yes, six each, 12 in all. I wouldn't ask, Charles, if it wasn't very important."

(Pause.)

"Thank you, Charles. We appreciate it. And Charles, if you can look at how soon you can retire the sum? It will help a lot."

As Bronfman, Wexner, Tauber and Lender began making calls, confirmations came quickly. Breakfast participants Henry Taub, Peter May, Charles Goodman, Max Fisher, Harvey Meyerhoff, Jerold Hoffberger, Alan Greenberg, Joseph Wilf and Lewis Rudin said they would be present. So did Pearlstone, Arlene Zimmerman, Raymond Zimmerman, Lester Crown, Richard Goldman, Stanley Chesley, Donne Hess, Ronne Hess, Holocaust survivors Erica Jesselson and Ludwig Jesselson of New York, William Rosenwald, Elizabeth Varet and Michael Varet, Susan Gelman of San Francisco, Milton Gralla of New York, William Weinberg of Baltimore, Richard Scheuer of New York and Herbert Mendel of Miami.

Several who would be out of town made qualifying pledges including Lynn and Charles Schusterman of Tulsa, Jacob Feldman of Dallas, Rowland Schaefer of Miami, Emanuel Rosenfeld of Fort Worth, Leonard Davis of Palm Beach, Irving Schneider, Bernard Marcus, Harold Grossman, Stanley Hirsh, the Strauss Foundation and the Magbit Foundation.

From abroad, Julia Koschitzky, Avie Bennett and Alex Raab of Toronto said they would be present, and Eric Samson of South Africa said he would qualify, their gifts to be credited to Keren Hayesod.

Some could not attend but made pledges after the event including Ronald O. Perelman, Henry Kravis, Michael Steinhardt, Joseph Gurwin, Donald Newhouse, Samuel I. Newhouse, Jr., Arthur Belfer, Robert Belfer, Jack Weiler, Robert Arnow, Larry Silverstein, Irwin Hochberg, Lester Pollack, Maurice Greenberg, George Klein, Leonard Stern, Jack Nash, Fred Rose, Jerry L. Cohen, Ronald Stanton and Sanford Weill of New York; Lew Wasserman, Bram Goldsmith, Syd Irmas, David Karney, Ted Mann, Stanley Chais, Alex Deutsch, Lester Deutsch and Dr. Sigi Ziering of Los Angeles; Sumner Feldberg, Shirley and Edgar Grossman, Steven Grossman and Paul Fireman of Boston; Arie Halpern and Sam Halpern of Central New Jersey; Mason Rudd of Louisville; Donald Zale and Eugene Zale of Dallas; Robert H. Smith of Washington, D.C.; Samuel Heyman of Connecticut; Zanvyl Krieger of Baltimore; Stephen Lieberman, Arnold Lifson and Helen Bigos of Minneapolis; and Jay

Schottenstein of Columbus, as well as the Pritzker family, Norman Braman, Alfred Taubman and Carroll Petrie and Milton Petrie.

On August 12, Rabin arrived in Kennebunkport, where he personally assured President Bush he would end settlement building on the West Bank and seek a peace agreement with the PLO. The two leaders addressed a news conference during which Bush announced that the United States would provide $10 billion in loan guarantees for settlement in Israel of Jews from the Former Soviet Union. Rabin flew to New York City where he spoke to the Conference of Presidents the next day and received Wexner, Bronfman and Fisher over hors d'oeuvres in his suite in the Plaza Hotel.

Rabin and the three Americans entered the second floor cocktail area at 5:10 p.m.[4]

There, as Michael Fischer recalled, "The Prime Minister mingled with the participants, puffing constantly on a cigarette. He stood patiently while he was photographed individually with each participant. He smiled and shook hands with every donor. He hid the cigarette away from the camera, then puffed away again. He was in a very good mood."

An hour later, Bronfman opened the meeting, Fisher introduced the Prime Minister and Rabin addressed the group. The Prime Minister said, "Israel today has a new order of national security policies, based on jobs and education and aliyah." He said an improved economy was necessary to fully absorb the 400,000 Soviet Jews who had arrived and the hundreds of thousands more expected. "This is what is important to Israel," he asserted, "more than three settlements or 10,000 units in the Territories." He said an improved era in Israel-United States relations was beginning, as evidenced by the loan guarantees Bush had announced in Kennebunkport the day before. And he sounded the campaign theme UJA asked him to include, thanking donors graciously for their past gifts and encouraging their future support.

Wexner thanked the Prime Minister, turned to the participants and said,

> Even though we have had two years of wonderful news about the rescue of Jews, it is important to remember that Operation Exodus is not over. Thousands of Jews are still waiting to get out of Russia. I am pessimistic about their fate there: Russia has been dangerous to the Jews for centuries. We have to help them get to Israel where they can live in freedom and help build the Jewish State. For them, Operation Exodus

---

4 Hours earlier, I was in the meeting room, which overlooked Central Park, for an event dry run. There, an Israeli security agent overruled placement of the podium near a window. Questioned, he said Rabin needed to be shielded by the walls since a sniper might climb a nearby tree in the park and fire a shot.

is their hope for the future. We are its leaders. I gave $6 million at the beginning of Operation Exodus. Tonight I pledge $7 million more.

Bronfman, like Wexner seated next to the Prime Minister, rose and said, "We have to do all we can to keep this great historic movement of Jews to Israel moving. We pledge $12 million. Six million from me, six million from my brother Edgar." That was it. Wexner had spoken for a minute; Bronfman distilled the speechmaking even more. Fisher shortened it further, remaining seated and stating only, "This campaign is still very important. I'll give another $3 million."

Lester Crown, speaking on behalf of the Crown and Goodman families, pledged $4 million. Lew Rudin, for his family and his brother Jack Rudin's family, $3 million. Peter May pledged $1.5 million for himself and his family; Richard Goldman, $1.5 million; Jerold Hoffberger, $1.25 million; Joel Tauber, $1.2 million; Marvin Lender, $1 million; Richard Pearlstone, $1 million; Henry Taub, $1 million; Joseph Wilf, $1 million; Ludwig Jesselson, $1 million; and Arlene Zimmerman and Raymond Zimmerman, $1 million. Hardly a word was spoken except a succinct sentence ending in a gigantic sum. The donors themselves knew something astounding was happening around them even if many had experienced it at the Breakfast.

Not all announced their gifts, in respect to the Prime Minister's long day, but the atmosphere among the UJA leaders in the room was, as one person present said, "controlled euphoria." Shortly after 7 p.m., Bronfman concluded the program by thanking the donors and inviting them to enjoy the dinner. Four or five remained for the appetizer; none stayed longer.[5] A million-dollar-a-plate dinner and no one remained for the meal. There was joy in a food pantry somewhere in Manhattan that night.

The Rabin Dinner, as it became known, raised $67.3 million, even more than the record shattering $58.7 million at the Breakfast of Champions. Tauber's risk had paid off. The Dinner brought in an enormous sum that would help tens of thousands make aliyah, and provided a thrilling lift to the Campaign. It proved there was life in Operation Exodus as stimulated by leadership from the top.

Word of UJA's single greatest fundraising achievement spread throughout the American Jewish community and into the mass media such as *The New York*

---

5 Bronfman left immediately too, to begin a series of interviews about the event. That night he was interviewed by Leon Charney for his television program, *"The Leon Charney Report."*

Times, and the achievement bolstered events recruitment and fundraising. One immediate effect was that it inspired ten more prospects to join the Prime Minister's Mission for $100,000 donors, bringing enrollment to 75 when the mission left the next week for Moscow and Israel. In an interview for this book, Rani Garfinkle, a participant, recalled the mission:

> I had been to Moscow in 1990 and by 1992 the aura of crisis had eased. However, the desire of the Jews to get out and go to Israel was still strong. We heard about incidents of anti-Semitism and discrimination, but the word that best described their feeling was no longer fear but uncertainty. Of course, as Jews they knew anything could happen. But by 1992 they seemed more motivated to leave by a desire to build a better life for themselves and their families. The living conditions in the homes we visited were still poor.

Participants who came to learn about the aliyah got to accompany immigrants as they actually made aliyah. They were booked on the same chartered El Al jet that departed, according to the schedule provided by Moscow authorities, at 3:20 a.m. Some of the older Soviet Jewish men wore their war medals, as they often did on special occasions, and some aged widows who had lost their husbands in the Battle of Stalingrad in 1940 wore medals given to their husbands posthumously. On board they screened a joyous welcome video, with Russian narration, showing scenes of Israel and footage of typical apartments and absorption centers. Natan Sharansky came on screen, welcomed them to Israel, and said life in Israel would be challenging, sometimes difficult, but very good. He encouraged them to speak up for what they want and need, have hope and leave fear behind.

They arrived as a strong early morning sun warmed Tel Aviv. The immigrants were escorted to a processing center on the second floor of the international terminal. There, Russian speaking Jews who had been absorbed in earlier months helped them complete brief paperwork and answered their questions. They sat around tables in small groups, drinking fresh orange juice and tasting warm cookies. The small children were taken to the next room where Russian speaking counselors played games with them and told them about Israel. The infants were in cribs, fed according to their mothers' instructions. At a table with one couple where I sat and listened, a Jewish Agency official took out several hundred dollars in shekels, counted them aloud in Russian, explained the conversion rate, and placed the money in their palms as their mouths dropped open.

Mission participants boarded buses for Jerusalem, 45 minutes to the southeast, where they checked into the King David Hotel, Jerusalem's most luxurious, which retained its colonial charm from the British Mandate period. Later they met with Knesset members to whom they expressed their views on various issues. They enjoyed a plush cocktail hour near the hotel's poolside in sight of the inspiring illuminated walls of the Old City. Dinner was with Avraham Shohat, Israel's Finance Minister, who explained that the hope they had seen in Russia, and the joy of successful immigration depended on funding, Israelis' and theirs.

In subsequent days participants met with immigrants rescued from Ethiopia, Sarajevo and the Soviet Union. They received background reports and insights from Cabinet ministers, generals, journalists and the United States Ambassador to Israel, William Harrop. They enjoyed "home hospitality," as UJA called it, at the residences of prominent cultural figures. They visited the Western Wall, the Tower of David, Ammunition Hill, the Israel Museum and the Bible Lands Museum. Tauber, Lender, Pearlstone, Garfinkle and others moved among the participants, heard their amazement at what Jews had accomplished, and discussed the role played by Operation Exodus in ongoing achievements. The Jewish Agency's Kaplan, JDC's Hassenfeld and United Israel Appeal's Norman Lipoff framed the appeal from the podium.

Shevach Weiss, Speaker of the Knesset, was their caucus host in front of the majestic Chagall tapestries; and Yitzhak Rabin, two months into his tenure as Prime Minister, delivered the caucus address, expressing his hope for peace and a completed aliyah. As donor after donor took the microphone to address the Prime Minister, $100,000 seemed more and more paltry. The Prime Minister's Mission raised $12.2 million for Operation Exodus.

The International Leadership Reunion with Keren Hayesod for $250,000 donors was held in Paris weeks later. Along the delightful Champs Elysees, amidst the fragrant Tuilleries, on the glorious Eiffel Tower, at an elegant cocktail hour in a private room at the Louvre, and at the opulent Palace of Versailles, participants renewed friendships and learned more about the Campaign. The 44 American donors gave $19.5 million to Operation Exodus, more than the $16.4 million the 58 American donors gave to that campaign on the previous reunion, possibly demonstrating an effect of the Rabin Dinner achievement.

The President's Mission for $10,000 donors offered a range of pre-missions to attract donors who seemed to have traveled everywhere. Pre-missions offered opportunities to meet with Jews in Greece, Italy, Morocco, Poland, Spain and Turkey as well as Russia and Ukraine. There was even a pre-mission to Israel with a cultural theme that featured a discussion with the artist Yaacov Agam, a behind-stage visit at the Israel Philharmonic Orchestra and front row seats for a concert at the Jerusalem Theater. Federations liked the pre-missions, which enabled them to gather local donors in smaller and more intimate contingents before the main plenary events. Those included Israeli entertainment at Sultan's Pool, at the foot of the walls of the Old City, for the 2,000 donors. Fundraising remained strong.

The UJA Women's Campaign mounted a Lion of Judah mission to Turkey and Israel, attracting scores of new $5,000 members. In Turkey the participants, mostly Ashkenazic, followed in the footsteps of Dona Gracia Mendes Nasi who helped Jews fleeing from the Inquisition in 1492; explored the ancient cities of Izmir and Sardis; learned about Sephardic Jewry; met with Turkey's President and Mrs. Targut Ozai; visited the Covered Bazaar in Istanbul; and enjoyed an elegant dinner cruise on the Bosporus Sea.

In Israel they visited Safed, which has a strong Sephardic dimension; met with immigrants and Jewish Agency and JDC officials; and cruised on the Mediterranean with Israeli Navy officers. Programming concluded with a reception hosted by Lea Rabin at the Prime Minister's Residence, where the Prime Minister's wife mingled graciously in the crowded reception room and posed for photographs with guests.[6] In the presence of Lea and Yitzhak Rabin, Yona Goldberg and past Women's Campaign Chairmen inaugurated the Lion of Judah's Zahav club for $50,000 donors. The mission raised $768,000 for Operation Exodus as the Women's Campaign moved farther into the forefront of UJA giving.

As Women's Campaign left Jerusalem on November 2 the Chazak Mission, consisting of 700 Young Leaders including 200 first-time visitors to Israel, arrived from Russia. The "Baby Boomers" exuded substantial energy throughout 14-hour days of visits with new immigrants and others aided by UJA-Federation Campaigns, meetings with officials and stops at inspirational sites. Then they partied well into the night. The participants were exhilarated by everything they heard and saw, especially by the courageous new immigrants they met, and gave $693,000 to Operation Exodus.

The missions proved yet again the value of bringing prospects into the environment where they can discover for themselves why they should give maximally, the ideal fundraising idiom.[7]

---

6 In a UJA footnote to history, the Prime Minister's plans to stop by before going upstairs for the night were delayed for two hours when the King David Hotel, where he had been meeting, was surrounded by angry West Bank residents. The police were summoned. I was standing next to Lea Rabin when she learned of this. Visibly angry, she said, "They think they are going to tell us what to do, the settlers? We will do what we want, what we have to do." When Rabin arrived later I asked him about the confrontation. His comment was, "Not so bad. I understand why they are upset."

Meanwhile, in the United States, UJA flew a score of leaders into communities at federation request to close nettlesome major gifts solicitations. Prospects were impressed that solicitors knew so much about the cause and that they had made the effort to learn about them and their concerns. They invariably increased their gifts. When someone who was or had been UJA National Chairman would think their gift was important enough to fly into town to ask for it, it was virtually impossible not to agree to the sum requested.

Major gifts programs and services like these were central to the love part of the love-hate relationship of federations with UJA. UJA imposed impossible demands on federations and ran roughshod over local sensitivities. But for exposing donors to experiences that made them want to give, and for closing gifts at levels the federations could not reach, UJA was indispensable. In major gifts fundraising, UJA was in a league of its own.

In December UJA rewarded senior level donors with the pièce de résistance, a visit to Leslie Wexner's ranch in Aspen. That was as exclusive an invitation as you could get, to the place to be for the highest echelons. Bunny Adler, Michael and Judy Adler and Donald and Judy Lefton of Miami; Michael and Debra Feiner of Englewood, Colorado; Herbert and DeeDee Glimcher of Columbus; Senator Frank Lautenberg; Zygmunt and Audrey Wilf of Springfield, New Jersey; Steven and Toni Sandler of Virginia Beach; and Preston and Joan Tisch of New York City were among those who joined Tauber, Lender, Pearlstone, Irwin Levy and other UJA senior donors in a day of relaxation.

Meanwhile, UJA pressed forward in aiding federations at all levels of support. It mounted a tour of American Jewish communities by 29 Jewish immigrants to Israel, including 16 rescued from the decaying Former Soviet Union, nine from chaotic Ethiopia and four from the disintegrating former Yugoslavia. Billed as a "Thank You, America," tour, the immigrants visited 123 communities in pairs, where they addressed audiences, met donors and were featured on local media. For example, Svetlana Goldes, rescued from Ukraine, and Sissy Wondie, from Ethiopia, visited Northeastern cities such as Boston, where they spoke for the Combined Jewish Philanthropies at nine synagogues, eight community meetings, five parlor meetings, three schools and a family gathering.

Molla Mengistu from Ethiopia (no relation to the dictator) and Anna Goren from Uzbekistan visited the Southwest with a similar itinerary. Molla, who had earned two degrees from Addis Ababa University, said his family was

---

7 All UJA events continued to raise funds for the Annual Campaign as well as Operation Exodus. The Lion of Judah Mission, for example, raised $1 million for ongoing needs. The Chazak (Strength) Mission raised $2 million.

given only hours to decide whether to leave, and left with only the clothes they wore. Anna described the religious harassment that forced her family to flee in fear from Ukraine, leaving behind all they knew for a country they had never seen. "When my son was born in [the] Soviet Union I looked into his eyes and I saw no future for him," she told an enraptured Tucson audience. "I said to my husband, 'Let's live in Israel, as Jews.'" General Campaign Chair Carole Levi of Tucson, where 65 solicitations alone led to average gift increases to Operation Exodus of 21 percent, said, "Hearing the speakers reawakened feelings of love for the Jewish people."[8]

As the third extraordinary year of Operation Exodus neared its end, Jews remained in danger abroad and continued to be rescued with funds from UJA Federation Campaigns. Even the news media were amazed. John F. Burns wrote in *The New York Times* on Nov. 15 about yet another rescue operation from Sarajevo:

Jews Evacuate 200, Muslims Included, in Bosnia

Sarajevo, Bosnia and Herzegovina, Nov. 14--With Jews and Muslims seated side by side on chartered buses and ducking at the sound of sniper fire, more than 200 people escaped this cold and hungry city today in an evacuation effort by Sarajevo's small Jewish population. [They passed] between the sniper and tank positions of the two opposing armies....

The evacuation, financed by the American Jewish Joint Distribution Committee, a relief organization with headquarters in New York, left only 500 Jews here, down from more than 1,300 when the siege by Serbian nationalists began in April.... Among those who packed into the buses were scores of Muslims . . .

No group has been more successful than the Jews, who have now organized seven convoys that have taken 800 Jews to safety. Unlike others, these evacuations have been accomplished without a single injury or death . . . Only this week, an evacuation by the Bosnian Red Cross that was to have taken 6,000 people to safety collapsed in chaos after only 1,000 people got out.

So successful has the Jewish operation been--and so effective in sustaining the Jews who remain here with food, medical supplies and other scarce essentials — that the phrase "becoming Jewish" has passed into the argot of Sarajevo.

Several hundred people who were not known to be Jews before the

---

8 Quoted in a UJA internal document. UJA also launched its first initiative into television, establishing a weekly syndicated cable television program, "UJA Update," hosted by Joel Tauber. Each week Tauber interviewed recent immigrants, JDC or Jewish Agency officials, or heads of UJA programs to highlight the importance of giving.

siege have appeared at the Jewish center on Drobrovoijacka Street and produced documents showing that they had a Jewish grandparent or, in some cases, great grandparent.

The Sarajevo rescues were funded through JDC from the Annual Campaign, which regained its footing and would exceed $750 million, but they also contributed to the image of Operation Exodus as an unfinished rescue campaign. The image was well founded: Operation Exodus brought 64,790 Jews from the Former Soviet Union in 1992 for a total of 397,144, not counting others as from Bosnia and Herzegovina and Albania. For them, Operation Exodus raised $117.4 million, for a jaw dropping three year total of $776.2 million. That may have been down from the phenomenal $503.4 million raised in 1990 and the breathtaking $155.4 million raised in 1991. But few philanthropies raised over a hundred million dollars in a year, let alone in the third year of a campaign and in addition to an Annual Campaign. Moreover, nearly all pledges were paid, the national collections program having been led by Edgar Goldenberg of Philadelphia, founder of Goldenberg's Peanut Chews.

All the sums exceeded the most optimistic projections of what could be inspired, invited, motivated, encouraged, persuaded, enlisted, enticed, induced, coaxed, urged, prodded, exhorted, inveigled or cajoled from the American Jewish community. The Soviet Union had given up along the way, but not the UJA. Communism fell but Operation Exodus went on.

Nevertheless, a sequel can add features not in the original but rarely exceeds it. The Rabin Dinner was not the Breakfast of Champions and could not, and did not, have the same far-reaching and sustained implications. Events overtook the Dinner's potential. As Wexner reflected in an interview a decade after the Dinner:

A lot changed between the Breakfast of Champions and the Rabin Dinner. I remember thinking at the time of the Dinner that the first campaign was more speculative, that we didn't know if we could get the Jews out, or how many, or what it would finally cost. We hadn't yet acted as leaders or as a community to make the aliyah happen. We were still tortured by the memories of American Jewish inaction to save Jews in the Holocaust.

But so much happened in that short period between the two events. Even though by the time of the Dinner there was evidence from experience that the gifts were being put to good use, people were less inclined to give. They heard that more wanted to leave Russia, but felt they had helped hundreds of thousands get out already. For the many Jews who had given at the beginning because of inaction in the Holocaust, Operation Exodus was an act of repentance for those who had not done enough. But by 1992 those donors achieved closure on that issue and didn't feel they had to give any more.

They were beginning to raise other questions, like whether we should rebuild the Jewish institutions in Russia. And whether the Jewish Agency had enough efficiency. And whether the resettlement effort was proceeding in exactly the way they liked. And whether Israel had become self-sufficient and didn't need our help any more. By the time of the Dinner they had plenty of excuses and reasons for not giving.

How much more could be wrung from donors? Tauber knew that the orange was just about squeezed dry.

CHAPTER TEN
The Oslo Effect

We are destined to live together, on the same soil in the same land.

We, the soldiers who have returned from battle stained with blood, we who have seen our relatives and friends killed before our eyes, we who have attended their funerals and cannot look into the eyes of parents and orphans, we who have come from a land where parents bury their children, who have fought against you, the Palestinians-- we say to you today in a loud and clear voice: enough of blood and tears. Enough.

We harbor no hatred towards you. We have no desire for revenge. We, like you, are people who want to build a home, plant a tree, love, live side by side with you—in dignity, in empathy, as human beings, as free men. We are today giving peace a chance and saying to you: enough.

Let's pray that a day will come when we all will say: farewell to arms.

Prime Minister Yitzhak Rabin, speaking to
the Palestinians upon signing the Oslo Accords
White House Lawn, September 13, 1993.

In Jewish history, 1993 will forever be known as the year of the Oslo Accords. Whatever they meant in the eons of struggle of Jews to be accepted by their neighbors, the Accords sealed the fate of Operation Exodus. In themselves, they would not have been enough. But following the sensational scale of the aliyah, the remarkable Campaign achievements, the terror of the scud attacks, the ecstasy of Operation Solomon and the stunning collapse of the Soviet Union whose repression had motivated the Campaign from the start, they were enough. The Accords were signed in the warm sunshine of Washington in September but the signs had been increasing all year that Israel's long diplomatic isolation was over and that a new era of worldwide Jewish security might be in store.

Of course in Israel, as in other democracies, the signs of progress were difficult to see under the layers of domestic distraction. Despite the image of Yitzhak Rabin upon his death as a transcendent leader with a noble universal vision around whom Israelis rallied, what the Israelis wanted from him in early 1993 was jobs. The unemployment rate stood at eleven percent, and Rabin was viewed as so inept at bringing it down that even the Russian immigrants, whose freedom and aliyah he had supported, formed formidable interest groups to demand work. In coffee shops and stores, Israelis debated whether Ethiopia's Falash Mura, whose forbears had converted away from Judaism but who considered themselves Jewish, enjoyed an automatic right, as Jews, to become Israeli citizens (the Cabinet voted in January that they did not). They argued whether Messianic Jews, who wanted to move to Israel to evangelize for Christianity, had forfeited that same right (the Israeli Supreme Court ruled in February that they did). The only relief for Rabin was a sex scandal involving Knesset Member Benjamin Netanyahu. As for concessions to the Palestine Liberation Organization, the Likud had no lack of candidates in its nationwide primary coming up in March, each of whom swore to block anything Rabin might have in mind.

The new American President, William J. Clinton, was beset by domestic problems too, as he struggled to establish himself, but Clinton invited Rabin to the White House on March 15 to ascertain if the old warrior was serious about peace. Clinton wasn't sure. After all, Rabin was a military man, having been a young brigade commander in Israel's War of Independence, Chief of Staff in the Six Day War and a general in the Yom Kippur War. When the Intifada broke out in 1987, with Palestinian youths throwing stones at Israeli soldiers, he was the Defense Minister who had warned the PLO, "We will break their bones." But Rabin impressed Clinton with his commitment. However, four Israelis were murdered by Palestinian gunmen and Rabin quickly returned home. There, he ordered retaliatory attacks on Gaza that killed two Palestinians and wounded 70. Within a few days, thousands of Israelis staged a vehement anti-Rabin rally in Tel Aviv to pressure him to choose a different path toward peace and security. The Israeli right rallied in Jerusalem the next day to harden Rabin's hand.

The peace camp's main victory of the season came on March 24 when Ezer Weizman, a former general and Defense Minister who had evolved from hawk to dove and stood to the left of Rabin, was elected by the Knesset as Israel's seventh President. The President's functions were mainly ceremonial, but Weizman was given a platform to represent Israel to other heads of state, the power to break electoral deadlocks and the mantle of national moral authority. The very next day Netanyahu, on the right within Likud, was elected as its Chairman. Rabin was being repositioned by others.

Some of Rabin's worst political problems were within his own coalition, even of his own making. By trying to force free market principles onto a largely socialist economy he alienated Histadrut, the powerful union, which staged national strikes in response. He moved to develop high-tech industry in the Hula Valley in Israel's Galilee but suffered the wrath of the agriculture-based kibbutz movement. He fended off challenges from former generals Ehud Barak and Amram Mitzna on his left, as he battled Likud members of his Cabinet on the right. He began to dismiss dissident Cabinet members one by one and take over their portfolios himself. In May he found himself as Minister of Defense, Minister of Religion, Minister of Education and Minister of the Interior as well as Prime Minister.

All this gave Shimon Peres, Rabin's Labor Party rival for decades and the Foreign Minister, a free hand in shaping foreign affairs. Publicly, Peres appointed his close associate, Colette Avital, as Consul General in New York, a key position for influencing American Jewish opinion and obtaining private funding for his own future political campaigns. He persuaded the Pope to recognize Israel. And he achieved a diplomatic breakthrough in India, receiving an official welcome in a country that had shunned Israel for years over the Palestinian cause.

Privately, though, Peres did much more. In January, his protégé, Yossi Beilin, told him that Terje Rod Larsen, Director of the Institute for Applied Social Science in Oslo, learned from his contacts in the PLO that it was tiring of the Intifada and might be willing to talk secretly with Israel[1]. Peres authorized Beilin to meet with those PLO representatives under Larsen's auspices. Beilin did so and confirmed that there was interest in a peaceful settlement. Peres agreed to meet with higher level PLO representatives in Oslo to pursue the possibility. Before leaving, Peres informed the news media he was going to Oslo for consultations and invited them to come along. As he had expected no one was interested. He just did not tell them -- consultations with whom.

Peres also did not tell Rabin with whom. Rabin was furious when Peres briefed him on the secret negotiations in late February. Nevertheless, Rabin allowed the negotiations to continue, with the goals of an explicit recognition of Israel's right to exist in peace and security, a PLO renunciation of violence, and a change in the PLO charter calling for the destruction of Israel. By late spring, Yasser Arafat was Peres' negotiating counterpart, although Arafat remained in

---

1 See Howard Sachar, *A History of Israel From the Rise of Zionism to Our Time*, New York: Knopf, 1996, pp. 991-1001.

Tunis, even when Peres was in Oslo, communicating through messages.

Peres found Arafat obstinate, even on procedural issues. He confided in President Mubarak of Egypt, who moved Arafat along, and enlisted Secretary of State Warren Christopher and his aide, Daniel Kurtzer, who moved Arafat along more. By early August, the basic outline of a Declaration of Principles, a structure for peace that was to form the core of the Accords, took shape. However, Arafat was still resistant. Finally, Rabin and Peres agreed to recognize the PLO as the official representative of the Palestinian people, giving it the status Arafat had long sought for his 30–year-old guerilla movement. Still Arafat refused to agree. In mid-August, Rabin and Peres contemplated what, if anything, would achieve a breakthrough.

American Jews did not know about the Oslo negotiations, but they were reading in the newspapers, hearing on radio and viewing on television the gradual steps that were ending Israel's isolation, at least in the non-Arab world. The decline in strength of the Intifada seemed to indicate that Israelis were no longer in such danger. Considering what American Jews had achieved through Operation Exodus, and because the news media were paying less attention to instabilities in the Former Soviet Union, it seemed as if the need for the Campaign had ended. It had not. On the contrary, more Jews from the Former Soviet Union had made aliyah in the first eight months of 1993 than had in the corresponding months of 1992[2]:

	1993	1992
January	5,950	6,282
February	4,616	4,280
March	6,082	5,013
April	4,849	4,686
May	4,989	3,542
June	5,105	3,908
July	4,185	5,025
August	6,072	5,080
	41,848	37,816

For each new immigrant, arrival in Israel was the beginning of the promise

---

2 Jewish Agency documents.

of the aliyah, the singular moment of achieving a place in a land of freedom. Beyond the 41,848 were thousands more, with airplane tickets, exit visas, applications for exit visas or who were at another stage in the still cumbersome emigration process. For them, Israel meant hope and security, better than the despair and anti-Semitic terror they left behind. *For them*, UJA kept the Campaign going.

A glimpse of the mindset that Russian Jews continued to be up against was provided to 25 federation communications directors whom this writer took to Russia in January 1993, to expose them to the continuing need for Operation Exodus. The mission participants met with Russian Jews who spoke of their fear of remaining, and with valiant Jewish Agency and Joint Distribution Committee emissaries striving to aid Jews amidst the bleakness and cold of the unforgiving Russian winter. They saw President Clinton's noon inauguration live by satellite -- at 8 p.m. Russian time -- a stark reminder of Moscow's geographical distance from America. Then they met with the Director of External Relations for the City of St. Petersburg -- an obscure former KGB operative named Vladimir V. Putin. After Putin laid out how St. Petersburg was making progress in improving local residents' lives, a participant asked him bluntly, "Are the Jews singled out for discrimination in St. Petersburg?" Putin paused, then said:

No, the Jews are not singled out for discrimination. We treat all minorities the same. There is the majority and then the minorities. If someone doesn't get something because he is a Jew, he would not get it if he was from another minority group. The Jews are not singled out: that is the way with all of them.

The participants were shocked by the content, and boldness, of the answer. They asked the translator to restate the question and be especially careful in the translations. He asked the question again. Putin tilted his head to the side, lifted his eyebrows slightly, curled his lower lip a bit, paused and nodded. "They are not singled out as a group alone. All the minorities are treated the same."

It was against this background of international hope and Russian Jewish despair that Operation Exodus was pursued. The United Jewish Appeal's Prime Minister's Council sponsored a gathering in January at the beautifully appointed Ocean Grand Hotel in Palm Beach that attracted 277 donors of $100,000 and more, and their spouses. Many were already in Palm Beach, where scores of them owned luxurious vacation homes, for their mid-winter holiday. UJA sprinkled an international flavoring into the event, borrowing from the International Leadership Reunion motif for $250,000 donors worldwide, by persuading Baron David de Rothschild of Paris and Sir Trevor Chinn of London to serve as Co-Chairmen with Max Fisher. UJA, never missing an opportunity to add to the pot, encouraged donors, at Andrew Tisch's suggestion, to recommend the event to their adult children. Many adult children attended, and they were welcomed with a special round of applause, participating too at $100,000 a couple.

Participants enjoyed an opening cocktail reception late Friday afternoon at the home of Abraham D. Gosman, Chairman and CEO of Meditrust, the nation's largest health care and real estate investment trust. They enjoyed Shabbat dinner at the homes of people like Arlene Zimmerman, the event chairman. Although they themselves lived in luxurious winter and summer homes, they found it fascinating to note the grand waterway views from others' living rooms and bedrooms, the deluxe furnishings and the marble lavatories. UJA offered optional programming on Saturday as expert academicians and Clinton administration senior advisors like Steven Spiegel provided insight into the Middle East peace process. The finest in afternoon wear was on display. Saturday night's black tie dinner, featuring Itamar Rabinovitch, Israel's Ambassador Designate to the United States and Chairman of Israel's delegation seeking peace with Syria, was resplendent; the thousand dollar tuxedos (none rented) and pastel gowns were worthy of a red carpet at the Academy Awards. Sunday featured a delicious brunch of fresh warm muffins and breads, herring, lox, caviar, fresh fruits and a variety of gourmet coffees and teas. Many opted for afternoon tennis and other recreation in the area, at facilities owned by some of them.

Tisch, Zimmerman and Fisher as well as Joel Tauber, Marvin Lender, Richard Pearlstone and Irwin Levy moved through the crowd throughout the weekend, closing gifts. UJA had no particular dollar goal for the group, so the event leaders created one. They totaled the previous giving by those present and asked them to strive to bring their cumulative giving to Operation Exodus to $50 million. Everyone was a good sport. The stretching enabled UJA to obtain a few million dollars more to begin the fourth year of the originally planned one year Campaign.

UJA expanded its King David Society by founding chapters in several cities and sponsoring events in Palm Beach in February, in Hartford in April, in Virginia Beach in June, and on the Jersey shore in July[3]. Pearlstone, UJA Chairman of Regions, reported to the Campaign Executive Committee in

August, "More than a million dollars in 'new money' was raised for Operation Exodus at those four KDS events."[3]

UJA pursued its popular Fly-In program in which experienced UJA solicitors met with major local prospects when federations needed help in closing gifts. Tauber was on the road three to four days a week, and each member of his Campaign Executive Committee was on the road at least once a week. Henry Taub, Norman Lipoff and Shoshana Cardin, who had served as United Israel Appeal presidents, were particularly effective in documenting the need to skeptical businessmen. Lois Zoller, Carole Solomon, Jane Sherman, Norman Tilles, Larry Hochberg, Vic Gelb and Yona Goldberg, experienced travelers, enhanced solicitations with reports of what they had seen and heard in remote lands. Tauber, Lender, Mort Kornreich, Marty Stein, Alex Grass, Bob Loup, Herschel Blumberg and Irwin Field carried great weight having served as National Chairmen.

UJA sponsored a cadre of Resident Solicitors, Israelis who were informed about needs abroad, fluent in English and trained in solicitation techniques. Resident Solicitors remained in communities as long as a few months, enhancing federation-led solicitations with a stronger overseas dimension. From January to August, Resident Solicitors participated in 963 solicitations in 18 cities.

The UJA Women's Campaign held a Lion of Judah event in Palm Beach; a Western Region Mission at a $1,000 minimum to raise funds and build toward the $5,000 level; and regional conferences. UJA's Young Leadership Cabinets, Rabbinic Cabinet, Women's Business and Professional Council and University Programs Department held similar fundraisers.

The UJA Speakers Bureau provided speakers for nearly 1,500 engagements from January through August, featuring Israeli diplomats, Jewish Agency and JDC leaders, academicians and journalists as well as immigrants from the Former Soviet Union, Ethiopia and the former Yugoslavia who brought vivid testimony about the problems in their home countries and described how they were being successfully absorbed in Israel. These speakers captivated audiences, motivated professionals and authenticated solicitations.

UJA continued to provide federations with inspiring videos, brochures,

3 In addition to their value to Operation Exodus, these events broadened the foundation for an important major gifts program within UJA. Whereas UJA efforts to establish giving programs at the $18,000, $25,000 and $50,000 level had failed in the 1980s because they merely sought to persuade donors to achieve an arbitrary gifts level, the King David Society succeeded because it was a bona fide "club" with a clear sense of group identity. King David Society members earned access to private events with movers and shakers in government, business and the arts, and made new friends of means. A quarterly newsletter promoted elite events and featured new members. VIP courtesies such as access to the El Al business class lounge even when flying coach, telephone calls and notes from Society leaders just to keep in touch, a membership card and newspaper coverage reinforced the Society's exclusivity.

direct mail letters and other materials they could use as is or adapt with a local message. It offered federation leaders background reports, briefings and sample speeches. It kept the aliyah front and center in the Jewish media with a steady flow of news articles, feature stories, photographs and graphics.

In May, Carole Solomon, incoming National Women's Campaign Chairman, and Martin and Heidi Damsky led a mission to Azerbaijan and Uzbekistan that featured a helicopter landing of participants, with retired General Nehemia Dagan, founder of the Israeli Air Force helicopter division, who was UJA Missions Director, at the controls. The landing took place in a field in Baku, Azerbaijan where participants were overwhelmed by a joyous welcome from thousands of Jews singing songs and bringing flowers. That night, participants learned that 1,046 Jews had emigrated from Azerbaijan to Israel so far in 1993 and heard from some of the thousands who wanted to do the same.

In August, Richard Pearlstone led a Prime Minister's Mission pre-mission to Tblisi, Georgia, in the Former Soviet Union, where the mood was grim. The participants learned that 2,113 Georgian Jews had emigrated so far that year. However, few Georgian Jews came out to welcome the visitors: the locals feared for their lives. Street fighting was heard in the distance. Participants left for the airport the next day with 85 Georgian Jews and were the last Americans to visit Georgia for months as the simmering civil war erupted.

In Israel, Pearlstone reminded the full mission at a dinner at the King David Hotel of the continuing precariousness of Jewish life in the unstable Former Soviet Union with this vivid description:

> Imagine a city that looks like Paris, a river running through it. Tree-lined cobblestone streets, beautiful buildings—this is Tblisi. You suddenly turn a corner — bombed out buildings, bread lines, empty stores, private militias — this too is Tblisi, the other Tblisi, where our Jewish brothers and sisters live. There is no overt anti-Semitism, but this is civil war. Mobs rule the streets. Roadblocks are placed in the paths of motorists and pedestrians, so that cars and money can be stolen, so that cameras and other valuables can be confiscated. It could be the police as easily as it could be gangs. There is no nightlife. There are no streetlights. Nothing moves at night through the darkness and desolation, except the gangs.

Ever the architect of access, the UJA arranged for participants on the mission, which was under the Chairmanship of Richard Spiegel, to meet with

Rabin, Peres and Mayor Teddy Kollek of Jerusalem. They also met with Uri Lubrani, who had negotiated the freedom of Ethiopian Jews in Operation Solomon; General Antoine Lachad of the Southern Lebanon Army, Israel's ally in the north; and Muhammad Bassiouny, Egypt's Ambassador to Israel. The participants visited new immigrants, from many countries now, where they lived and worked. They rested at Taba, a tiny strip of luxury hotels near Eilat that was the last parcel returned to Egypt under the Camp David Accords. Then they flew in small Arkia Airlines planes to Jerusalem to pledge, in front of Rabin at the Chagall tapestries in the Knesset, more for Operation Exodus.

As Tauber continued to lead all UJA fundraising, he maintained publicly that Operation Exodus would continue until the last Jew was out. However, privately he could not ignore increasing signs that the Campaign could not be sustained much longer. UJA knew of no one else of means to invite onto missions or to major gifts events. Federations had no one on their lists they had not approached. Donors at all levels had been drained again and again, already having given more than anyone – even the donors – had ever imagined. The news media that fostered Campaign growth seemed to have abandoned it. Operation Exodus was trapped by success. There was no more money tree to shake.

Every week brought new signs that Operation Exodus had largely run its course. For example, following UJA meetings with the Campaign Directors of Midwest federations in January, Tauber received this staff memorandum:

> Cincinnati feels that it is finished with Operation Exodus.

> Cleveland is planning on running a separate fall OE Campaign. However, they are expecting that the campaign will yield about half of what the UJA is hoping for. There is lukewarm interest, at best, in another mission.

> Columbus is open to the idea of a continuing Exodus Campaign. However we would have to crystallize that interest.

> Detroit has the feeling that Exodus is dead. The Board there voted to continue Exodus at your urging, but Detroit thinks that for all intents and purposes there is no Exodus Campaign left there.

> Milwaukee thinks Exodus is dead there.

Pittsburgh is finished except for Super Sunday level gifts.

Minneapolis is finished with Exodus.

Simply calling national meetings or missions is no longer going to do the trick. This is the mood in communities that are all UJA supporters, sensitive to overseas needs and with good fundraising operations.

In the early months of 1993, a clamor grew from federations across the country for UJA to set a concluding date for the Campaign. Tauber was compelled to address it, not simply to appease federations, which it was not in UJA's institutional makeup to do. Rather it was born of the reality of the Campaign. Donors were numbed emotionally by the successive surprises of triumph and near tragedy and exhausted by relentless appeals. No one, at UJA or federations, believed the Campaign could be viable for more than another year. The insiders who favored an ending date thought that it would not only relieve them of the need to continue two simultaneous campaigns indefinitely but also invigorate Operation Exodus if donors thought that the next "ask" would truly be the last. Many advocates of this view favored the naming of a Chairman for the concluding phase, to enhance fundraising results and demonstrate that UJA was serious about issuing no more Campaign extensions.

Tauber was loath to end the Campaign. He had devoted much of his life since 1990 to Operation Exodus and it was the centerpiece of his National Chairmanship. He had donated generously to it and was giving it virtually all his time. He knew the cause inside and out from countless treks to the Former Soviet Union and Israel, and hundreds of meetings and briefings, and felt an enormous obligation to future immigrants to keep the Campaign going. He was not a quitter.

Tauber held to this position, but began to reconsider it as the idea of change took hold at UJA over several weeks. Marvin Lender, the architect of Operation Exodus' remarkable opening years, who had become one of Tauber's closest personal friends, persuaded him that it was in the best interests of Operation Exodus, and the larger UJA enterprise, if the Campaign would end. At a riveting Campaign Executive Committee meeting in the National Chairman's Office, Lender urged Tauber:

Joel, it's time. Declaring an end to Operation Exodus will help everyone focus what is left of their energies on it and is the best way to maximize its ultimate results. The Campaign will run out of steam if we don't shore it up soon. The lack of an end game will work against us.

Appointing someone to chair the concluding phase is also a good idea, although I am the last person to say that you shouldn't lead both OE and the (Annual) Campaign at the same time because I myself did that and you have been great at it. But it will show everyone we are serious that this is our last trip to the well.

You would not be abandoning OE. You would be making it stronger. You would remain in overall charge and be indispensable to a strong finish. You would not be quitting. You would be ensuring the best results by getting everyone to focus on the remaining challenge.

Tauber agreed[4]. On his recommendation, the UJA National Officers set May 31, 1994 as the closing date for Operation Exodus. Tauber began consultations on whom to appoint as Operation Exodus Chairman. He offered the position to Richard Wexler, whose achievements in Jewish life, intimate knowledge of the cause and strong leadership skills made him a logical choice.

Wexler possessed considerable understanding of federations, having served as Chairman of the Jewish Federation of Metropolitan Chicago and its Jewish United Fund, and as Associate Treasurer of the Council of Jewish Federations. He knew UJA thoroughly as a National Vice Chairman, and as Chairman of its Campaign Budget and Finance Committee. He was an effective major gifts fundraiser for Operation Exodus as he demonstrated as Chairman of the Dor L'Dor Mission in 1990 and the President's Mission in 1992. He carried special knowledge having served as Chairman of the National Conference of Soviet Jewry. He evinced a lawyer's critical eye in private policy debates and was a zealous advocate in public for Jewish freedom. Wexler accepted and became Chairman of Operation Exodus officially on June 1.

In these months, as part of the effort to spur federations on, UJA mentioned higher and higher Operation Exodus goals and at one point set a $1.2 billion goal in the hope of motivating fundraisers and donors. However, the environment for Operation Exodus was not the same as it had been in the beginning. Moreover, whereas Herculean goals earlier in the Campaign encouraged donors to stretch to give more than they themselves thought they might, in the later stages of Operation Exodus the goal had no effect. Ironically,

---

4 Tauber also felt an obligation to shore up the Annual Campaign, leave the organization in a strong position for his successor, and implement other ideas. One initiative he soon pursued was the enhancement of UJA campaigns in 400 small cities and towns, a fundraising bedrock that was often overlooked by UJA in the attention it had paid to federations. UJA formed the Network of Independent UJA Communities to organize an increase in services and bring the widely dispersed small communities into association with one another. Marty Stein, who had visited many of these cities and towns over the years, chaired the Network, and Russell Robinson, who helped form the King David Society, provided crucial professional support.

talk of it, among the relatively few who paid attention to it, overshadowed the surprising strength that UJA and federations were still teasing from the Campaign. For despite all handwringing Operation Exodus, which had raised $776.2 million through 1992, rose to $820 million on June 1, 1993 and, after the Prime Minister's Mission ended on August 13, 1993, to $842.6 million. Sixty-six million dollars were raised in the first eight months of 1993, $2 million dollars a week, for a second line campaign. That was still a lot of money.

By mid-August, a structure for peace with the Palestinians had been negotiated. However, Arafat could not bring himself to recognize unequivocally Israel's right to exist, renounce violence and agree to void sections of the Palestinian Covenant hostile to Israel's existence. Peres and Rabin's decision to offer Arafat recognition of the PLO as the official representative of the Palestinian people, providing him with the legitimacy he had long sought, was their final concession. Still Arafat refused. With the approval of Rabin, Peres telephoned Norwegian Foreign Minister Johan Jorgen Holst, a key intermediary, and declared that if Arafat could not accept the pact by that very night Israel would break off talks with the PLO. Instead, Peres threatened, Israel would negotiate exclusively with Syria, which meant that its attention would shift to the Golan Heights, and that it might not offer concessions on the status of the West Bank and Gaza for years. Holst telephoned Arafat in Tunis with the ultimatum and, following an extensive conversation with him, held alternating telephone calls with Peres and him. Finally Arafat relented. On Rabin's and Peres' authorization, Uri Savir, the Director General of Israel's Foreign Ministry who had conducted much of the negotiations for Israel, signed the tentative agreement in Oslo on August 20. Ahmed Qurei and Hassan Asfour, Savir's negotiations counterparts, signed for the PLO[5].

The Palestinians were eager since they stood to gain recognition, some land and a new public strategy from Israel, but the Israelis heatedly debated whether the PLO could be trusted. Many Israelis feared that the Accords would place their country's security in jeopardy. Israelis across the political spectrum found it abominable to recognize the despised PLO, which had murdered thousands of innocent Jews including children in schools, families in their homes, shoppers in stores and travelers on buses and hijacked airplanes. After debate, the Israeli Cabinet approved the draft agreement on August 30 with two abstentions, but a later debate in the Knesset, a better representation of Israeli society, showed that the Israelis were deeply divided. Rabin warned the Knesset

5 Sachar, p. 992.

that the alternative to the pact was bloodshed:

> Members of the Knesset: we cannot choose our neighbors, or our enemies, not even the cruelest among them. We only have what is there. The PLO has fought against us, and we have fought against them – and with them we are today seeking a path to peace. We can lock every door, thwart every attempt at peace. We have the moral right not to sit at the negotiating table with the PLO . . . not to shake the hand that pulled the trigger. We have the power to reject with revulsion the PLO proposals– and then to be unwilling partners to the continuing cycle with which we have been forced to live until now: war, terrorism and violence[6].

Revulsion there was, but Rabin prevailed in the 120-member legislature. However he obtained a slim majority of only 61-50 and depended on the votes of the five Israeli Arabs to achieve it[7].

Before Israel would sign, Rabin required a written statement from Arafat that he was personally committed to the Accords. Such a letter arrived at the Prime Minister's office on September 9. Upon receiving it, Rabin telephoned President Clinton who offered to host the signing on the White House lawn at noon on September 13. Israel and the PLO accepted, but it was not yet determined whether Rabin or Arafat would attend personally. It wasn't an easy decision for them. Arafat was purporting to renounce everything his life had been about and Rabin found it noxious to recognize the PLO, the instrument of so much Jewish death and suffering. Neither had gone to Oslo nor negotiated directly with the other side. They had fought each other bitterly for decades, reviled each other and hated to meet. They knew the troubled history of the region and that future events could make them look at the ceremony like Neville Chamberlain at another Munich. They knew that their presence would inflame their domestic opponents, who already had denounced them as spineless traitors. Yet each had faced worse, including military and political defeat and had looked many times into the barrel of a gun. Each told Clinton he would be present. In the hours prior to the ceremony there were massive demonstrations in every Arab country, including hundreds of thousands of enraged protestors in just one public square in Syria. There was clamor for Holy War against Israel, the severing of Arab ties to the PLO and demands for the assassination of Arafat as well as Rabin.

The Accords were not a peace treaty but a Declaration of Principles, a

---

6 Sachar, p. 993.

7 Eight legislators abstained and one was absent.

platform for peace. They were based on confidence building steps in a five year transition period, during which talks on a permanent solution would begin. The Accords provided for immediate creation of an interim elected self-governing body, the Palestinian Authority, empowered to establish and maintain an armed police force and to take control soon in Jericho and Gaza. The Palestinian Authority would have responsibility over Palestinian health, education, welfare, taxation, tourism and culture. Israel would begin to redeploy its troops immediately and begin to extricate its soldiers from Palestinian daily life, although it would retain the right to defend itself and protect Jews in the Territories. Mechanisms were established for peaceful resolution of disputes. There was a reference to a Marshall Plan to build the West Bank and Gaza. The more difficult issues such as the status of Jerusalem, the rights of refugees, the future of settlements, detailed security arrangements, the delineation of borders, and relations with other neighbors, both sides had agreed, would be addressed in permanent status talks.

Former Presidents Bush, Carter and Ford and hundreds of diplomats from around the world gathered, along with leaders of UJA and other organizations, in the warm sunshine and crisp Washington air, while a billion people observed the unbelieveable development on television. At the signing, Clinton stated:

> For too long the young of the Middle East have been caught in a web of hatred not of their own making. For too long they have been taught the chronicles of war. Now we can give them the chance to know the season of peace.

Mahmoud Abbas, the PLO International Relations Chief, said:

> We are looking to the world for its support and encouragement in our struggle for growth and development which begins today.

Arafat said:

> We will need more courage and determination to continue the course of building coexistence and peace between us. This is possible.

Peres said:

> Let all of us turn from bullets to ballots. We shall pray with you. We shall offer you our help.

Rabin delivered his unforgettable testament to the ideal of a lasting peace including the words that made headlines worldwide, "(E)nough of blood and tears. Enough." Then Rabin and Arafat shook hands.

The Oslo Accords were signed in a world moving with rapid speed toward reconciliation. They overshadowed the season's other unbelievable event, the formal end of apartheid in South Africa. The Rabin-Arafat handshake instantly became a towering symbol in a momentous century. Even in a supremely optimistic era, the handshake made concrete and credible the fantasy that global peace could soon be achieved.

With the Soviet Union dead and Rabin and Arafat shaking hands, was it any wonder that American Jews thought the need for Operation Exodus was over[8]?

Nevertheless, UJA continued to succeed at what it did best: raise vast sums through major gifts. It provided prospects with still more portals to exciting, exclusive experiences if they promised to put forth plenty of money.

In recruiting $10,000 donors for the President's Mission, UJA knew that most prospects had not only visited Israel several times but also Prague, Budapest, Warsaw, Vienna, Rome and other standard pre-mission cities. So UJA came up with a pre-mission idea that had never been offered before by an American Jewish organization: Berlin. The decision to bring a large delegation of wealthy Jews to the former nexus of Nazi Germany was made after surprisingly little debate. Although many American Jewish organizations referred to the Holocaust, few had anything directly to do with Germany. They left that especially to Israel, with important roles played by the World Jewish Congress, Holocaust survivors organizations and Yad Vashem. After all, it was a tricky area to enter for, while some felt Germany had changed, no one wanted to be confronted by survivors who had lost everyone and maintained it had not[9]. UJA, never an organization to pay attention to subtleties, sometimes seemed oblivious to the issues of the

---

8 Before Peres returned to Israel he sat down in his hotel suite for a private videotaped interview with this writer during which he declared that American Jews should continue to support Operation Exodus. He stated that the Campaign was helping make possible "a wonderful immigration that is bringing about medical, cultural and educational achievements that show Israel as a contributing people to all the nations." He said the immigrants were making Israel "a more attractive partner for regional peace," and by aiding their aliyah American Jews were helping build "a new and peaceful Middle East."

9 Although UJA often referred to the Holocaust to remind donors of Jewish vulnerability, it was careful not to exploit it in any way. For example, in the 1980s UJA mounted an historic exhibition, with riveting evidence of the Holocaust that it had borrowed from the Auschwitz State Museum, and sent it on a two-year tour across the United States. Alex Grass, then UJA National Chairman, had the idea to bring the Holocaust evidence to hundreds of thousands who would not likely visit Auschwitz. This writer negotiated the agreement by which UJA borrowed the materials, with Andrej Dobrzynski, the Polish Ambassador to the United States. In it Poland recognized for the first time that the Holocaust was preeminently a Jewish catastrophe, not something that mainly harmed Poles. UJA did not conduct or permit any fundraising in conjunction with the exhibition.

day. Without any substantive discussion whether a pre-mission to Berlin should be undertaken as part of a post-war healing process, or not offered because it was premature and might offend Holocaust survivors, UJA sent invitations to all $10,000 donors it knew asking if they would like to visit Berlin. The decision was taken solely to recruit donors so as to increase fundraising results. Fortunately for UJA the pre-mission garnered substantial enrollment, and considerable news media attention, but little criticism.

Three hundred and three American Jews from 59 cities were aboard the Lufthansa flight from John F. Kennedy International Airport to Tegel International Airport in Berlin on October 17; more of the mission's 673 participants would have been aboard but registration for the Germany pre-mission closed at 303. On their first day, the participants visited Berlin synagogues and Jewish community centers and met with local Jewish leaders. Then they arrived at the Brandenburg Gate, which was earlier a symbol of Nazi power and later a sign of a reunited, free Germany when the Berlin Wall behind it was torn down. Guides pointed out a huge unmarked mound of soil near the Gate that covered Hitler's last bunker.

The next morning, participants visited the scene of the notorious Wannsee Conference, half an hour's drive from Berlin. There, in small groups, they entered a small conference room furnished with fourteen chairs around a tawny board of directors table. Expansive floor–to-ceiling windows encompassed most of the far wall and overlooked a bucolic lake, the sun glistening on the water. On January 20, 1942, Adolf Eichmann met there with thirteen other powerful Nazis and told them that Hitler had just informed him of his new decision. The Fuehrer had determined it was no longer enough to banish the Jews from Germany and Nazi-occupied countries. Eichmann handed out folders containing sheets of paper listing countries, regions, cities and towns and estimates of how many Jews were living in each, openly or in hiding. Every Nazi present found his name on the top of one sheet. Eichmann gave them their orders: find the Jews and kill them. The Final Solution to the Jewish Question was to kill every Jew in Europe.

Hours later, participants were stunned when they met with some of the thousands of "New German Jews," Soviet émigrés who had spurned opportunities to live in the United States or Israel since 1990 and chose Germany instead. In small group discussions, moderated by German Jewry experts like Edward Serotta, the new German Jews said Germany offered better economic prospects than the United States and was safer than Israel. They said they were aware of the Holocaust but did not think it had much to do with them. The exposure was sobering and troubled the participants. Some said they would write bigger checks to Operation Exodus and urge UJA to build programs in the Former Soviet Union to discourage immigration to Germany.

Leadership has its privileges, and UJA arranged for nine mission leaders to be received by Germany's President Richard Von Weizsacher at the Presidential Residence in Bonn. For Von Weizsacher, who had been instrumental in building German-Jewish relations, this was a chance to cement his efforts as his ten year term ended. For the American Jews, led by Roberta Holland, the Mission Chairman, and William Shure, the Germany Pre-Mission Chairman, it was a moment of unforgettable access. In preparation for the meeting, this writer had obtained substantive questions, nine it turned out, from Malcolm Hoenlein, whose knowledge of the political contexts for Jews in many countries was encyclopedic. This enabled each participant to engage the President in a meaningful way. It was vintage UJA. As Holland said to me as we left the Presidential Residence, "I will treasure this day for the rest of my life. How else, except for UJA, could I have had this experience?"

The pre-mission participants were pensive on their flight to Israel but became joyful, even exuberant when, soon after their arrival, they were on the tarmac to greet a plane filled with new immigrants from Russia. "I am so relieved to see them coming here," said one mission veteran. "In Jewish life you can't take anything for granted, even what Jews do."

That evening all participants joined together at Sultan's Pool, also known as the Hassenfeld Amphitheater. There, at the foot of the illuminated walls of the Old City, they enjoyed a festive concert of Israeli music. The next day, they heard briefings by Jewish Agency officials on the need to continue to support Operation Exodus, visited settlements on the West Bank near Jerusalem where residents feared their homes would be lost as part of the Oslo process, and met with Foreign Minister Shimon Peres. In groups of three and four, they were guests of recent immigrants in their apartments and learned of their hosts' experiences in the Former Soviet Union and Israel.

A mission innovation was an emphasis on youth, with many of the participants' adult children, and Israeli high school and college students, traveling with the mission. As Tauber told the mission, "We have to learn more about the life of everyday Israelis and they have to learn more about us. We have to build bridges between our children." Lewis Norry of Rochester conceived of this initiative, put it together for the UJA Young Leadership Cabinet, and chaired the Young Leadership contingent of $10,000 donors, many new to UJA giving.

The mission culminated with a colorful pre-departure dinner, with a delightful smorgasbord of culinary treats indigenous to America, Israel and Morocco, in a gaily decorated hangar at Ben Gurion Airport that featured Prime Minister Rabin. The Prime Minister spoke of his hope for peace and prosperity after the Oslo Accords that he had signed in Washington thirteen days earlier. Rabin reminded those present that Jews still faced danger in the Former Soviet Union and thanked them for supporting Operation Exodus. Holland announced that $15 million had been raised for the Annual Campaign and Operation Exodus, the division to be announced later, including $2.7 million from UJA Women's Campaign, and $541,000 from UJA Young Leadership.

Rabin mingled freely with the guests for an hour after his speech, initially greeting Tauber, Lender and Pearlstone whom he knew, and offering participants who had never met him the opportunity to speak with him. Participants loved it. Having been cleared through customs and baggage check-in earlier under special arrangements UJA had made with El Al, they partied until half an hour before their flight's departure. Then they merely stepped outside the hanger where the shiny Boeing 767, glistening in the floodlights, stood only a few hundred feet away, fueled and ready, the crew at its stations. Feeling good about whom they had just met, what they had seen and learned -- and proud that they had the money to give away and had given it away, they ascended the silver staircase to the aircraft cabin. In a few minutes they were airborne, feeling richer for the experience. Many of them glanced at the Tel Aviv nightlife below before settling in for the overnight flight home to the United States.

A few days later, the International Leadership Reunion gathered in San Francisco, under International Co-Chairmen Melvin S. Cohen of Washington, Jack Rose of Toronto and Eric Samson of Johannesburg, with the minimum gift increased to $275,000. Rhoda and Richard Goldman chaired a Host Committee consisting of Barbara and Gerson Bakar, Hanna and Alfred Fromm, Mimi and Peter Haas, Elinor and Eugene Friend, Roz and Merv Morris, Barbara and Bernard Osher, Madeleine Russell, Carol and Harry Saal and Roselyne and Richard Swig. UJA participants pledged $13.8 million, including an overall increase in gifts to Operation Exodus. Before the Reunion, the Swigs brought 20 participants to Uzbekistan where they met Jews in Bukhara, Samarkand and Tashkent who wanted to make aliyah.

UJA's biannual Lion of Judah Conference, under Women's Campaign Chairman Carole Solomon, further established UJA Women's Campaign as the fastest growing division in Jewish life. More than 1,100 women assembled in Washington to explore Jewish needs, learn about politics and enhance the status of women in Jewish life. The Conference raised $4 million for

Operation Exodus, including $1.5 million beyond what the donors had pledged to it previously. (Annual Campaign giving also rose, to $8.2 million.) Demonstrating formidable growth at all levels, 95 women qualified as new Lions, 51 as Ruby, 19 as Sapphire, 23 as Emerald and eight as Zahav (Gold), reflecting respective advancement to the $5,000, $10,000, $18,000, $25,000 and $50,000 levels.

Federations mounted major gifts events in partnership with UJA. For example, the Combined Jewish Philanthropies of Greater Boston sponsored a successful Prime Minister's Council dinner for $100,000 donors that was chaired by Michael Bohnen, Jay Fialkow, Ted Benard and Thomas Lee and under the professional direction of Barry Shrage.

To energize the effort to retain and enhance major gifts after nearly four years of grueling double campaigning, Tauber assembled a group of experienced solicitors. Each was an experienced traveler for UJA in the Former Soviet Union and Israel and knowledgeable about the financial case. Each was a skilled solicitor, and had recently increased his or her own major gift. Each was willing to drop everything at business or home and fly for hours on airplanes to close gifts. Tauber called them the Dream Team. They played the role of a relief pitcher, coming into the game when it was on the line, in this case when the donor believed a lesser gift was sufficient and UJA believed it should be more.

When federations asked UJA to fly into their communities, onto their own turf, it was the moment of truth in their complex relationship. They persistently condemned UJA for insensitivity, condescension, brusqueness and making them feel parochial when they advocated for local needs -- and UJA leaders had to laugh sometimes because they knew that characterization of UJA was well founded. But when they needed someone to close major gifts, they knew that no one could do it like the UJA.

The Dream Team consisted of Melvin Alperin, Stanley Chesley, Joseph Cooper, Rani Garfinkle, Alex Grass, Thomas Green, Donald Hess, Larry Hochberg, Marvin Lender, Stephen Lieberman, Arnold Lifson, Richard Pearlstone, Arthur Sandler, Richard Shenk, Mark Solomon, Richard Spiegel, Martin Stein, Joel Tauber, Andrew Tisch and Arlene Zimmerman. Tauber and his Campaign Executive Committee meticulously matched them with prospects based on donor and prospect giving levels, prior associations, business similarity and common interests. Tauber's achievement was not so much in initiating the Fly-In program since UJA had previously used the initiative. Rather, he enhanced the program and made it much more effective. In a baseball analogy, he assembled a broad and deep bullpen of the best righties and lefties in the league, who knew every hitter and how to throw every pitch. They knew how to win in the bottom of ninth inning. In a solicitation, that was the moment of truth when the passion had played out and the donor was deciding whether to go up or down in his gift.

Tisch, Pearlstone, Sandler, Garfinkle and Cooper also solicited on the Prime Minister's Mission, as did Zimmerman at the International Leadership Reunion and several others did so on the President's Mission, but they and the rest of the Dream Team were additionally valuable at Fly-Ins. There, there was no Prime Minister present, no worried Jews in front of prospects in a hostile land and no jetliners streaming in with new immigrants aboard. In the last half of 1993, the Dream Team closed 83 gifts on Fly-Ins for Operation Exodus that totaled $10.1 million.

Here are excerpts from a UJA memorandum dated November 1, 1993 that illustrates the role the Dream Team played in enhancing Operation Exodus (and the Annual Campaign). A report to the Campaign Executive Committee by Morris Sherman, it shows that the orange squeezers kept at it to the end:

Atlantic City	In July a solicitation Fly-In and training session for Campaign leadership was held at a retreat at Princeton University. Rabbis from CLAL [The National Jewish Center for Learning and Leadership] held workshops on the religious obligations of giving to Jewish causes. During the retreat every leader was solicited.
Boston	We participated at a Boston Fly-In in October, soliciting mostly campaign leadership (whose higher gifts placed them in a stronger position to ask others to renew or increase their gifts). Our most vital work in that community was the initiation of a one million dollar gift from Tommy Lee.
Central New Jersey	We helped plan the major gifts caucus for the Central campaign. Marvin Lender ran the caucus. After doing so, Marvin secured an appointment for Joel Tauber to solicit Joe Wilf [a Breakfast of Champions donor]. This led to a $50,000 increase by Joe Wilf for this year.

Charlotte	Andrew Tisch is going into Charlotte on December 13th to solicit their top three gifts and to speak at their major gifts dinner.
Chattanooga	We arranged for Don Hess to solicit 40 percent of the campaign with three solicitations.
Chicago	We have set an appointment for Richard Pearlstone and Ed Cadden of Chicago to solicit a $250,000 gift and have provided extensive research and leads for their campaign.
Cleveland	We were in Cleveland in July. UJA arranged for Natan Sharansky to speak to donors and participate in solicitations. Marvin Lender solicited the top givers.
Columbus	We arranged for Richard Spiegel to solicit the top gifts in Columbus.
Des Moines	We arranged to solicit gifts at the UJA King David event in Washington.
Detroit	We were brought in to train chairpersons in various divisions of its campaign. We also created a Fly-In for the Max Fisher Dinner in which several members of the Dream Team played important roles in solicitations. We motivated and trained local solicitors in connection with the Max Fisher Dinner.
Fort Lauderdale	We met with the federation Executive Committee, have done extensive research, and will be using the Dream Team to implement solicitations.
Greenwich	We spoke at their first meeting of the year. We have created a profile on twenty of the prospects in Greenwich with the highest potential. This community is extremely wealthy and has potential for giving similar to the Florida Gold Coast. We

are attempting to make appointments for Mendel Kaplan, Andrew Tisch and Richard Pearlstone. We successfully recruited the new president, Steve Levy, for the Prime Minister's Mission.

Hartford

We solicited the new Campaign Chairman, Lou Green. We were invited to speak at their goal setting meeting in September. We are supposed to secure some [names for] solicitations.

Indianapolis

We have been asked to arrange a solicitation with Mel or Herb Simon. We also arranged to solicit one of their top givers, Jack Larman, in Israel.

Kansas City, Mo.

Steve Lieberman, a Dream Team member, is going into Kansas City to solicit some of their lead gifts.

MetroWest

We have several programs going at once with MetroWest. We are working with the Achim [Brotherhood] Division, that's the $100,000 group, to arrange for solicitations where appropriate. We have profiles on all the members of this division and have solicited several of them. We are working with MetroWest's ABC Division, which is searching for prospects to upgrade to the $100,000 level. MetroWest has also completed one of our most successful VIP missions, a UJA mission tailored to select major donors, and we are planning another one this spring. Finally, we are working together to develop a large contingent for the UJA Palm Beach Gathering.

Miami

We are intimately involved in the major gifts aspect of their campaign. We are working on several major solicitations with them.

New York

We are working in close cooperation with New York in several areas . . . soliciting major donors that need a national solicitation. The most prominent of these is the 500K donor, S. Daniel Abraham [developer of Slim-Fast]. We have trained staff and several divisions in the campaign. Furthermore, we initiated and have developed an ongoing relationship with their Long Island Campaign. Marty Stein of the Dream Team has done many solicitations in the community at two Fly-Ins. We have also had the opportunity to solicit their Chairman.

Palm Beach
We have researched many prospects for them and we are cooperating to achieve some important solicitations. Much of our work will be centered around the Palm Beach Gathering this January but we have already participated in their campaign planning. We have initiated a formal process to identify and develop strategies for creating new 100K givers.

Pinellas County, Fl.
We ran their Major Gifts Caucus and solicited four of their top gifts. One of them became a new member of the Prime Minister's Council.

Portland, Ore.
We helped arrange for a visit by Mendel Kaplan immediately after the International Leadership Reunion to solicit one of their top gifts, who is a business partner of Mendel's.

Rhode Island
We have researched their top gifts and leading prospects. I have participated in their campaign planning and assignments. Arlene Zimmerman was brought in for certain solicitations and we are planning other key solicitations with her. Andrew Tisch and David Hirsch [a UJA National Vice Chairman from Pawtucket, Rhode Island] are working on a major upgrade prospect that we found through our research.

San Diego
We have arranged for Marty Stein to solicit a group of their top gifts. They have been cooperating at the King David level and we have worked on solicitations there.

Seattle	We have worked closely with them at the 100K level. We have provided research on their top givers and have cooperated in the solicitation of these gifts. Marty Stein was brought in for a Fly-In and Richard Pearlstone is going to solicit some of their top gifts and address their major gifts dinner.
South Broward	We ran a major gifts training program for their board. Marty Stein has already spent one day soliciting there.
South Palm Beach	We have developed a working relationship with the campaign director that will result in our involvement in their major gifts campaign.
Springfield, Mass.	Andrew Tisch solicited some of their top gifts. We are cultivating others.
Washington, D.C.	Joel Tauber closed several solicitations. Stanley Chesley, a Dream Team member, is working there. We have created a great amount of research on the donor prospects.

Bruce Hoffberger gave his second $1.25 million gift and Sanford Goldberg of Minneapolis, Lee Coplan and Joseph Wilf each gave their second gifts of $1 million to Operation Exodus as part of the Fly-In program. Meanwhile donors gave at all levels as part of other UJA and federation programs.

In 1993, Operation Exodus raised $83.9 million to bring the total to $860.1 million. Donors redeemed more than half a billion dollars in pledges, remitting $511.2 million to the special Campaign by year's end. Most of the balance was expected within the next two years. Eleven percent of the revenues was retained for local absorption. It was a good thing too that so much had been raised and received. More Jews made aliyah from the Former Soviet Union in 1993 than in 1992: 66,035 compared to 64,790. The monthly rate in 1993 mirrored that of 1992 and remained within a narrow range, 4,185 to 6,817, indicating that fundraising needed to continue. But federations believed that the aliyah could be funded effectively through the Annual Campaign. Tauber yielded to the inevitable. He reconfirmed that the concluding date for Operation Exodus would be May 31, 1994, on federations' assurances that they would campaign for it to that date, and provide for the aliyah from future Annual Campaigns.

As 1994 began, the attention of Americans, including American Jews, shifted to domestic affairs: public, private and sexual. As the final winter and spring of Operation Exodus unfolded, the Clinton Administration's main domestic initiative, a plan to insure the health of every American, was comatose. On January 8, Attorney General Janet Reno reluctantly named a special prosecutor, Robert Fiske, to investigate allegations of wrongdoing in the first couple's business activities in Whitewater, Arkansas in prior years. Soon, Paula Corbin Jones, a former Arkansas state employee, filed suit against Clinton for making unwanted sexual advances when he was Governor of Arkansas. The scent of scandal overtook policy issues. The country was treated to tales of marital fights and lamp throwing in the White House. Focus on foreign affairs, and economic issues like how to spend the "peace dividend," economic benefits Americans expected from shrinking military expenditures in the New World Order, were overtaken by the politics of personal destruction and saucier stuff.

The country became infatuated with extraordinary technological advances. A new medium took hold, the Internet, and tens of millions logged on for the first time. Users were bombarded by a staggering array of gloves-off misinformation, distortions, absurdities and lies amidst information. The number of 24 hour a day cable stations multiplied, with boisterous talking heads ranting on every political, economic, religious, educational, military and social subject. Televisions, or videotape monitors, sprouted in restaurants, doctors' waiting rooms and the rear seats of automobiles. A cell phone seemed to be in everyone's hand and a computer on millions of laps. Perpetual distraction became becoming a way of life.

Like others, American Jews were ebullient over the apparent triumph of the American ideals of peace and freedom around the world and fascinated by the new instruments for work and play. They were hopeful, perhaps even presumptuous, about a peaceful future for Israel. With them, as with others, the euphoria over the signing of the Oslo Accords gave way in their attention to the rising stock market, including on the previously little-noticed Nasdaq. After all, like others, they had to earn a living, pay college tuition and prepare for retirement. The rising tide of intermarriage, assimilation and alienation from Jewish institutions at home, brought to the surface in the CJF Population Study in 1990, was not yet stemmed. Anti-Semitic incidents were down worldwide. Had Operation Exodus been sold on anti-Semitism in 1994 as it had been in

1990 it would have had few takers.

From most headlines, Jews abroad seemed more secure, but Jews abroad were not so sure. Israel's pariah status in the world community lessened as more countries recognized Israel diplomatically and a few Arab countries began public contacts with it. Rabin met with the Pope at the Vatican on March 17, where the two laid the final foundation stones for the Roman Catholic Church's recognition of Israel. But Israel remained largely shunned by other countries. John Paul II, who as Father Karol Wojtyla in Krakow had saved Jewish lives in the Holocaust, bestowed papal knighthood on Austrian President Kurt Waldheim, a former Nazi collaborator; and established a Holy See embassy in Jaffa, a mainly Arab town in the Tel Aviv municipality. Nothing for the Jews was ever easy.

Implementation of the peace process envisioned by the Oslo Accords alternatingly lurched forward and fell back, faltering on transfer of power issues such as where, when and how the new Palestinian Authority would gain control of border crossings. Jews were killed in scattered incidents and Israel responded to restore order. Then a Palestinian blew himself up in order to kill eight Jews standing nearby, escalating the terror with a new form of violence. As Rabin struggled to deliver on his peace initiative, he was besieged at home by the left that said he was not giving in enough, and by the right that said he was giving in too much. Despite his halo in foreign capitals, Rabin's standing in the polls at home fell at Passover 1994 to its lowest point since he had been elected in 1992. When Israeli troops withdrew from Jericho in May, Palestinians danced in the streets as music blared all night, but the mood among Jews was somber.

Rabin became the first Israeli Prime Minister to visit Russia, where nearly every Jew just a few years earlier had been virtually a prisoner. Yet the Jewish future there remained uncertain. Vladimir Zhirinovsky, whose anti-Semitic Liberal Democratic party had received 24 percent of the vote in the country's legislative elections four months earlier, declared he would run for president of Russia. As economic reforms foundered in every Republic, and the promise of a post-Soviet era remained unfulfilled, many Jews felt exposed to scapegoating.

Yet the inspiring drama of daring rescues had not yet played out. After all those who had been saved by aid of American Jewish largesse, the incredible JDC mounted its eighth rescue from Sarajevo in the Campaign's closing weeks. This time it was 74 Jews along with 222 Muslims and Christians whose bus bypassed yet another exploding mortar shell that killed 68 people. Among those rescued was Zajniba Hartaga-Susie, a Muslim who had saved Jews during the Holocaust and who had been honored as a Righteous Gentile by Yad Vashem.

The thrill energized the Campaign but only momentarily, and numbing set in once more. The world was rapidly changing, and American Jews were already weary from the demands of the Campaign. Many felt, perhaps rightly, that they had done enough for Operation Exodus.

Even UJA insiders could not wait for Operation Exodus to be over. For them, the UJA National Conference in May, when it would end, began to look like an oasis to desert travelers. But they were not there yet. They were good soldiers in a humanitarian army, and there was probably still some juice left in that orange. They squeezed on.

A UJA mission visited Uzbekistan and Israel and raised some funds, but it was preaching to the choir. Thirty leaders participated under Wexler's chairmanship, every one of them a generous giver, proven solicitor and experienced mission traveler. There simply was not much room for campaign growth from them; they participated to obtain the freshest testimony from the field to enhance their final solicitations. They met with Jews in Tashkent, Samarkand and Bukhara who were interested in aliyah for economic reasons, and not for fear of imminent danger because they were Jews. The mission highlight was completely unexpected. The visitors were invited to a wedding about to take place of a young Bukharan Jewish bride and groom who hoped to make aliyah within the year. The wedding was held indoors but without indoor heating, the warmth provided by fires flaming from charred barrels encircling the wedding canopy. They joined in the traditional Jewish dances and songs remaining, like the locals including the bride and groom, in their hats, coats, scarves and gloves. The mission reminded UJA leaders that the cause of Operation Exodus needed to be pursued through the Annual Campaign as long as there were Jews who wished to move to Israel. But it had the feeling of a final Campaign swing for a retiring politician, a final swish at the tee for a golfer retiring in his prime. The sense of urgency was over but Operation Exodus was not yet history.

A mission that took place days later included no fundraising at all. It was a solidarity mission, led by Marvin Lender, to show Israelis that American Jews stood with them after a car bomb planted by Hamas exploded in Afula and killed eight Jews. UJA chartered an El Al 747 and brought 365 American Jews from 57 cities on a two day visit to Afula, where they made shivah calls to every family, including three that had lost children. The mourners were overwhelmed that hundreds of American Jews, whom they had not known personally, traveled so far just to console them. "No one can know the pain of a parent who loses a child," said Lender, visibly shaken, as his daughter Sondra, a mission participant, stood at his side. Participants wept as the Afula Choir sang songs dedicated to a choir member who was murdered in the terrorist attack. Then they proudly joined in the singing of Hatikvah, "The Hope," Israel's national anthem.

Fundraising took place at other UJA events to close the campaign strongly. The Prime Minister's Council held its winter weekend in Palm Beach in January under Ronne and Donald Hess' chairmanship and they, Tauber, Lender and Pearlstone closed several gifts. The King David Society firmly established the $25,000 giving level UJA had long sought as it raised funds at events in January, February, March and April in different parts of the country. The Women's Campaign held successful Lion of Judah programs for Emeralds in Washington in January, Sapphires in Palm Beach in February and Rubies in Palm Beach in March; and mounted a mission to Poland and Israel for Lions at all levels in April. The Business and Professional Women's Council under Sandra Cahn produced good results as well.

The biannual Young Leadership Conference, organized by Robert Max (Skip) Schrayer and Emily Zimmern and coordinated by Yael Septee, Young Leadership director, was held in Washington in March and drew 2,600 Jews in their 30s and 40s. At the closing plenary, ten successfully absorbed Jews from the Soviet Union, Ethiopia and Sarajevo described their suffering in their old country and how much better their lives were in Israel. Participants were asked to give yet again, $100 in honor of each speaker to aid future immigrants. Another million dollars was raised.

UJA continued to provide important services to federations, securing speakers and organizing missions. Former Prime Minister Yitzhak Shamir was persuaded to visit the United Jewish Federation of MetroWest where he addressed 600 donors and met privately with 40, events that brought the cumulative MetroWest Operation Exodus Campaign to $19 million. The last Operation Exodus mission UJA organized was for the Jewish Federation of Metropolitan Chicago, to Russia and Israel, from April 21 to May 3; it boosted Chicago past the $49 million mark.

Federations mounted local programs that raised funds for Operation Exodus such as UJA-Federation of New York which sponsored events from major gifts, including in the crucial Real Estate and Wall Street divisions, to Super Sunday. Striving to the last moment, Peter May completed four stunning years as UJA-Federation Operation Exodus Chairman and James S. Tisch provided strong leadership and support as Campaign General Chairman. New York achieved a four-year total of $177.5 million.

On May 15, the 500,000th immigrant from the Soviet Union or Former

Soviet Union arrived in Israel. That immigrant, never formally identified, arrived during the ripe old age of Operation Exodus. But for that woman, man or child who descended the stairs of the shiny El Al jet and stepped onto the tarmac, it was the first day of the aliyah.

The Campaign formally ended on May 31, 1994, but it was already spoken about in the past tense during the three day UJA National Conference, held at the Grand Hyatt Hotel in New York City from May 22 to 24. Chaired by Lois Zoller, the Conference included panel discussions with political leaders and academics, planning sessions for UJA divisions and departments and a joyous celebration of Tauber's triumphant two year term as National Chairman. Although technically there were a few days left, Operation Exodus ended when Pearlstone succeeded Tauber at a joint meeting of the UJA Trustees and National Officers on May 23. Tauber received a standing ovation with a thunderous round of applause for his outstanding leadership of Operation Exodus and for his role in sustaining the Annual Campaign in two years of uphill struggle. Pearlstone thanked Tauber for all he had accomplished and promised to do everything in his power to maximize funding for immigrants in future Annual Campaigns.

EPILOGUE

Operation Exodus was pursued from January 15, 1990 to May 31, 1994, a period of four years, four months and 17 days. In selfless support of it, 1.2 million Americans, overwhelmingly Jews but not only Jews, contributed $882.9 million. Their generosity enabled 502,218 Jews from what was the Soviet Union when the Campaign began, and 20,630 from Ethiopia, Sarajevo, Bosnia-Herzegovina, Syria and Yemen, to escape from persecution and hardship and begin lives of freedom and opportunity in Israel. The Americans gave freely, in idealism, solidarity and hope. They helped make a miracle happen.

The world was almost unrecognizable in 1994 from what it had been in 1990, and Israel, a country not much larger than New Jersey, was transformed as well. The population increase alone was staggering; it was as if the entire population of Spain had immigrated to the United States in four years. Yet the Israelis greeted the newcomers with open arms. Unemployment, inflation, social dislocation and daily inconveniences increased for the Israelis but their welcome mat always remained out. Refugees carried from planes on stretchers, who walked with canes, who were blind, ill or mentally feeble were embraced along with the educated physicians, brilliant scientists, skilled engineers and talented artists and writers. Immigrants unable to support themselves, and with no person to support them, became citizens upon arrival just like the few who had family members or friends already in Israel. Even at the fabled Ellis Island those who might be a burden had been turned away. The government's policy matched the people's aspiration: not one major demonstration was held anywhere in the country, at any time, to limit the immigration. Israel proved yet again it was the sanctuary for all Jews.

Life was not easy for the newcomers, but they adjusted. They found jobs, usually within a year. They learned a new language. They became accustomed to new foods. They blended into the fabric of the country while maintaining, as did other immigrant groups, dimensions of the culture of their native land. They were amazed by their ready access to goods and services that improved their lives. They discovered they could express their views, publicly as well as privately, without being arrested. They began to learn about their religion. And they treasured the opportunity to live openly as Jews.

The greatest voluntary movement of Jews since the Exodus from Egypt continued even after Operation Exodus. By the end of the decade, 827,425 had made aliyah from the Soviet Union or its successor states, more than 955,000 by the end of 2005. American Jews visiting Israel beamed when they met immigrants in stores, or heard Russian chatter in cafés and on the streets, knowing that their own generosity had helped make the new Israelis' journeys to freedom possible. They swelled with pride as the new immigrants established themselves in Israel as cancer researchers, professors, social workers and conductors of symphonies.

On November 4, 1995, Yitzhak Rabin was assassinated by a Jew who disagreed with his policies. It was the first political murder of the leader of the Jewish people by a Jew in 25 centuries. From 2000 until early 2005, a new Intifada raged in which 1,050 Israelis were killed and 7,176 were wounded, mostly civilians. Later in 2005, Israel unilaterally withdrew all its citizens, troops and settlers alike, from Gaza. But Hamas, which was dedicated to Israel's destruction, was elected to lead the government there in early 2006. Danger remained the companion of every Israeli, sabra and immigrant alike.

In America, on November 17, 1999, the United Jewish Appeal and Council of Jewish Federations merged. The new organization was named the United Jewish Communities. UJA had valiantly served the Jewish people for 60 years, ten months and seven days, and raised an astonishing $18 billion. Over the years, UJA rescued hundreds of thousands of Jews, kept millions more alive in lands of distress, and made Jewish life possible in cities and hamlets around the globe — wherever a Jew could be found. UJA possessed the uncanny ability to reach into the essence of every American Jew's heart, and make people happy to give their money away. It promised donors nothing material in return, but gave them something priceless: an opportunity to shape Jewish destiny. No one could tell the story of the economic, scientific, cultural, educational and social achievements of Israel, and the modern survival of Jews and Jewish life around the world, without paying tribute to the indispensable role of the UJA. UJA enabled millions of American Jews for generations, from billionaires to schoolchildren, to sustain and save Jews abroad.

Operation Exodus was conducted in an era of breathtaking surprises, not all of them on the international stage. One was that Operation Exodus would turn out to be the last hurrah of the United Jewish Appeal. The Torah states, in its last line, "And there has not risen a prophet since in Israel like unto Moses." Perhaps it might also respectfully be said that never has there been an organization like the United Jewish Appeal.

INDEX

OPERATION EXODUS

INDEX